Pett in Sussex

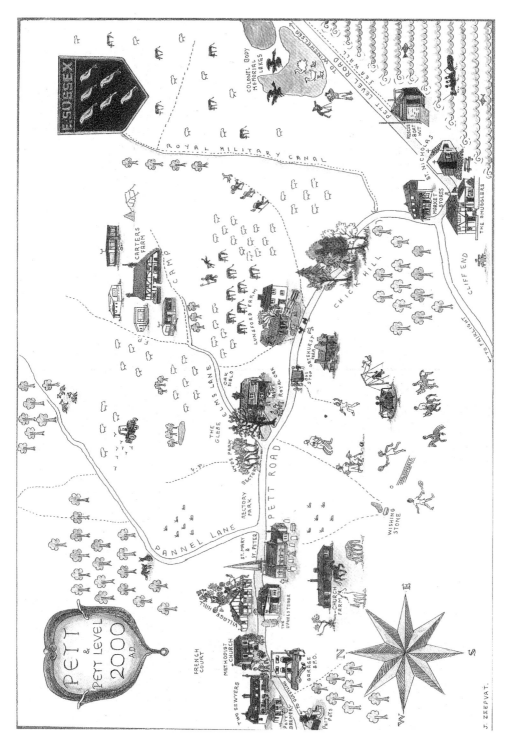

Pett and Pett Level. Millennium Map – drawn by Joan Zeepvat

Pett in Sussex

The Story of a Village, its Church and People

(Nearly a Thousand Years of History)

By

John N C Taylor

Edgerton Publishing Services

Pett, East Sussex

First published in Great Britain in 2004 by
Edgerton Publishing Services
Jasmine Cottage, Elm Lane, Pett, Hastings, East Sussex TN35 4JD
Tel. +44 (0) 1424 813003
Email enquiries@eps-edge.demon.co.uk

ISBN 0-9548390-0-5

A CIP catalogue record for this book is available from the British Library.

Typeset in Garamond by Edgerton Publishing Services.

Printed and bound in Great Britain by Antony Rowe Ltd, Chippenham, Great Britain

Acknowledgements

It is with gratitude that I thank the many people who have helped in the course of preparing this book. Without their assistance and support the book would not have been written; without their reminiscences some of the tales could not have been told but would have been either lost or forgotten, maybe for all time.

First, I must record my thanks to, and warm appreciation of, the staff of the Reference Section of the Hastings Central Library. The service and encouragement given to me was superb and the content of the library was an essential and most informative part of my research. My thanks too, to the staff of the East Sussex Records Office, where documents on Pett Church are kept with other invaluable material.

To each of the following I offer my thanks, not only for the assistance given but also for the great pleasure I had in obtaining material or help from them.

- The Royal Institute of British Architects for information on Benjamin Ferrey.
- The Hastings Observer Group for permission to reproduce an article by Reginald Cooke.
- Rev. Robin Balch and Ken Holmes for permission to peruse and copy some of the Church documents and Parish Records.
- Alfred Close for a copy of St Mary & St Peter, Pett, Monumental Inscriptions.
- Lawrence Cooke for his reminiscences about Pett Level and his family.
- Décor Art Creations Ltd for permission to reproduce drawings of six porcelain plates.
- Evelyn Darnell for information about The Two Sawyers.
- Members of the Dunlop family for information and tales about farming.
- Jillian Green for the histories of the Hills and Colegate families.
- Robert Heather for permission to use his engraving of Pett Church.
- Kay Jury and the Pett Women's Institute for permission to use information from their Pett History.
- Winifred Lovejoy for information about Carters Farm.
- Joan Medlock for permission to reproduce the comprehensive botanical survey of St Mary & St Peter Churchyard.

- John and Rosemary Moon for the history of the Cooke family and details about some of the artists who worked at Pett Level.
- Eric Newton for details about the Church Clock.
- Richard A. Parkins for his encouragement and for the use of various documents associated with Pett Church.
- Cicely Perring for her help, kindness and the loan of several old guide-books.
- Rev. John H. Read for the story of the aumbry in Pett Church.
- Marjorie Rowson for information about the Bexhill Charter.
- Brian Scott for various documents associated with local history.
- Ron Steer, my good friend, for his help in my research at the East Sussex Records Office.
- Philip and Peter Taylor for computer wizardry far beyond my poor capabilities.
- Robert Taylor for information on Frankpledge and the Lucas-Shadwell family.
- Avril Thurley for her encouragement, stories about Pett people, information about the History of Parish Councils, and for reading through the draft and correcting many of my typing errors.
- Joyce Wheatley for her detailed research into various facets of life in Pett and for permission to use much of her material.
- Members of the Young family for permission to use photographs, letters and family history.
- Charlotte Zeepvat for her photographic skill and encouragement.
- Joan Zeepvat for permission to reproduce her Millennium Map.
- The many contributors to the Pett Parish Magazine from 1915 to 2000.
- The many folk in Pett who shared information and stories with me and always supported me in this venture.

My thanks go to Graham Fitton for assistance with the printing of the book, and especially to David Penfold, whose expertise and goodwill enabled this book to be published.

The whole project would not have been possible without the help and support of my wife, Ray, who put up with me during the time spent on the research and writing of this book. She also helped to formulate some of the paragraphs, read and corrected the many mistakes in the first draft and proof read the final text. Any errors, grammatical or otherwise, that remain are solely mine. I am indebted to her for all her encouragement and help, and I dedicate this book to her.

John Taylor
Pett, June 2004

Table of Contents

1

Introduction

Every English town and village has its own story to tell. This is Pett's story. Pett, the very name conjures up images of happiness: a name that implies the presence of people. This has not always been the case. Near the sea in East Sussex, about five miles from Hastings and seven from Rye, and between the high down of Fairlight and the orchards of Icklesham lies the low hill of Pett, falling abruptly to the marshes of Pett Level at the seaward end. Pett sits on a ridge of sandstone and clay and from the earliest of times has had an affinity with the land and the sea. There are a number of pits on both sides of the ridge, some of which are Roman or earlier iron workings.

Some say that it is from the word 'pit' that Pett gets its name. It certainly evolved from the 13th century spelling 'Pette' or 'Putte', the 14th century 'Potte' and the 15th century spelling 'Pytte'. Before that, at the time of the Norman Conquest, it was probably called 'Luet' or 'Ivet'. At the time when the Domesday Book was written (1086) the manor of Pett lay chiefly in the parishes of Guestling and Pett and is mentioned among the possessions of the Earl of Eu. The entry in the Domesday Book reads:

> In Guestling Hundred William de Septimus holds Luet: Leuret held it of Earl Godwin. It is one hide, and never paid land tax (geld). There is land for two ploughs. In demesne is one plough, and a villein and three cottages with two ploughs. There are three acres of meadow. Twenty shillings have been the value under the Saxon government (King Edward), and at the present day. It has been desolated.

Since the Normans, no Baron raised a castle in the parish nor did any wealthy individual or aristocrat build a grand house. So in that sense history passed Pett by; though the chronicles of England have played their part in the development of this village. The character of Pett lies more in its people than in any building and there has always been a rare individuality in the village among the young and the old – a factor fast disappearing from many places in England. Pett is, above all, a companionable place.

Christianity came to these shores in the 1st century AD and it has been said that Britain was converted in the 2nd century. However, Christians were not well understood by many people in Roman Britain at that time. They worshipped in private houses, were sometimes accused of being subversive and were often persecuted. Nevertheless, Christian roots, though thin, became established and as the centuries rolled by more and more people living in the towns followed Christ. In 597 a mission from Pope Gregory, headed by Augustine, arrived in Kent intent on converting the Anglo-Saxons. In 600 Augustine won a great prize when he baptised King Athelbert of Kent. Augustine became Archbishop of the Anglo-Saxons and later, by 682, Wilfred, former Bishop of York, began a crusade to convert that still largely heathen part of the Anglo-Saxon kingdom – Sussex. He arrived at a time of great famine caused by drought, and it is said that when Wilfred began baptising converts it began to rain and the new harvest was saved. Wilfred was hugely popular and the king gave him an estate at Selsea to build a new monastery.

By the middle of the 8th century Christianity was well established in England, though not at Pett, which was a very wild place – mainly woodland. In 771 King Offa, after a victory at Hastings, controlled the whole of Sussex. The following year, probably to curry favour with the Pope, Offa issued a land grant to Oswald, Bishop of Selsea, witnessed among others by King Cynewulf of Wessex. This is probably the first time that Christianity came to this area. The Charterlands given to Oswald for Christian use extended in pockets from Barnhorn Manor (near the Pevensey Marshes) to Icklesham. The area given at Icklesham was three hides (a hide being about 80 acres), and the one at Blackbrookes and Foxham one hide. St Peter's Church in Bexhill Old Town is built in the centre of Offa's Charterlands. Because Pett was not even a hamlet in those days, it is not mentioned in the Charter, but there is no doubting the fact that Christianity was now being practised in this part of East Sussex and places of worship were in use not too far from this still desolate place. At this time there may have been one or two folk scratching out a living from the land or digging up the local clay for pot making, and a few may have been collecting salt from the sea-shore as well as endeavouring to catch fish for food.

By 960 Dunstan had established the supremacy of the monastic order and after the Norman Conquest, and the crushing of various rebellions, many abbeys and churches began to appear in Sussex, as in most other parts of the country. Pett still remained isolated and mainly wooded.

In 1071 William I divided Sussex into six rapes, each with a castle, a port and a river. To rule these divisions William appointed his trusted followers, who started to build castles, churches, dwellings and ports. This continued right into the Middle Ages and for a time in the 12th century Hastings became the most important of the Cinque Ports.

There were enough people in the area for Pett to have a church of its own late in the 13th century, as records mention a Pett parish in the taxation of Pope Nicholas in 1291. It is probable, therefore, that Christians have worshipped at Pett for about 750 years and many of them devoted much of their lives to the church here. It is the village of Pett, its church and the people who lived and worshipped here that this book is about. The endeavours of many Christians over hundreds of years have left a legacy of great spirituality in this parish, a place of great beauty and serenity for us and future generations to use and enjoy.

The complete tale about Pett begins long before the Romans invaded Britain, when dinosaurs roamed the land. Our story, however, is associated with people and really starts well after the Normans arrived and changed our history after the Battle of Hastings. We shall begin 200 years later when the first church was built at Pett.

2

The Guestling Hundred and Early History

Pett is a very old parish with a fascinating past. It lies under the high Fairlight ridge and close to the Level, named after it. Pett is a village in East Sussex on the edge of the High Weald, an area that is rich in ancient woods and coppices. Pett Level is on the edge of the marsh and wetlands that extend towards the Romney Marsh. Pett was part of the Hundred of Guestling, which lay in the southern portion of the Rape of Hastings and comprised four parishes: Fairlight, Guestling, Pett and Icklesham. The Hundred was bounded on the east by the town of Rye and the River Brede; on the south by the sea; on the west by the town of Hastings and part of the Hundred of Baldslow; and on the north by part of the Hundred of Baldslow and the River Brede. By 1296, Winchelsea (which was originally included) ceased to be part of the Guestling Hundred. Relics of the former character of the village are few though some survive in such charming roads as Peter James and Rosemary Lanes, or that other lovely lane which meanders through woods, crosses Pannel Sewer and then mounts up to Hog Hill on its way to Winchelsea. To this ancient Cinque Port there is no approach quite so attractive as the road from Pett that enters the town under New Gate.

The earliest mention of the 'fee of Pett' is late in the 12th century, when it was held by Gilbert de Ore. He was probably the same Gilbert de Petti who in 1196 granted to the Abbey of Robertsbridge various marshlands held in his estate of Pett. Some six manors are associated with the history of Pett, none of which remain today though some of the local farms in the area retain links with the old names, such as Stonelynke and Mersham (Marsham). These manors changed hands many times over the centuries and some of the owners held the advowson of the village church (see Table 2 in the Appendix).

The meeting place of the Hundred Court may have been a spot near Fairlight Church called 'Hundred Acre' and it was here that the Manor Court (or Court Baron) would have been held. At this the customary tenants of the manor usually surrendered or were admitted to their holdings, paid their quit-rents and transacted all business relating to their tenures, through a homage, or a selected body of tenants, chosen at the meeting of the court. The Steward presided, and looked to the Lord of the manor's interests. The bailiff collected the fees and any fines (or amercements) that were imposed by the homage. The homage also heard and dealt with civil actions of debt or damage to the amount of 40s (shillings), punished all trespassers on the Lord's soil or waters, on the deer in his park, or the hares, conies or pheasants in his warren. They likewise determined cases of waifs and strays and of villeins absenting themselves or marrying their daughters without the Lord's consent. This court was generally held twice a year.

The Knight's Court was usually held at the same time as the Manor Court, but occasionally on different days. At this court the gentlemen and any nobles were bound to attend either in person or by proxy, to do their service and pay rents. The Court Leet, or View of Frankpledge was usually held twice in the year. At the court the Tithing-Man attended with the entire Tithing, including the twelve principal inhabitants, who acted as a jury. The absence of any inhabitant duly summoned to attend was reported, and he was fined 2d (pence), as also was the tithing-man for not producing him. The tithing-man was also bound to collect from the tenants and pay in at each of the two principal courts 1d for each yardland and one halfpenny for each half-yardland and cottage.

'Frankpledge' was the system in old English law by which units or tithings of ten households were formed. Every male of 12 years and over was obliged to be a member of a group of ten or twelve, also called a tithing, and members of the group were corporately held responsible for the good behaviour of one another. A member of such a group was bound in pledge for his neighbours. The tithing list of the manor was checked at each View of Frankpledge, and all boys who had reached the age of 12 were enrolled. The elected representative of the tithing was the tithing-man, and he was responsible for presenting to the Manor Court all misdemeanours committed by members of the families within his tithing.

One of the early records of Views of Frankpledge in the Guestling Hundred is from the 17th year of the reign of Richard II in 1392. The jurors were Robert Zellyngh, John Lydham, John Waryn, Robert Tornour, William Norton, Henry Steuene, John Neplysham, Thomas Gybbe, Thomas Grofherst, William Hykke, John Asshe, Thomas Watte and Thomas Smyth. For Pette, 'Henry Taylour, tithingman presents the default of John Baker, 3d, Gervase Fyne, 2d, Thomas Honhom, 3d, therefore in mercy. Item John Bakere, 2d, Thomas Henhom, 20d, because they have brewed and have broken the assize, therefore in mercy. Item that their watch is not kept, therefore in mercy, 6d. And the whole tithing, for concealment, 2d. (Amercements 3s 8d) Sum (total) 19s 3d, wherefore 12d belongs to the Abbot of Fescamp. Approved.' Note: in mercy meant a punishment imposed by the Court – usually a fine.

Other items from records of that court include: For Fairlight: 'Robert Alard broke the arrest of the constable, therefore in mercy, 3d. And Randulf atte Holte, because he was seen in Court to be rebellious at coming to the meeting, in mercy, 4d.' For Guestling: 'John Huchon unjustly raised the hue upon William Saylham, therefore in mercy, 3d. That the bridge at Pykhamemell is noxious by default of the whole tithing, therefore in mercy, 6d.' For Icklesham: 'That the highway in le Parkstrete is noxious by default of the Lord of Iklysham, therefore in mercy, 12d.' Spellings of names and places vary considerably and sometimes the name of a person may be spelt in more than one form in the same set of records.

The earliest record of a church in Pett appears in the taxation by Pope Nicholas of 1291, when the value of the tithe was £1 6s 8d and it was noted that the marsh was 'submerged by sea'. At the time when the first church was built, sometime in the late 13th century in the reign of Edward I, Pett was not an easy place to live in. Life was hard. Food had to be coaxed from the land, violence was never very far away and even the weather made life difficult. Events that must have affected Pett at this time surely include the terrible storms that swept along this part of the south coast. In October 1250 old Winchelsea was partly submerged by a phenomenal high tide and in 1287 the town was virtually destroyed by the greatest storm this part of England has ever witnessed. Most of the Romney Marsh was flooded and the course of the River Rother changed. It must have been a dreadful time and the tempests changed the nature and shape of the coast. King Edward I helped to plan and build a new Winchelsea on a hill, which at that time was nearly surrounded by sea. The new town was to be a port, well above all danger from high tides and linked to Pett by the narrow neck of land that was an ancient coastal road to Hastings; part is still used as Pannel Lane. The rebuilding of Winchelsea could have involved some of the men of Pett, few though they may have been. It is certain that talk of the storms and the building of the new town took place around the fires of the local dwellings here.

The first church in the small village may well have been a wooden building, as there were so few people here. There is no record of that first church, though Robert de Hastings is listed as being the priest in 1285. The area served by the church was not dissimilar to that enclosed by the pre-1894 boundaries. The parish priest reigned within the walls of his church and there he said Mass, attended on Sundays and Holy days by the majority of the villagers. It was the heart of medieval religion. The peasant as he stood or knelt on the earthen floor, each Sunday, could not follow the Latin words of the service but could well understand the fear of hell that was exploited by the priests of the time, both to enrich the Church and to call sinners to repentance. The people would hear the familiar but mysterious sounds of the Mass and might know some of the stories about God and his Son. It was a time of faith by fear.

By 1291 many of the woodland areas had been cleared and crops suited to the local soil planted. Manors in this region grew oats as well as some wheat, barley and rye. Large flocks of sheep were kept on the Winchelsea marshes, though the main livestock on the hill smallholdings was cattle. Sheep were only kept where there was access to pasture in the river valleys or marshland. Deer were kept in some parks, the nearest to Pett being at Beauport. Rabbit warrens were managed and provided food and fur for landowners and their tenants.

At this time most farmsteads and cottages were built of logs or planks, or of uprights and beams supporting rubble and clay. The floors were usually bare trampled earth, and the roof thatch. People's bread and ale depended on the uncertain harvest and in bad seasons there were local shortages of food – almost famine. Meat, cheese and vegetables made up an important part of their diet and many folk kept poultry and ate the eggs. If you were well off you might have a cow or a pig, and bacon was a common dish in the villages in the 'good times'.

In the fourteenth century many things happened that touched the people in the whole area. Winchelsea, which had been growing in prosperity, had 15 ships of between 83 and 190 tons involved in the wine trade with Bordeaux. It is highly likely that men of Pett and Pett Level were associated with this or with the fishing industry along the coast. It was also at this time that smuggling began to be recorded after Edward I introduced the customs system. The inhabitants of the Cinque Ports had acquired the reputation of being the most infamous of all European pirates, killing and looting as much as they pleased. There was a warrant from 1301 to search for wool, hides, bales and other merchandise that had been pirated. Timber and dairy products were among the goods exported from the port of Winchelsea and no doubt some were supplied from this area. Then came famine, the outbreak of the Black Death and the Hundred Years War (1337–1453).

In 1315 England suffered a great famine, which resulted from a second dreadful harvest. In 1320 the Black Death first struck the area and raged across the kingdom between 1348 and 1350. It is said to have claimed the lives of about half the population engaged in agriculture. How this affected the few folk of Pett we do not know, but it must have been a terrible time for all who lived hereabouts. The Black Death seems to have cleared Winchelsea by 1350 when the Battle of Winchelsea, also known as the Battle of L'espagnol sur Mer and fought off the shore at Winchelsea, could be seen from the hills above the coast. This was a victory for the English and more than half the Spanish ships were captured. The Black Prince took part in this fight and the excitement among the local people must have been great.

Raids by the French started in 1337. Winchelsea suffered a severe raid in 1359 and another in 1360. In 1377 Rye was burnt to the ground, but Winchelsea was saved as a result of the defence set up by the Abbot of Battle. He and his men defended Winchelsea and its surrounds so well that when the attackers arrived and found such formidable opposition, they retreated to Rye and set fire to that town. Between 1337 and 1380 the fires in Winchelsea would have been seen from Pett and the people living here would have been very much afraid.

The men of Rye and Winchelsea retaliated with a raid to France, during which they got back the church bells carried away by the French in 1377. Many Channel ports were subjected to disastrous raids by the French during this period, and Hastings, Winchelsea and Rye, among other places along the south coast, were attacked many times and were seriously damaged. Mind you, the English ships raided the coast of France too during these savage years. It was a time of much violence and bloodshed.

Pett at the time of the Hundred Years War was still little more than a hamlet. It now had its church and there were landowners in the village whose names are recorded as Non-Resident Barons (of the Cinque Ports) and whose lands were exempt from tax contribution in 1343. They include such fine names as: Agatha Robynhood, Thomas Thonder, Richard Herde, John Jakeman, Agatha Clyveserve, Robert Clerk and John Crouhurst. In the Nonae of 1340 taxes granted by Parliament to King Edward III were ascertained by commissioners to be a ninth; namely the ninth lamb, the ninth fleece and the ninth sheaf. The ninth in 1340 was accepted as being the equivalent to the tenth in 1292 and for Pett amounted to £1 11s 0d.

There are some interesting records from this period in the 'Feet of Fines'. The Feet of Fines comes from the Latin *finis* meaning 'conclusion' and in this context was a formal conveyance of land, the practice dating from the reign of Henry II (1154–89). Each party received a copy of the agreement and a third copy was filed by the Treasury. Two such conveyances are:

1 Edward III (1327) *(i.e. the first year of Edward III's reign)* 'Stephen Alard of Winchelse v Sampson de Stonlynk and Denise his wife: 13 acres in Pette by Winchelse: to Stephen for 20 marks.'

18 Edward III (1345) 'John Hughes of Promhille and Isabel his wife v William Joseph of Pette and Helewise his wife: a messuage, 10 acres of land, 4s rent in

Pette: to John and Isabel and heirs of their bodies to hold by render of a rose at midsummer, contingent reversion to William and Helewise and heirs of William.' What a lovely way to seal a transfer of property and build up a friendship.

Some of the names of Pett landowners and tenants who appear in the Sussex Subsidy Rolls for the period around 1330 include: Rico Gylot, Willo ate Ok, Roger Coleman, Relicta Rogi de Pette, Bartholemew ate Carte, Alano de Ferne, Agnes Godeloue, William de Redwyssh, Jake Coleman and Stacio Brounyng. Most of these names would not be recognised in the village today, but these are a few of the people who began to build up the village life here and who most likely worshipped in Pett's first church.

One of the early Rectors, William Baron, must have had lands nearby as he is recorded as receiving 'a messuage of land, 6 acres of meadow, 7 acres of wood in Westfield, Buxle and Halyton' from Reynold de Regge and his wife Joan for 20 marks. William Baron was Rector in 1365 (see Table 1 in the Appendix), though he probably came to the village just to conduct the occasional service.

Though Pett was only a small village at the time of the Hundred Years War, it is possible that some of its inhabitants were woodcutters who supplied the oak beams to shipyards from Rye to Chichester. These beams were cut from the oaks felled from the remains of the forests that covered much of Sussex in the early centuries. Some people may have been involved with the iron industry that had undergone a revival in Sussex, but most would have been working the land. As Winchelsea declined as a port from the end of the 14th century, resulting from the silting up of the land around the town, so the town became less important; trade dwindled as the sea withdrew. We can only guess how this affected Pett.

In the rolls of Parliament for the 13th year of Henry IV (1412), it is recorded that the House of Commons granted to the King a subsidy or tax. In this area, 'William, Lord de Echynghame, had manors and lands worth yearly, £58 13s 4d made up from: manor of Echynghame £30, manor of Edmere £10, manor of Pette £8 13s 4d, manor of Pekedene £10'. Lord Echynghame would have paid tax on all this except any lands tithes that were paid to the clergy. Then in 1427 the Corporation of Winchelsea collected a levy of one penny on each hundred pounds of corn purchased in or outside the town. The rate was fixed and roads were so bad that no horse could be expected to carry a greater amount. This would have affected the farmers at Pett and caused considerable consternation.

In 1439 there were two Rectors and it would be interesting to know why one of them resigned. Could it be because the village was too small and scattered, and that the tithes paid to the clergy were too meagre? The vacancy occurred due to the resignation of James Chestre. William Halle of Ore was the patron and held the advowson. It was he who chose William Russell as the next Rector, whose induction was carried out by the Archdeacon of Lewes (Lewis Coychurch) on 30th April. Five years later William Russell was replaced by Walter Nicholl (6th April 1444).

A 'tithe' was a tax of one tenth. Specifically, a tithe was a tenth part of the annual produce of land or labour, levied in a parish to support its priest, to maintain the fabric of the church and to provide for the relief of the poor. Payment was compulsory and could be enforced by both the civil and ecclesiastical authorities. Various acts of parliament changed the nature of tithes over the centuries but they were not completely eliminated until the Tithe Act of 1936. Many people objected to the payment of tithes, either in cash or kind; however it was often necessary because the income received by many parish priests was inadequate and was the cause of considerable poverty and hardship. This frequently led to a priest augmenting his pittance by cultivating his own crops in addition to the produce of his glebe – land set aside for the maintenance of the parish priest. There is an old rhyme that sums up many folk 's feelings about tithes:

> We've cheated the parson
> And we'll cheat him again,
> For why should the vicar
> Have one in ten?

More records from around the mid-15th century show that the Guestling Hundred 'Views of Frankpledge' were still dealing with the same type of misdemeanours as half a century earlier. For Pett, in the last day of March in the 25th year of the reign of King Henry VI (1446): 'Thomas White, tithingman, presents the default (absence) of Nicholas Stokker, 2d, and John Moger, 2d, from their view. Therefore they are in mercy.' 'And that Robert Farnham has brewed twice, 4d, and has broken the assize. And that Nicholas Stokkere unjustly took from the goods of Robert Farnham one pair of "Trays" value 1d, against the peace. Therefore in mercy, 4d. And that Thomas Goldhord has brewed and has broken the assize. Therefore in mercy, 4d. And a "mast"and 2 pieces of timber which came from a wreck of the sea *(prouen' de Wrakko maris)* are in the custody of Robert Taillour. (Wreck of the sea 6s 8d)'. There are equally long lists for the other three villages, Fairlight, Guestling and Icklesham.

In the Hundred Court of 1447, 'Nicholas Stokkere has unjustly detained 1 "mattock" found by him, after proclamation had been made thereupon. Whereupon the 12 Jurors say that he is not guilty therein. Therefore the whole tithing except the 12

Jurors are in mercy, 6d.' Later, in 1462, on 8 April in the second year of the reign of King Edward IV, 'Thomas White head tithingman and ale tester there (Pytte), sworn, with his whole tithing, presents that John Roo, 3d is a common huckster of ale and has broken the assize. And that the King's way over against the tenement formerly Colmanez is noxious through default in cleansing the ditches of John Ichynton. And he has a day before the feast of the Nativity of St John the Baptist to well and sufficiently amend it, etc. under penalty of 40d etc. (amercements 3d penalty).'

These courts dealt with all kinds of offences, and some of the record entries around this time make interesting reading. For example: Icklesham – 'And the 12 (jurors) say that Alice Taillour is a common "scobe" and uses "sorserie" against the form of the statute, 4d. And Joan Danyell, wife of Thomas Danyell conspired with the same Alice to carry out certain magic arts against Babilon Grauntsort, to the hurt of his body. Therefore she is in mercy, 12d.' Guestling – 'And John Podelonde is a miller and takes excessive toll, 6d. And the highway between Dolhambregge and Haltonthorn is noxious by default of the whole tithing, 6d. And that John Wyterhese made an assault on William Morys against the peace, 2d. And that William Morys made an assault on John Wyterhese against the peace, 2d.' (I wonder what caused the row that led to the fight?)

Local justice in the Hundred worked and the well-being of the people in the community was very important. Village life was well ordered in the 15th century.

3

The 15th and 16th Centuries

Though village life was well ordered in the 15th century, there was much turmoil across the country. In 1450 the rebellion led by Jack Cade was one of the most serious uprisings to take place in England between the Norman Conquest and the Civil War. Unlike Wat Tyler's Peasants' Revolt some 70 years earlier, the rebels included members of all social classes. In 1449 Rouen fell to the French and only Calais was left in English hands. The French lost no time in increasing their raids upon the Kent and Sussex coasts and in attacking the English herring fleets. There was great unrest in Sussex and murder, rape, robberies and burnings pervaded the county and beyond. The whole country was discontent with a king and authorities who were unable or unwilling to enforce the law and protect their people, and angry at the widespread corruption in the government. Jack Cade, who falsely claimed descent from the powerful Mortimer family, raised an army of insurgents dissatisfied with the political situation and living conditions.

Trouble began in July when, during religious gatherings in Kent, Sheriff Cromer threatened to lay waste the whole county as punishment for the murder of Henry VI's long-time servant, the Duke of Suffolk, William de Pole, whose headless body was found on Dover beach. Unrest soon became a full-scale rebellion and thousands of armed men marched on London to put their grievances to King Henry VI. He responded by sending troops to crush the rebels.

In Sussex the rising was treated in much the same way as an authorised levy. In many of the Hundreds the constables called out the musters. Even though it was harvest time, many East Sussex parishes sent every able-bodied man. Guestling was one of those parishes and, as the Guestling Hundred was involved, it is certain that men from Pett were included among the rebels. The gentlemen of Sussex included the Abbot of Battle, Lunsfords and Oxenbridges.

Cade had James Fiennes, Lord Say and Sele, and William Cromer executed. At Whitechapel Cade ordered an old friend, Thomas Bayly, to be beheaded, because he feared his own masquerade as a Mortimer might be revealed and his identity made known. After his initial successes, Cade's headquarters were set up in Southwark and on

5th July the rebels were routed after a bloody battle on London Bridge with a joint force of citizens and the Tower of London garrison. On the following day 3,000 pardons were granted, among which were those for 18 squires, 74 self-appointed gentlemen, 500 yeomen and hundreds of tradesmen, brewers, innkeepers, butchers, tailors, sailors and agricultural workers. Cade was left with a small nucleus of loyal supporters and he fled. He was mortally wounded near Heathfield and tradition has it that he was caught and killed at Cade Street. His head was fixed upon London Bridge. What happened to the men of Guestling and Pett who were part of Cade's force is not known; they probably lay very low if they managed to escape back to the villages. Grim tales would have been told back in the Guestling Hundred after this most exciting and terrifying venture. And what did the rebellion achieve? It certainly had no immediate effect upon the lives of the people of Pett, who continued to struggle for a living.

The inside of the church at Pett would quite possibly have been brightly coloured during the last half of the 15th century. Churches at that time had brilliantly coloured wall paintings in which the glory of redemption was contrasted with the horrors of hell and eternal damnation. The mass was incomprehensible to most who attended it and wall paintings and sometimes play-acting were intended to instruct and to edify. There are no records of how the church in Pett looked then and we can only surmise that it was well supported as the village grew and spread. Throughout the Middle Ages the Church had occupied a very important place in society. Everyone belonged to the Church and recognised the right of the Church to control his or her life in both this world and the next. Everybody expected the Church to levy a tax on his income, and acknowledged its right to do so, even in those rural areas that disliked the tithing system. All people accepted the fact that if he or she were guilty of a breach of one of the Church's laws they would suffer the penalty, be it fine, imprisonment or even a flogging. Everyone looked to the Church to provide education, leadership, poor-relief, sick-nursing and all other social amenities. The Church was a very powerful force.

Things were now happening in the country that would alter life everywhere, though changes were slow to occur. In 1476 William Caxton set up his printing press in Westminster and in the next hundred years the printed book started to make its mark throughout the land. Henry Tudor defeated Richard III at the Battle of Bosworth Field in 1485 and so began the House of Tudor.

Transcripts of Sussex wills at the end of the 15th and beginning of the 16th centuries reveal some fascinating aspects of the relationship between local people and the church at Pett. In the 1400s both Amicia and William Halle of Ore bequeathed money to the church (William Halle was the patron). In 1523 Thomas Ashburnham bequeathed to the church of Pett 5s 7d, and Richard Cheeseman 2s 3d. Robert Crowche of Rye gave 5s 7d to the church for general repairs in 1497 and Denis Ive of Guestling gave the same in 1509, while John Tayler gave 2s 7d 'towards the reparacions of the sayd church of Pett' and also gave 2s 3d towards the repair of the church at Icklesham. Between 1540 and 1550 Thomas Bakeholder, Richard Cheesman, Elizabeth Firlow, John Jones and John Teyler mentioned in their wills that they wished to be buried in Pett churchyard, though there are no church records as early as this that could verify whether or not these burials took place. In 1545 Thomas Edwards of St Giles, Winchelsea, bequeathed 'one torche, price 5s 7d to the church of Pett'. Thomas Bakeholder willed 1s 'to the poore mens boxe' in 1548 and in 1551 John Jones stated 'I will to the poore mens chest 2s 3d'. John Jones went on to state, 'I will for two sermons to be preached within the Parishe churche of Pett within 11 months next 5s 7d and I will that either Mr Thomas Rose or Mr John Madewell preache theym yf they come into these parties within that space.' William Lonsforde (Lunsford) was a wealthy landowner and was generous in his will, which states:

> I wyll and gyve to the mendyne of the hye waye between Wyckham gate and Pannell brygge 10s wher need ys as is aforesayed . . . I wyll to be bestoyed at my buryenge to the poore and other charitable works 10s at the dyscrecon of my executors. And lyke manner at my monthes mynde to bestoyed 10s. And at my yeres mynd in lyke manner to bestoyed 10s. Item I give to 4 men that shall bere me to church 6d a pece. Item I gyve and beqweth to everye one of my poore neybours beynge howsholders within the paryshe of Icklesham 12d a pece. Item I wyll and beqweth to 20 poore folks in Winchelsey by the dyscrecon of my executors 8d a pece. Item I gyve and beqweth to the poore people of Geslynge, Pett and Farleygh (*Fairlight*) to every paryshe 5s at the dyscrecon of my executors.

These wills give colour to the picture of how people lived in the rural society of the 16th century.

The priests at that time often witnessed wills, and records show that in 1543 'John Crowche, prest' witnessed the will of Richard Cheeseman; in 1545–1546 Sir John Foster witnessed Elizabeth Firlow's will; Mr Thomas Rose and Mr John Madewell witnessed that of John Jones in 1551; Sir Richard Daughty, parson, witnessed for John Teyler and Symon Suder 'Parsonne of Pett' for Nichlas Peccam of Arlington in 1559. Also in 1551 John Jones willed to Thomas Blackburne, Curate of Pett, five shillings.

One will, late in the reign of Henry VIII, dated 7th March 1545–1546 provides a real mystery about the dedication of Pett Church. In the will of Elizabeth Firlow, she states, 'My body to be buryed in the church yard of St Stevyn of Pett'. The authenticity of ancient church dedications can often be traced through the last wills of the parishioners. In this case 1545–1546 is the earliest date for which there is documentary evidence for a dedication of a church in Pett, even though it may well go back much earlier than that.

The Sussex Record Society gives the following dates of the earliest wills establishing the dedications:

Ore	St Ellen (Helen), 21st December 1421	
Guestling	St Lawrence, 12th February 1503–1504	
Icklesham	All Saints, 12th April 1497	
Rye	St Mary, 1473–1474	
Winchelsea	St Thomas the Martyr, 1397–1398	
	St Giles, 1471	These two churches
	St Leonard, 1451	have now disappeared.
Pett	St Stephen, 7th March 1545–1546	

So what should the true dedication of Pett Church be? Should it be St Stephen? Could Elizabeth Firlow have been mistaken? There was no other church at Pett. When did the dedication to St Mary and St Peter first occur? The parish records begin in 1675 and earlier entries (1606–1674) for Baptisms, Weddings and Burials are taken from Bishops' Transcripts; in these the dedication is to St Mary and St Peter. Many dedications were changed in the Middle Ages and it is possible that the dedication of the church at Pett was changed at the time of the Reformation. The mystery remains with us until more documentary evidence turns up. There is only one other church in the Diocese of Chichester dedicated to St Mary and St Peter and that is at Wilmington. There are, however, two churches dedicated to St Peter and St Mary – at Fishbourne and at Southwick.

When Henry VIII became king (1509) England was still a Roman Catholic country and the Pope in Rome ruled the Church. Then came the Reformation. This was not a natural fulfilment of what had gone on before but was rather an act of state. Reform was precipitated by papal procrastination concerning the divorce between Henry and Catherine of Aragon. Henry repudiated Papal authority in England and, in a series of Acts of Parliament, severed links with Rome. In 1531 Royal Supremacy was imposed on the clergy by King Henry VIII; many suffered death for refusing to acknowledge it. The Act of Supremacy of 1534 led to the birth of the Church of England. Miles Coverdale produced the first complete English Bible for the King and in 1541 a royal proclamation was made ordering that the Bible, in English, should be in all parish churches. However, because of arguments about translation and politics associated with it, the Bible did not appear in most churches at that time.

The Catholic Church was not very popular in much of England and a survey carried out in 1535 showed that many priests were rich and lazy. Henry now set about getting rid of, or 'dissolving', the monasteries. Stones were taken from many abbeys and monasteries and used to build houses. Whole libraries of books were burnt. By 1547, the year of the King's death, the Reformation was well under way. Traditional ceremonies of the medieval church were abolished and an order made to remove all images from 'wall and window'. This resulted in the lime-washing of wall-paintings, the destruction of religious statues and the smashing of windows. It was in Edward VI's short reign that doctrinal Protestantism became official policy. In 1549 and in 1552 the Acts of Uniformity require that the Book of Common Prayer should be used in Anglican worship. The death of Edward VI in his sixteenth year was a great blow to the reformers and Queen Mary's policy was to undo all that had been done by her father and brother and restore the Church in England to communion with Rome. Between 1553 and 1558 the restoration of the Roman Catholic form of worship resulted in fierce persecutions of the Protestants by Queen Mary. Many priests in Sussex were replaced and 41 Protestants in the county were burnt at the stake; the nearest to Pett being in the parish of Mayfield, though there was a Protestant martyr in both the parishes of Catsfield and Rye. In Pett, during the reign of Queen Mary, there were two Rectors, Richard Dounton and Simon Suder. Richard Dounton became Rector in 1554 and may have been a deliberate replacement for Thomas Stunt, who preceded him.

How much of this religious turmoil affected Pett is not known. People here still continued to follow the seasons. Men and women worked the land and the local salt-pans, kept livestock and lived their lives much as they had before the Reformation. Gradually things would change: a new Queen ruled England and her name was Elizabeth.

Some of the names that are associated with Pett around this time are recorded in the Subsidy Rolls as paying tax. They include Richard Barton, Robert Beale, Robert Hall, Humffry Adams, George Homan, John Lewes, Anne Wetheris, John Mershe, Robert Weller, Thomas Reve and others; alas, the families with these names do not appear in today's civil Electoral Roll. Elms farm and Carter's farm were now established in the village and parts of the farmhouses were built in the 1500s. Common houses and cottages were still made of timber, or of 'half timber' with clay and rubble between the wooden uprights and crossbeams. Stone was used in the better houses and brick was gradually being introduced. The stone and timber church in Pett would have been the most important building in the village.

Over the last two hundred years the harbour at Winchelsea had started to silt up. By 1561 there were no ships at Winchelsea and the silting worsened. In the first thirty years of the 16th century the commercial centre of the town was almost non-existent. Many people moved away from the town and by 1575 there were only 60 houses inhabited. Rye began to prosper at the expense of Winchelsea, as it was not affected by silting. It was not a very happy time in this part of Sussex.

By the time Queen Elizabeth I (1558–1603) came to the throne, the whole county was in a most unhappy state. Tyranny and brutality at home combined with an unpopular foreign policy had bred much dissatisfaction. Ecclesiastically the country was divided into three groups. First, there were those who had supported Mary in the return to Rome, and who were now in power; the parochial clergy who had not been turned out were all pro-Roman. Second, among those who had been deprived of the 'living' was the nucleus of the Protestant party and, finally, between the two groups was a middle party that was the Church of England, truly catholic in all essentials but cleansed from the abuses that had gathered around it during the Middle Ages. Church life was at a very low ebb in the early part of Queen Elizabeth's reign but began to improve steadily as time went on. Churches were restored and refurnished. Services were more reverently said and the clergy showed increasing signs of responsibility and conscientiousness. At the beginning of the reign there were many vacant benefices and for some time pluralism continued as before. Some parishes were entrusted to the care of ill-paid and ill-educated stipendiary priests.

Normally the priest would conduct Morning or Evening Prayer from a seat in the nave and was ordered to say the offices without mumbling. The clergy were encouraged to preach, if licensed to do so, otherwise to read one of the Homilies that were available in 1562. The Eucharist was celebrated, usually at the end of Morning Prayer: in places like Pett this occurred about four times a year at major feasts. Bells were to be rung regularly, so towers had to be added to many village church buildings.

We know nothing about the first two Rectors during the reign of Queen Elizabeth. William Garret was Rector in 1560, but an Elizabethan return on the state of the Diocese of Chichester dated 1563 shows 'The parish of Pett havinge neither parson or curat'. However, this was rectified in 1569 or 1570 when Richard Gowge was inducted. (See Table 1 in the Appendix for a complete list of Rectors.)

An exciting event that must have caused much joy and anticipation in the area was the visit of Queen Elizabeth I to Winchelsea in 1573. As the news of the impending visit spread round the villages, most would have made an attempt to see 'their Queen' as she made her way through Northiam to Winchelsea. The cheers could have been 'heard in London'; even though the town of Winchelsea was declining, it was not every day that the monarch visited a town in Sussex.

One effect of the Reformation was to turn the parish into a unit of local government and it heaped upon the incumbent and churchwardens a whole range of new secular responsibilities. The churchwardens had the greatest burden to deal with. In addition to their traditional responsibilities for the maintenance of the parish church, its services and the enforcement of ecclesiastical law, they were now men of considerable authority in the parish. They were accountable for the Parish Constable; supervision of the education and relief of the poor, the sick and the needy; maintenance of public buildings, fences and boundaries; the removal of vagrants; the extermination of vermin and much more. The churchwardens also represented the views of the parishioners in parochial matters and were responsible for encouraging church attendance and ensuring that the young were baptised. At the annual audit, the churchwardens took possession of property left to the parish in the previous year, received contributions from the people, each according to his occupation, and arranged for the distribution of surplus goods to those believed to be in greatest need. Churchwardens were expected to be rigorous in upholding the standards of behaviour, and parishioners who transgressed and were guilty of moral crimes were reported to the Archdeacon's Court. It was not until 1571, well into Queen Elizabeth I's reign, that the churchwardens were required to 'set up' the 'Bishop's Bible' in their churches. However, it was later that King James I ordered a new translation and in 1611 the 'Authorised Version' or 'King James Bible' became the familiar form for people in churches across the land for the next 350 years.

In June 1581 Thomas Mawdesley was granted a faculty from Edmund Grindal, Archbishop of Canterbury, to hold the rectory of Iden with that of Pett in plurality. Mawdesley was chaplain to Viscount Montague (patron of Iden) and was allowed to be Rector of both parishes, 'being not more than 20 miles (apart), provided that in each parish 13 sermons a year are preached and residence is kept for two months in the parish of non-residence'. An extract from a Liber Detectorum, which illustrates the state of East Sussex churches in 1586 and 1587, has the following entry for Pett: 'There are no sentences of holie scripture written upon the walles of the churche. Item, There lacketh the table of the ten commandments'. This shows that Pett church was fairly insignificant and there was little money to spend upon things such as these.

In 1588 the mighty Spanish Armada was smashed by the English ships led by such men as Lord Howard of Effingham, John Hawkins, Martin Frobisher and, of course,

Sir Francis Drake. The sounds of the battles and the sight of fire ships being sent among closely packed Spanish ships in the English Channel must have been heard and seen by many along the coast from the Isle of Wight to Dover and beyond. Beacons would have been lit on the hills above the coast and those at Fairlight and Hastings would have been kept alight by local folk. The defeat of the Armada would have resulted in the church bells being rung in every village and much ale being consumed. Every parish, including Pett, would have celebrated such a glorious victory.

Thomas Mawdesley was Rector when Joan Brecher of Pett was, in 1597, whipped at the cart tail, half naked, for petty larceny. He was also Rector in 1603 when an ecclesiastical return for 81 parishes in East Sussex was made to John Whitgift, Archbishop of Canterbury, via Anthony Watson, Bishop of Chichester. This document was drawn up in the first years of the reign of King James VI of Scotland, now King James I of England, and two years before the Gunpowder Plot that is still vividly remembered and celebrated throughout the land.

Mawdesley answers questions put to him and each reply concerns both his livings.

1. Communicants: Iden, about 120   Pett, about 70
2. (Popish) recusants: Iden 9   Pett nil
   (*N.B. recusant – a person who refuses to attend Church of England services*)
3. All of these people actually receive the Holy Communion, except the nine recusants quoted.
4. His two benefices are each with cure (of souls). He is a Master of Arts, and qualified to hold two livings by the late Lord Montague (this implies that he had been chaplain to that person who lived at Battle Abbey), with confirmation under the Broad Seal. Iden and Pett are given as five miles apart, but this is an understatement. The King's Books value Iden parsonage at £18 and Pett at about £4 18s per annum.
5. & 6. These questions 'concern him not'.
7. The patron of Iden is 'L. Vicount Montague'. This clearly refers to the son of the Lord Montague previously mentioned. Note that there is no 's' in Viscount, showing that the word was pronounced in 1603 as it is today. Pett has for its patron James Thatcher, esquire.
   (*Note: See Table 2 in the Appendix for a list of Patrons and those who held the Advowson*)

Thomas Mawdesley, Rector of Iden and Pett, was instituted in Iden in 1576 and in Pett in June 1581. He was presented by George Courthope, by virtue of a lease to him of the advowson for 21 years from James Thatcher, of Priesthawes. Mawdesley was described in 1600 as aged 50. A reference in one of the volumes of the Sussex Archaeological Society states that he was buried at Pett on October 18th 1615. There is no record of this in the parish records as they do not start until 1675, nor is the burial recorded in Bishops' Transcripts, which commence in 1606. It does seem surprising that a Rector of 34 years at Pett is not mentioned in these records as being buried in the village churchyard.

By the end of Queen Elizabeth's reign the pulpit had become a feature in the nave of all churches, though seats in a church had not become commonplace and Pett would not have had any at all. People stood or knelt during the Sunday service. The Creed, the Lord's Prayer and the Ten Commandments had replaced the wall paintings in many churches and the communion table was moved from the east end of the church, where it normally resided, to the centre of the church for the occasional Eucharist. Metrical versions of the Psalms were now being sung and the church was still the religious, social and cultural centre of the village community. Pett being a poor place had no 'Holy' sentences on the walls, even though the church provided the main focus for village life.

4

The 17th Century

The 17th century very nearly began with a big bang. Shakespeare wrote *Twelfth Night* in 1601 and *Hamlet* in 1603, the year the great Queen Elizabeth I died. Then King James 1 became monarch and disappointed the Puritans by failing to resolve religious conflicts. This led to the Catholics' plan to destroy the King and Parliament and of course to the Gunpowder Plot (1605), which, if it had been successful, would have changed history. Gradually things settled down.

During the first 15 years of the new century Thomas Mawdesley was still Rector of Pett, as we have seen. However, it is debatable how much time he actually spent in the village. If we examine the Bishops' Transcripts of the Baptism Registers from 1605 to 1754, we can see exactly how plurality affected Pett (see Table 3 in the Appendix). With few exceptions the named rector had a curate, probably poorly paid, who took the services in the village. These would have included Matins, weddings and funerals, as well as the baptisms from which these records are taken. It is fortunate that these show the names of the churchwardens of the time, some of whom could not write their name. They were men of power in the village and these were the men who devoted much of their lives to the church in Pett and kept it alive.

Griffin Flud was curate during Mawdesley's incumbency and lived in the village. In 1615 he became Rector, though in the baptism record of his son Edward in 1617 he is noted as being the 'parson of Pett'. In 1622 a daughter Elizabeth was baptised and in the burial record of 1623 it stated that on 6th January 'Mr Griphin Flud' was buried at Pett. Griffin Flud's name is spelt in different ways in various documents associated with him. He himself signs as Griffin Flud in a very flowery signature on a hand-written document of 1615. The document is in connection with a Glebe Terrier, which was an inventory of possessions, the size of the parsonage, profits and endowments associated with a benefice. It was first required in 1571 and thereafter compiled periodically in each diocese. The document is a declaration on parchment and states:

We the Minister and Churchwardens of the parish of Pett in Sussex do signify unto who it shall concern that we know of no Terrier of the parsonage and house and Glebe lands thereunto belonging in — aforesaid in any Bishops Register and therefore as followeth unto this fourteenth Articles concerning Church possessions and thus certify and inform.

Pett

We have a parsonage house and Barn with nine acres of land thereunto belonging, pastures and arable ground. One Close with two gardens joyning unto the parsonage – as for Outhouses Stocks* Implements Tenements and know none thereunto belonging or any profits but only all Tythes of the parish paid thereunto.

George Wright – Churchwarden George Swane – Churchwarden

Griffin Flud – Minister

(*Note: * Stocks – term applied to wool, flax, hemp, wood, thread, iron and other necessary ware and materials to set the poor to work provided by the overseers and churchwardens at the expense of the parish.*)

This parchment is the oldest handwritten document that exists in English giving a small glimpse into the history of the Pett Parish Church and looks as if it has actually been written by the Rector. What pressure was put on him to write it and what help he had in doing so we can but guess. What we do know is that, small though Pett was, the village was important enough to require information to be passed on to the Bishop of Chichester through the Archdeacon of Lewes. By early 1620 Pett church was said to be 'somewhat ruinous' and it was little better for the next hundred years.

The greatness of Sussex in the Elizabethan era, and even the greatness of the country in general, depended to a large extent on iron. Had not our ordnance kept pace with the foundries of Spain, we should probably have become a vassal state. Michael Drayton (1563–1631) wrote a long poetic topography of England, which he completed in 1622. In it Drayton laments the iron-makers' ruination of the woodlands, which included many in Sussex – some not so far from Pett. In his poem *Polyolbion* Drayton writes:

> There iron times breed none that mind posterity.
> Tis but in vain to tell what we before have been,
> Or changes of the world that we in time have seen;
> When, now devising how to spend our wealth with waste,
> We to the savage swine let fall our larding mast,
> But now, alas! ourselves we have not to sustain,
> Nor can our tops to shield our roots from rain.
> Jove's oak, the warlike ash, veined elm, the softer beech,

Short hazel, and smooth birch, supplies the forger's turn,
When under public good, base private gain takes hold,
And we, poor woods, to ruin lastly sold.

The remains of hammer ponds can still be found in Pett, and charcoal for the furnaces of forges would have been made from timber felled from local woodlands as they were cleared for increasing the amount of arable and grazing land.

Peter Theobald followed Griffin Flud as Rector and his name first appears as signing the Baptism records of 1622. He was Rector right up to the Civil War (1642) and he too must have lived in the village. He and his wife Ann had two daughters baptised in the church, Anne in 1624 and Eleanor in 1628. There were two other Theobalds in the village in the first part of the 17th century, Samuel and his brother George. The Rector was officially associated with these folk in the following manner. Peter baptised three of Samuel's daughters, buried his first wife Mildred and sponsored Samuel's second marriage, by licence, to Alice Relf of 'Maighfield' – a widow. In the Calendar of Sussex marriage licences recorded in the Consistory Court of the Bishop of Chichester for the Archdeaconry of Lewes there are more than 25 occasions when licences to marry were granted to people of Pett. Samuel's second marriage did not take place in Pett. Peter's relationship with George is uncertain; they may have been brothers. George must have been a fairly wealthy man because a brass in the church declares that he gave a bell 'to grace the new steeple'; we will learn more about this bell later. George died on the 10th March 1641 and was buried at Pett on the 13th March.

Charles I came to the throne in 1625 and life in Pett continued much the same as it did before. One interesting fact emerges a few years later about Peter Theobald. In the 'Contrebution of the Clergie within the diocese of Chichester towards the repairing of St Paule's Church in London' in 1634, 'Peter Theobalde, parson of Pett', is shown to have given '£00 06 08'. St Paul's Cathedral had suffered a severe fire in 1561 when the roof and spire were destroyed. The roof had been repaired, Queen Elizabeth I being a major benefactor, but extensive repairs to the spire did not begin until 1638 (*Note: This was the St Paul's before the great Fire of London and the Christopher Wren Cathedral*). It was on these repairs that the money from Chichester would have been used, together with that given from other dioceses. One wonders if any pressure was put upon the local clergy to make a donation of this sort to a church in London when many churches in this part of Sussex were in a great state of disrepair.

Under Charles I's authoritarian High-Church Archbishop Laud, altar rails were introduced and the communion table was now positioned in the east end of the chancel. Box pews were becoming common and Pett Church had such pews, some of which were allocated to the various local farmers. People were encouraged to make bequests to the church, though there are few of these recorded for Pett.

Records show that Thomas Springett, knight, died on 17 September 1640, in the 15th year of the reign of Charles I. His son and heir, Herbert Springett aged 24, inherited lands in: 'Sokehouse and Leadam alias Leydham Hill in Guestling and a mansion in Icklesham, half of Gatehurst and Carters in Pett and Fairleigh, etc. etc.' Both Gatehurst and Carters farms were well established as were Lunsford and Knight's farms. The village was an expanding community, though the state of the church at Pett left much to be desired. In 1641 the Churchwardens' Presentment says: 'There is nothing special' and goes on, 'there is noe scholmaster, physicians, & chyrurgians', and 'we have a Register duly kept'. The presentment bill is mutilated on one side and has a portion missing. It is signed by Thomas Crowherst (with an X) and William Boorder. Churchwardens' Presentments were handed over to the Archdeacon and his Registrar at the time of a visitation to the church. It is from these visitations that we can learn much about the church buildings and furnishings, and the village as it existed so many years ago. It was still a very small place with no doctor and no school.

On the bell in the steeple of the present church is an inscription that reads, 'Robert Foster gave XV(L) towards me, 1641'. There is a brass in the church, also dated 1641, which states that George Theobald gave a bell 'to grace the new steeple'. It may be that there were two bells in the church in 1641, but it is more likely that there was only one, as the steeple at that time was just like a pyramid on top of a small tower, and it is unlikely that there would have been room to house two bells in it. It is probable that Robert Foster, together with George Theobald paid for the new bell, or that Robert Foster's gift enabled the existing bell to be recast. There is no mention of George on the bell. Robert Foster, the son of another Robert, was born in 1620 and died in 1668.

In 1633 gangs of unemployed men roamed this part of East Sussex and the Poor Relief mounted sharply. Pett was still a dangerous place to live, and it has been said that in March 1642 not a single gentleman (apart from the clergy) was resident in the five marshland parishes of Pett, Icklesham, Iden, Playden and East Guldeford.

The Civil War arose from constitutional, economic and religious differences between Charles I and the Long Parliament that he summoned in 1640. The war started in 1642 and lasted almost ten years. It was the greatest domestic conflict in British history. Brother fought against brother, countryside and town were torn apart by divided loyalties, and the unthinkable happened when the king was executed by his people. There are no parish records between 1641 and 1666 (inclusive) or between 1669 and 1671. During the first of these periods the country was in turmoil. The Parliament troops were fighting against the King and the Church and there was much destruction of churches and church property. Stained glass windows were broken; church ornaments smashed, books torn up or burnt and vestments cut to pieces. Parliament forced Puritan incumbents on many parishes after 1648, a year in which the valuation of all property in Pett was £817 7s 4d. Fortunately for Pett, most military activity in Sussex was concentrated in the western side of the county, though there was fighting in Rye in 1648, when an attempt was made to seize the magazine of armaments and gunpowder.

King Charles I lost his head on 30th January 1649 and became as near to being canonized as it is possible to be in the Church of England; he stood as a symbol of the patient sufferer who lays down his life for his creed and his Church. After the restoration of the monarchy (1660), and from 1662 to 1858, the execution of King Charles I was commemorated in the calendar of the Prayer Book and special services were held each year on 30th January.

The new Prayer Book of 1662 was implemented, like its predecessors, as part of an Act of Uniformity. The Act required all clergy and schoolmasters to make a declaration that they believed it unlawful to take arms against the king, and that they would use the 1662 Prayer Book and no other. Some 2,000 clergy were removed from their livings for refusing to conform to the Act. The Church of England was restored and those who were not prepared to accept it had to go. John Easton (or Eston) received a dispensation from Charles II to hold the rectory of Pertenhall, Co. Bedford, with the rectory of Pett, and in 1662 'John Eason was ejected for non-conformity'. Though the spelling of the name varies there is no doubt that this priest was the John Eston who is recorded as being Rector in 1660.

In 1661 Zachary Cradock became Rector. He was born in 1633, had been a chaplain of King's College, Cambridge in 1650 and was also a celebrated preacher. He later became Prebendary of Chichester (and a Canon in 1669–1670), was a fellow of Eton College in 1671 and Chaplain in ordinary to King Charles II. He was acquainted with the diarist John Evelyn, died in 1695 and was buried in Eton College Chapel. Why did such an eminent man become Rector of such a small parish in rural Sussex? The Archbishop of Canterbury gave him dispensation for non-residence in Pett in 1669 and first Anselm Mathilry and then Thomas Brian acted as Cradock's curates in the parish during his incumbency.

Churchwardens' Presentments for the years 1674–1676 record that Zachary Cradock was Rector. In 1674 the Churchwardens report: 'Wee present our churchyard to be at present out of reparacions and some utensills are likewise wanting'. In 1675 they say, 'Wee present the fence of the churchyard as wanting reparacions: the steeple wanting two butterise to support it: bible wants new binding: surplice and a chest for the use of the parish'. Further needs were a carpet for the communion table and 'Our churchyard fence wants repayreing, which shall be done with all speed'. Nothing changed by 1676 when they present: 'The west end of our steeple wants a buttresse to support it. A new bible, or the old one bound. We want a surplice. We want a table-cloth for the communion table. We present our steeple to be out of repaire for want of 2 new buttresses, which we are taking care to have repayred'. In 1677 there is a blank space – perhaps they had given up! How difficult it must have been for Simon Sharuall (or Shervell), Lawrence Houghton, William Purfield and William Lunsford, who were all churchwardens around this time. The church was dilapidated, the Rector was rarely in the parish and, though all the inhabitants of Pett attended St Mary and St Peter's church regularly, they were not wealthy enough to pay the sums of money needed to carry out all the repairs and refurbishment necessary.

The Baptism, Marriage and Burial registers date from 1606 and give much information about the families living in and around Pett. We shall look at some of the details later as they help to colour in the picture depicting the social 'goings on' in a country village.

The ecclesiastical census of 1676, often called the Compton Census – after Henry Compton, Bishop of London, was carried out at the request of Archbishop Sheldon. Parish priests were required to return a census of parishioners, together with details of those who absented themselves from worship. These were the 'Dissenters', non-conformist members of Christian bodies that did not conform to the doctrines of the Church of England. Before the Act of Uniformity, dissenters or puritans were frequently persecuted. All those over the age of 16 were to be included in the 1676 returns, which vary considerably in their reliability. The return for the Guestling Hundred shows:

Parish	Conformists	Papists	Non-Conformists
Pett	49	–	–
Guestling	109	–	8
Fairlight (Furleigh)	65	5	–
Icklesham	84	–	–

In Pett, the difference between the number of conformists (49) in 1676 and the number of communicants (about 70) in 1603 could be accounted for by a reduction in the population in the village, or by the number of young people and children under the age of 16 that were not included in the Compton Census. It is probable that both sets of figures are approximate and that the under 16s were left out of the Pett return of

1676. One thing is certain: the village was still small and had not grown much – if at all – in seventy-odd years.

When Charles II was restored to the throne in 1660, part of the normal organisation and life of the Church of England was restored after the chaos of the Commonwealth years under Oliver Cromwell. However, there is a large body of evidence that shows that Sussex often moved more slowly than London and the Cathedral cities in changes to national and ecclesiastical affairs. Events too, like the Great Plague that devastated the population of London in 1665 and the Great Fire of London in the following year, had little effect in rural southern England. Things were so backward in Sussex that nearly 30 years after the Commonwealth some churches had not even a communion table or surplice (see the Churchwardens' Presentments of 1675). This was the situation when King James II came to the throne in 1685 and when John Lake was Bishop of Chichester. John Lake was a man of character and courage. He resisted the tyranny of James II and later refused to take the oath of allegiance to William and Mary. He was very active in the suppression of abuses in the Church and in 1686 sent inspectors to visit the churches in the diocese.

To put the situation at Pett in perspective, it is interesting to note the state of one or two other churches in the area. In Hastings, St Clement's, though in good structural repair, had 'its altar not railed in and not even in its proper place at the upper end of the chancel'. All Saints had its chancel 'out of repair, no altar rails, and two bells "crakt"'. All that was left of the great church at Winchelsea was two side aisles and, 'all the pavements much dilapidated, bells – all sold save one, hogs kept in the churchyard, parsonage house pulled down, no alms box, no Common Prayer Book, no surplice, no covering for the communion table – nor even a "linen cloth and napkin" for administrac(i)on of the most blessed Sacrament'.

And what about Pett? Obscurely situated under Fairlight Down and on a road that led to nowhere except the marshes at Cliff End; Pett, with its small church serving a few families – how did that fare? St Mary and St Peter Church was inspected by two local clergymen reporting to the Bishop. They were Mr Brian of Guestling and Mr Williams of Rye. No individual church sent in a report by its own incumbent, even though Thomas Brian had acted as Curate of Pett for over ten years. The report is quite short and reads:

At the parish Church of Pett. The Rector's chancel wants repaire viz: the windowes glaseing. The white limeing and the pavements mending. The Bells (want) new hanging. Carpet for ye Communion table, a poor box and chest, a book for stranger's names, the churchyard overgrown with bryers and bueshes.

There is a marginal note, 'Ye churchyard cleaned'. The 'book for stranger's names' was really a visiting book, intended to record the names of visiting preachers when any such appeared. It is obvious from the report that there were a number of windows broken or perhaps unglazed; this was fairly common and glass was expensive. The state of the churchyard has always been a problem and in the past a number were open to the wanderings of domestic animals, especially swine or sheep. Many church-yards were not enclosed by a wall at all, but by a wooden fence. Pett had a fence around its churchyard, which was much smaller in area than it is today, although it was not like the one at Dymchurch, in which the parson had erected a haystack and pas-tured his horse. Note that 'briars' had taken hold, and today they still require attention after hundreds of years. The chest was for church linen and the pavements would have been the tiles (or possibly flagstones) in the chancel. The report mentions that the bells want hanging, but we cannot be sure if there were one or more bells at that time.

One event that caused much excitement locally occurred soon after William of Orange and his wife Mary came to the throne. On 30th June 1690 a combined Anglo-Dutch fleet was soundly beaten by the French ten miles off Beachy Head. The English lost 350 men and eight ships. The *Anne*, a 70-gun ship of the line, was beached off Pett Level at the low-water mark on 3rd July having been seriously dam-aged in the battle. Captain John Tyrell wrote to the Admiralty, 'we have a 100 men killed and wounded. … our ship being so much battered God Almighty send us clear of our enemies'.

The French won the battle against the Anglo-Dutch fleet commanded by Lord Torrington. However, they were unsuccessful in helping the deposed King James II to recover his throne. The *Anne* had lost all her masts and, after it had been run ashore, Tyrell set fire to his ship to stop her becoming a French prize. He was later acquitted, at an inquiry, of any blame for losing his ship.

The warship *Anne* was 151 feet (46 metres) long and 40 feet (12 metres) wide; she had 70 guns ranging from demi-cannons (32 pounders) on the main deck to 3 pound-ers on the poop deck. She was a frigate (frigat) and a ship of the line. She had three masts with sails, a bowsprit with a sail and her figurehead was a lion. Many local peo-ple would have stood on the shore at Pett Level and stared at this tragic scene. The wreck of the *Anne* could be clearly seen and at low tides and in calm weather must have been a haven for the scavenging of artefacts and timber. I wonder how many houses in Pett have timber from the wreck of the Anne built into them?

5

The 18th Century

In 1702 Anne succeeded William III and soon became deeply concerned about the welfare of the clergy, many of whom were very poor. The old medieval dues of 'First Fruits and Tenths', which the Pope had always collected from the English clergy, had been annexed to the crown by Henry VIII and converted into a fixed tax. Anne, moved by two of the Bishops, Burnett and Sharp, gave this money in 1704 to form a fund known as 'Queen Anne's Bounty' from which the stipends of the poorer clergy might be augmented. It was not until 1948 that the Queen Anne's Bounty was amalgamated with the Ecclesiastical Commissioners to form the Church Commissioners for England.

As each Bishop was required to spend more than half the year in London, the administration of the dioceses had to be left largely to the archdeacons. Roads were bad and dangerous, means of travel slow and distances great, so places like Pett rarely saw their Bishop and Confirmations in the 18th century were done on a large scale. There were no suffragan bishops in those days, so it was customary to collect vast crowds on the day of the Confirmation from churches over one or more deaneries. It was almost an excuse for a holiday and many parishes turned the event into a party with much feasting and dancing. Life in the small parish church had not changed much and pluralism, non-residence (as we have seen), nepotism and sinecures all flourished, with disastrous results for the spiritual life of the Church. Because more than half the incumbents of English parishes in the 18th century were absentees, curates had to be employed to do the work. Many were poorly rewarded: £30–40 a year was considered to be good pay. In a country church like St Mary and St Peter in Pett a morning service took place on most Sundays. Holy Communion was usually celebrated quarterly at Christmas, Easter, Whitsuntide and Michaelmas. There was no organ in the church, but the singing of hymns had begun to be introduced, probably accompanied by some instrumentalist or 'musicker'. The sermon played an important part of the service and an hourglass was often prominent on the pulpit. There is no record, however, of an hourglass on Pett's old three-tier pulpit.

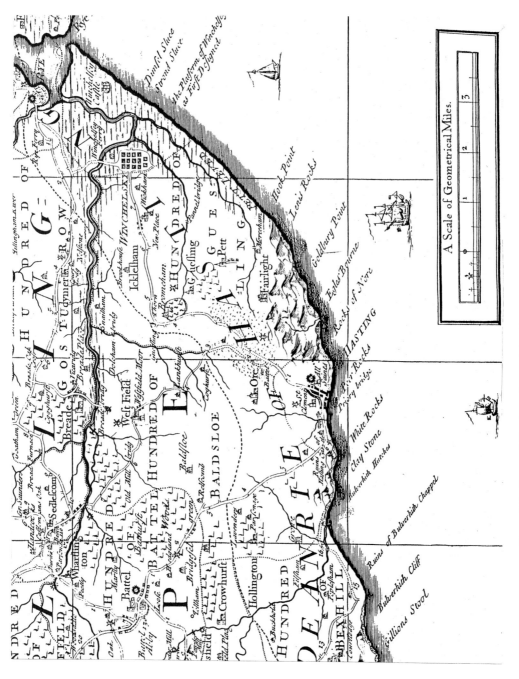

Part of the Rape of Hastings from Richard Budgeon's Map of Sussex – 1724

In 1702, the same year as Queen Anne came to the throne, Pett had a new Rector. He was James Cranston and resided in Hastings, where he was also Rector of the united parishes of St Clement's and All Saints. He was well educated and had some influential friends in Hastings, one of whom was John Collier, some-time mayor. In fact James Cranston's daughter Mary became John Collier's second wife in 1717.

By the time George I became King (1714–1727), things were beginning to improve at Pett. The churchwardens during the first quarter of the century were Nicholas Myles (Miles), Thomas Nabbs, Abraham French, John Marten (Martin), Richard Blackman and Joseph Rhodes. These men were responsible for putting right many of the deficiencies that were found at the inspections of the previous century. By 1724 a report on the Diocese of Chichester to Bishop Thomas Bowers gives a picture of a well-ordered and cared-for church. The church was inspected by the incumbents of Rye, Guestling and Fairlight. This is interesting because Stephen Frewen was the vicar of Fairlight and had been so from 1701; from about 1720 to 1723 he had also been the Curate at Pett. Stephen Frewen would have conducted a service in his own church each Sunday before making the journey down Peter James Lane to Pett. We do not know whether or not he rode a horse or walked, but the time taken on the trip back to Fairlight after the service at Pett would have given him much to think about, the road being winding and the hill steep. He might, of course, have just admired the lovely lane and superb scenery.

The parish of Pett was still part of the Rural Deanery of Hastings, quite a different area from Hastings' urban deanery of today. In those times the deanery was a long narrow strip of coastal land stretching from Bexhill to Rye. The three local priests reported to Bishop Bowers as follows:

The Return of the Commissioners to make a Parochial Visitation through the deanery of Hastings" (*Spelling below is as presented in the report*)

Patron	Mrs Elizabeth Denham (widow)
Incumbent	Mr James Cranston
Condition of the Church	In excellent repair. Bible very defective, the churchwardens promised a new one. Good Common Prayer Book. A pewter flagon, silver cup and cover, linen cloth for the Communion table. One bell.
Chancell	In very good repaire and handsomely beautified at the charge of the parish.
Rectory	In good repaire. The barn and stables covered with tiles and very well repaired.

Families in the parish	About 17 families, no papists or dissenters.
Value of Living in King's Books	About £5
Divine Service	Twice every Sunday by Mr Edward Dyson, curate.
Communion	3 times a year, about 12 communicants.
Glebe acres	30 plain, 6 acres rough, 4½ acres Woodland.

This is a very satisfactory report, especially so after the visitations in the previous century. It is interesting to see that the Bible was still defective, but the windows had obviously been glazed and the church had been cleaned and was in a good state of repair. The linen cloth would have been a 'fair' one for the Communion table and not an altar frontal, which in those days would have been called a 'carpet'. The beautification of the chancel included some degree of painting and the presence of the Decalogue (Ten Commandments), Lord's Prayer and the Creed. There were only three Holy Communions in 1702 and, if the number of 12 communicants is correct, the number had radically dropped from the figure recorded in 1603. All these numbers are a little suspect and care must be taken when using them. One thing is certain: when Stephen Frewen was curate there was only one service held on a Sunday. In 1702 when Edward Dyson, who had no other church, was curate both a morning and an evening service was held. Note that there were only about 17 families living in the parish.

James Cranston died in 1726 and was buried at St Clement's, Hastings on the 13th May. He was followed by Edward Levitt, who was Rector for five years before resigning, and then in 1731 David Denham resigned his incumbency at Upwaltham, between East Dean and Bignor in West Sussex, to come to Pett. A David Denham had been patron when James Cranston was instituted, and his wife Elizabeth was patron when Edward Levitt became Rector. They were probably related to Thomas Denham, who was a curate at Pett for about 20 years and who was buried in the churchyard. David Denham had been a scholar at Christ's College, Cambridge, was instituted on the 14th November 1731 and remained Rector of Pett until his death in 1745. He did have a curate for at least two of the latter years of his incumbency. An interesting memorandum in the East Sussex Records Office states that on the 23rd June 1735 George Martin (a Pett parishioner) had notice from the Rev. David Denham to pay his tithes 'in kind'.

Early in the 18th century the need for money to combat smallpox made serious inroads into parish funds and the disease was a constant threat to both towns and villages. It was a major killer for about a century and the incidence of the ailment was high, though the recovery rate favourable. By 1740–1750 inoculation against smallpox reached Sussex and by the end of the century places like Hastings, Winchelsea and Rye would have paid for the inoculation of their poor. Doctors' bills certainly appear in the Pett Poor Books, but there is no mention of payment for inoculation against smallpox.

In the 17th century Turnpike roads were built and travelling between the major towns in the country improved. At this time roads in Sussex had a particularly bad name. Highways were largely little more than cart tracks, rutted in summer and 'muddy up-to-the-ankles' in winter. A traveller in Sussex in 1752 maintained that 'a Sussex road is an insufferable evil'! Up to 1663, roads were entirely the responsibility of the parishes through which they passed, not those who used them. Until about 1840 all roads, except Turnpikes, were still rutted and even beyond the 1850s, when it was wet, local walkers in the villages would sink up to their calves in mud. Travel was not easy and it was not surprising that so many incumbents had curates living locally in their parishes.

In 1750 the patrons were William Hyland and John Alde. Both names have local connections, the former in Hastings and the latter in Fairlight, though John Alde lived at Telscombe near Brighton. They presented Augustin Diones Geere to be Rector in 1750. This gentleman had been Deacon and Curate at Westham in 1731, Curate of South Heighton, Tarring Neville and Denton in 1732, and the Rector of South Heighton and Tarring Neville in 1738. South Heighton, Tarring Neville and Denton, all near Newhaven, were villages in a united benefice and Rev. Geere remained incumbent of this and Pett until his death in 1765. He was a well-educated man having been a student at Christ's College, Cambridge and, though he did not spend much time in Pett, he has left a legacy in the form of the font. This is not only a beautiful object but it has had a chequered history over the years since it was given to the church in 1753. A description of the font appears later in this book, together with its strange story.

By 1738 John Wesley had begun to sound his trumpet-call and his life-long crusade as an open-air preacher (his last open-air sermon being at Winchelsea in 1790), and in both church and state vast changes were about to take place with the beginning of the Industrial Age. Coal, iron and steel, cotton, many new inventions and an increase in scientific knowledge meant a greater movement of people, new factories and new towns. Most of this seemed very far away from Pett, where there was not even a school for the children to attend in the 18th century, though it must be said that many children across the country did not go to school.

At this time an important job for the churchwardens and overseers was the upkeep of the Poor Book. The earliest Pett Poor Book, where details of both income and distribution are recorded, is dated 1723 and extracts from this and its successor are shown in Table 5 in the Appendix. We learn, for example, that in 1794 two hocks of mutton cost 7/-, a pair of shoes 3/6 and a pint of wine 1/3. Every entry could tell a story, but three items recorded during a month in 1762 need little elaboration: 'For sending man and horse to Rye for the Doctor to Dame Foster, 3/-. Foster's nurse, 12/-. Mrs Cramp for laying Dame Foster, 7/6'.

Johnson Towers succeeded Augustin Diones Geere as Rector in 1765. The patronage had passed on to the widow Grace Geere and three others. It is unlikely that Towers lived in the village as he had at least one curate during his incumbency in the person of a Mr B. Gibson. Sir William Burrell, a great antiquary of his day, visited Pett Church on the 28th May 1776. He said that in the early part of the reign of George II (1727–1760) the advowson had been purchased by an unlikely person who was a 'Perfumer in Fleet Street, London' and that, at the time of his visit to Pett, the living was estimated to be worth £180. When Sir William visited Pett, Diones Geere was Rector. He was the son of Augustin Diones Geere, who died in 1764, and he too was Curate of South Heighton, Denton and Tarring Neville. It was while the Rev. Diones Geere was Curate of Denton in 1793 that he took out an advertisement in the local paper to complain that the Rector, who lived in London, owed him arrears in salary. Diones expressed the hope that no other clergyman would accept this job as curate until he himself was paid. He was a young man when he obtained the living at Pett as he was Rector from 1774 to 1823, a period of 49 years, during which he was sometimes officiating in the benefice near Newhaven. He died at South Heighton on 20th December 1830 in his 82nd year. The *Sussex Advertiser* of the time said in his obituary that he was 'universally lamented'.

There are a few records worth mentioning that give a little more insight into local people at the end of the 18th century.

On 18th June 1784 John Reed of Pett was married at 'St. Margaret, in the London Parish of Westminster, to Elizabeth Paine, widow of this parish'. This marriage was by licence and appears in the London Parish Register though not in Pett's. We know little more of John Reed as he is not mentioned in the Parish Registers, though it is likely that some members of the same family lived in the village as ladies of that name were married in Pett church around this period.

In September of the same year (1784) in the Record of Deputations of Gamekeepers, George Medley, esq., of the Manor of Pett had John Thorpe of Fairlight, yeoman, gamekeeper, entered and certified. We shall look at the Medley family later as there is a window in the present church that was given in memory of the family and others. George Medley appears again in the East Sussex Land Tax returns of 1785 – a list of landowners, occupiers and rentals. Table 4 in the Appendix gives the names of these people, many of whom are from families with a long association with the village and the church. John Reed (mentioned above) was one of the assessors and collectors of rent, but we do not know if he lived in the area after his marriage in London.

Sir William Burrell made notes of many Sussex churches as he collected material for a history of Sussex, and was the first 'outsider' to give a brief description of the early church at Pett – and make a sketch of it. We will consider Burrell's description of the old church with others giving information about it in the next chapter.

6

The Old Church and the First Half of the 19th Century

From 1587 there had been various comments and statements about the state of the church. Churchwardens' Presentments, visitations and inspections provide a lot of information about the church building and its interior. However, it is Sir William Burrell in 1776, Sir Stephen Glynne around 1826 and Thomas Walker Horsfield in the 1830s who, between them, give a good description of the church. With these and with drawings, paintings and photographs it is possible to describe the old St Mary and St Peter Church fairly accurately.

Sir William Burrell (1732–1796) was a well-known Sussex antiquary and lived at Deepdene in the county. He collected materials for a history of Sussex and visited many churches. His notes and sketches (including those of Pett) are held in the British Museum. Sir Stephen Glynne (1807–1874) was brother-in-law to William Gladstone, Prime Minister. He too was an antiquary and made notes on 5,530 English churches. He left a great mass of manuscript notes that are kept in St Deiniol's Library in North Wales. Thomas Walker Horsfield (d.1837) was a topographer and in 1835 published *The History, Antiquities and Topography of the County of Sussex*. From these observant gentlemen we can produce the following description.

The medieval church was a small building with a nave, chancel and shingled bellcote. While Glynne calls it an 'uninteresting' building, Horsfield calls it 'small and neat'. Burrell says that the church 'is in tolerable repair except the altar piece, the boarding of which is entirely decayed, and ought to be new'. He goes on to state that the font was given by 'Mr Dyonisius Geere (*spelling incorrect*) 20th May 1753 at which time he was Rector. There is neither monument nor inscription in this Church'. Burrell's account ends with a drawing of the double-cross gravestone outside the north door. By the 1820s there had been some change as Glynne reports, 'the church is much modernised and devoid of architectural beauty. The arch between the nave and chancel is plain and pointed, and south of it is a smaller open arch. On the north side of the chancel are some square rectilineal windows of two lights. There is an obtuse lancet on the north side of the chancel – most of the other windows have been modernised. The buttresses are stone, and there is a shingled turret at the west end. The church is neatly paved and the pulpit and Communion cloth are of a rich crimson velvet. The earth is cleared from the Church wall and a drain carried all round. In the churchyard is a stone sculptured with a cross.' Horsfield says, 'the belfry being an obtuse spire erected on the roof of the church, having no separate tower. There were formerly three bells, but only one remains; the other two, being heavy and cracked, were taken down.' He goes on: 'The church is capable of containing 250 persons. The interior is particularly neat. A gallery was erected at the west end in 1824. A cast of the Royal Arms (corresponding in oak colour with the pews throughout the church and chancel) is placed in the centre. The aisle is cemented in imitation of stone, and the whole rendered dry and warm by means of a stove. The altarpiece is a neat design covered with crimson velvet; "I.H.S" is embossed in gold in the centre; the cushions and hangings of the altar, pulpit, and reading desk to correspond. The above, with the Royal Arms, stove, and ornamental painting, is the gift of the present Rector (Rev. Henry Wynch, M.A.). Few situations in the neighbourhood command more beautiful and varied views of the surrounding scenery than the churchyard, where there are some ancient tombstones.'

In 1776 there was no monument or inscription in the church, but in the 1830s there was at least one monument in the form of a tablet on the south wall of the chancel, to the memory of Cordelia Sayer. We will look at this in more detail later as it still adorns the south wall of the present church. Burrell seems to have missed the brass, dated 1642, of the gift of George Theobald, which is also in the present church. This brass may have been set in the floor or low down on one of the walls. As to the font, a handsome piece of Georgian furniture, this is the one given by Augustin Diones Geere that will be described later. The 'modernised' windows that Glynne mentions are those with wooden frames; sometimes they had sashes. The window-panes were made up of lozenge-shaped quarries (leaded lights) that were able to with-stand the strong winds that can blow around the church. The rich pulpit cloth is typical of the decoration of the period and was maintained in this manner until this church made way for a new one. By the time the church was pulled down and rebuilt there were other memorial tablets on the walls. Tablets in memory of Frances Pellew, George Wynch and his wife Mary and George Peter Baile Wynch were taken from the old church and repositioned in the new.

From drawings of the interior of the church it can be seen that there were box pews and a combined pulpit and reading desk. The pulpit appears to be a 'Three Decker' with a canopy above it. The Rector would have sat below the reading desk by the chancel arch. There were three large box pews on the north side of the nave and six on the south side extending right up to the chancel arch. Some of these pews were allocated to the families of local landowners or farmers. There were wooden altar rails

St Mary and St Peter Church, Pett, 1836

in the sanctuary and what appear to be (from drawings) more box pews or seats in the chancel itself. There was a place to hang hats and cloaks on the north side of the nave, nearest the north door and part of the nave looks as if it was carpeted. Above the pointed chancel arch was a large painted board on which (from left to right when facing the altar) were The Lord's Prayer, two panels containing the Ten Commandments and the Apostles Creed. The Royal Coat of Arms cannot be seen in the drawings (except for a small part of the crown above the tie beam in the nave), but would have been that of either King George IV or King William IV, as Henry Wynch gave it to the church during his incumbency between 1823 and 1852. Neither the painted board nor the Royal Coat of Arms has survived. The roof of the nave was of the barrel or wagon type and the internal panelling would have been made of timber, probably painted.

The drawings and photographs of the outside of the church are fascinating and, in addition to providing information about the church, show how the surrounds looked a hundred and fifty years ago. Burrell's sketch depicted a shallow north porch which had over the outer door a tablet inscribed 'I MOOD 1716'. In Henry Young's drawing there is no 'I' or 'J Mood', nor is there any mention of a person named Mood in the parish records. It could be that a Mr Mood was responsible for repairing the porch in

1716 – it remains one more mystery! The drawing on page 38 seems to be remarkably accurate and the cottages at the Pett Road end of Pannel Lane are well drawn. The chimney for the stove can be seen on the south side of the church roof and on some pictures an attractive weather vane is shown, though it varies in shape from sketch to sketch. It can be clearly seen from the photograph on page 48 that the shape of the church, apart from the tower, was little different from the present church and the size appears to be very similar. It seems unlikely that it could ever seat 250 persons as Horsfield says, even if it did have a gallery. It is a pity that there is no drawing of a gallery and the earliest vestry meeting records make no mention of it; however, the vestry meeting minutes of that time usually record just the names of those elected to office in the parish. The stone walls of the church look as though they had been rendered in some way and the rectangular windows look freshly painted, as does the stable-type door. The photograph also shows a door underneath the east window in the chancel. This is covered by crimson drapes in the drawing of the interior of the church (page 44). We have no pictures of the south side of the church, though there was probably a small vestry (or cupboard for vestments) on that side, entered through the open arch in the chancel.

The old church had probably stood in this spot for more than five hundred years and in it the good people of Pett had worshipped God, been baptised, married and buried. The building had undergone changes. It had been renovated and repaired many times, had gone through some good and bad periods, and had been the centre of the community of Pett. It is only through the devotion and dedication of some of the Rectors, Curates, Churchwardens and people in the parish that it served God's purpose in this parish for so long.

At the turn of the century and around 1801 the population of the village was 185 and the number of inhabited houses was 36. This was not to last, as once again the history of France became closely entwined with that of England and the population in and around Pett was to expand considerably. In the late 18th century, following the upheaval of a bloody revolution, the French began to acquire new territories. Under the brilliant Napoleon Bonaparte French armies rampaged across much of Europe. In 1793 France declared war on England. Not for the first time England faced the threat of invasion and the resulting defence initiatives affecting Pett were threefold. First, in 1801 there was a great survey taken across the south coast giving details of people, livestock, crops, wagons and weapons. This was to enable the King and his Ministers to provide for the defence and security of the realm against this very real threat. Table 6 in the Appendix shows the returns for the Guestling Hundred and gives much information about the state of the area at this time. It would appear that Pett had no

Photograph of a painting of St Mary and St Peter Church, Pett, painted in 1851 and owned by John Maclean of New Zealand

people willing to fight and that no folk had a weapon of any sort – or at least, none that they wished to declare! Some of the numbers are a little suspicious but the whole is a remarkable document that is only a small part of an enormous undertaking. The second and third defence projects followed one after the other; the first being the digging of the Royal Military Canal and the second the building of 73 Martello Towers along the coast of Kent and East Sussex.

The Royal Military Canal was the brainchild of Lt. Col. John Brown, who thought it would be a kind of moat defence barrier. It would run from Shorncliffe in Kent to the Rother at Rye, and it later would be extended to Cliff End at Pett Level. Pitt's government pushed on with the scheme and appointed Sir John Rennie as controller. The first soil was dug in 1804 and Rennie resigned a year later. Lt. Col. Brown was placed in command and he and Lt. Col. Nicolay supervised the section between Winchelsea and Pett Level. There were all sorts of problems and the whole canal was not completed till 1809, by which time the threat of invasion had largely passed. So this unique engineering folly, which cost over £200,000, was left as little more than a curiosity. It was rather naïve to think that the French forces, after traipsing round half of Europe would be thwarted by a canal less than thirty feet wide. Gun turrets planned along its length were never built and, apart from a shortish period when it was used for the transportation of goods, it remains a pretty canal in lovely country-side that has some good fishing and which has attracted some famous artists, including J.M.W. Turner.

In the spring of 1805 work started on the construction of the Martello Towers and by 1808 seventy-three had been erected along the south coast. Each tower was a cylindrical structure approximately 30 feet tall with walls 13 feet thick on the seaward side and 6–8 feet thick on the landward side. On top of the tower a 2.5 ton gun was placed, which could fire a 24 pound shot a mile out to sea. Eight of these towers, numbers 31 to 38, were built on the beach between the Rye end of Winchelsea Beach and Cliff End, the last of which was pulled down in the 1890s (long after the threat that had caused their building had passed). During the summer of 1805 the whole of the south coast was one gigantic building site as the towers began to rise. Then on 21st October Lord Nelson destroyed the combined French and Spanish fleet off the coast of Portugal at the Battle of Trafalgar, and it was only the death of Nelson that cast a shadow over the huge celebrations that swept the country, including Pett. Bells rang in the villages, work stopped and the feasting began. The construction of the Martello Towers continued and must have provided some much needed employment in the area and more people settled here. England now stood ready to face an invasion by Napoleon, but in 1815, after the Battle of Waterloo, the threat finally passed and the use of the towers changed. Because of rising taxes, the smuggling trade was rife along the coast and most of the population was involved in one way or another, enjoying the benefits of cheaper smuggled goods. There was much corruption among magistrates and officers appointed to enforce the law. Many were open to bribery and even the clergy turned a blind eye to it. The illicit trade reached a peak after the war with France and the towers were used by Customs and Preventive Services. The Coastguards used the towers as lookouts and as accommodation for themselves and their families until the late 1880s. We shall look at some of these families later.

There is a wonderful Hastings Guide by James Barry, dated 1804. This paints a lovely picture of a very rural area and it is worth quoting some short sections here.

> The vicinity of Hastings abounds with the most delightful walks and rides, the entrances are remarkably numerous, and it is impossible to select any road that does not lead to some scene of rural amusement: the lands are as beautiful as extensive, and the sea exhibits a continual round of passing variety. The Hop Gardens, Bohemia, the Old Roar (a cataract in the middle of a thick wood, that

Pencil sketch, drawn by Henry Young – October 1858

falls perpendicularly from a rocky precipice, about 40 feet), Bexhill, Pevensey, Broomham Park, Winchelsea, Rye and the surrounding villages all have charms to please the inquisitive mind, or curious or plodding eye. One circumstance must, above all others render Hastings dear to those who have a regard to morality – Vice has not yet erected her standard here: – the numerous tribe of professional gamblers, unhappy profligates, and fashionable swindlers find employment and rapine elsewhere. Innocent recreational delight, card assemblies, billiards, riding, walking, reading, fishing and other modes of pastimes banish care from the mind, whilst the salubrity of the atmosphere impels disease from the body. The society of Hastings are gay without profligacy, and enjoy life without mingling in its debaucheries."

Other writers have expressed a different view about the morality in and around Hastings at the beginning of the 19th century.

Later on in the book, Barry writes about the view from the fire beacon at the top of Peter James Lane, Fairlight – looking down towards Pett (a village too small to mention by name in this guide).

… From hence, the view on every side is scarcely to be paralleled in the kingdom. … but it ought to be observed, that in the evening, about an hour or two before sunset, is the proper time for enjoying views from this spot, in their greatest beauty. At this time, the lengthened sunbeams just gild the mountain's brow, and point where the steeple rises with majestic grandeur above the deep embosomed wood. Every house and cottage now rears its head amidst the surrounding verdure.

> 'Heavens! what a goodly prospect spreads around
> Of hills, and dales, and woods, and lawns, and spires,
> And glittering towns, and ocean wide, till all
> The stretching landscape into smoke decays!'

The towns of Winchelsea, Rye, Lydd, New Romney, Tenterden, and villages innumerable, may be seen from this spot on a clear evening. … Descend Fairlight Down, through some pleasant lanes, to the village of Guestling, near which is Broomham Park.

The scenery around Pett and the views from the top of Peter James Lane have changed little in the last two hundred years (except for more houses) and it is so very fortunate that much of the land remains unspoiled.

At the end of the Napoleonic Wars, Winchelsea stood independent of the County of Sussex because of its status as a Cinque Port, a privilege granted centuries before in return for ship service. Its liberty or area of jurisdiction stretched from Pett Coastguard cottages to Jury's Gap including parts of the parishes of Pett and Icklesham and all of Camber, an area ripe for smuggling. Then, between 1811 and 1817 there were riots against growing unemployment. Agriculture in the rural areas all over the country was in a far worse position than it was before the war. Many small farmers went bankrupt, particularly those who had bought their land at high prices during the long war. The new Corn Laws, designed to help farming profits by restricting foreign imports, had not worked in practice. The agricultural workers were in a worse state. The population had grown, wages were low and high taxes on staple items like soap, candles, sugar, beer, paper and tobacco made life very difficult indeed. The Poor Law relief rates had been drastically cut and the ever-growing number of paupers due to unemployment and depressed wages meant that most parishes had to find accommodation for them. Parochial officers were to provide 'convenient houses' for the impotent poor without any work provision. This must have affected Pett, which did not have its own 'Workhouse', the nearest being at Fairlight and Guestling. Registers of those receiving poor relief were kept from 1691.

Watercolour of the interior of Pett church by an unknown artist, about 1860

In 1825 the Stockton to Darlington railway opened and George Stephenson's triumph was complete. The opening up of the country began as the railway system gradually encroached upon towns across the land and the movement of people became so much easier. Two years earlier, in 1823, Henry Wynch became Rector of Pett. His father George, who had been living in South Wales, held the advowson and now resided at Winchelsea. Henry and his wife Charlotte came to Pett, where they were to stay for nearly 30 years. The Wynches lived in some comfort in the large Rectory, with their butler, cook and two other servants. The Rectory, two hundred yards from the church, was later destroyed in 1864. Henry's stipend was £460 a year, some twenty times the average earnings of the agricultural labourers who made up the majority of his parishioners. From 1831 he was also Rector of South Heighton with Tarring Neville, as were some of his predecessors, but this ended in 1838 with the new Plurality

Act forbidding clergymen to hold more than one benefice. Henry and Charlotte had two children, George Peter Baile – born on 27th June 1828, and Florentia – born on 27th June 1831. George died when he was only eight years old. This tragedy occurred outside the Two Sawyers Inn, when a groom stopped for a drink while in charge of a pony and the young boy. The pony shied and George was killed.

A more joyful time for the Rector was when he officiated at the wedding of his cousin, Peter Bourchier Wynch, to Charlotte Stovin, a Hastings girl, in 1830. Peter too was a clergyman and sometimes acted as Henry's curate, one of a number who assisted over the years. The curate received only £80 per annum in 1835. Another happy occasion was when Florentia, barely twenty, married William Drew Lucas-Shadwell. He was twelve years older than his new wife, who was to outlive him by more than forty-five years. William Drew was a J.P. for thirty years and in 1854 became High Sheriff. He built Fairlight Hall in 1849 and was interested in the Volunteer Movement, forming the 2nd Sussex volunteers with himself as Captain of the one hundred members. His greatest interest was in the Temperance Movement, and in this his wife led the way. At a time when some public houses were open for seventeen hours out of twenty-four there was a great need for reform and an encouragement to lessen drinking. William Drew became a total abstainer himself in 1862, following the earlier example of his wife. A Fairlight Total Abstinence Society was formed and 'The Hall' was the scene of temperance societies' gatherings every Whit Monday. Drew became a Vice-President of the National Temperance League and frequently spoke at their meetings. The Lucas-Shadwells had a son William and two daughters, another Florentia and Mary. The family continued to have connections with Pett, as we shall see later.

In an early volume of the Parliamentary Gazetteer, published between 1843 and 1844, there is an interesting report on Pett which reads:

A parish in Guestling hundred, rape and union of Hastings, county of Sussex; 3 miles south-west of Winchelsea. Living, a rectory, in the archdeaconry of Lewes and diocese of Chichester; rated at £4 15s 10d; returned at £150; gross income £547. Patron in 1835, the Rev. H. Wynch. This parish is entitled to one-third of the produce of £1,000, three per cents, arising from the property, bequeathed, in 1734, by the Rev. Robert Bradshaw, for medical attendance, & etc. On average of 7 years to 1835, hops have been annually cultivated in this parish to the extent of 10 6/8 acres; average amount of hops charged, 13,123 lbs; of duty paid, £109 7s 2d. Fairs are held for cattle and pedlery on May 27th and for pedlery on July 18th. Acres, 1,750. Number of houses, 49. Assessed property, £2,776. Population, in 1801, 185: in 1831, 297. Poor rates in 1838, £229 10s. (*Note: pedlery was a fair where travelling salesmen sold their wares.*)

7

The 19th Century – the Middle Years, Smuggling and Transportation

By 1844 a 'Confirmed Tithe Apportionment' showed that the Rector of the parish of Pett was 'entitled to all tithes arising from or accruing due upon all lands of the said parish'. There was an annual sum of rent charge of £480 instead of tithes (except for hops). This did not apply to the Glebe land, where there was a rent for £3. By 1857 the rents had risen to £507 16s 8d.

The earliest Pett Vestry Book is dated 1846, well into Henry Wynch's incumbency. In 1846 John Thorpe and John Waghorne were Churchwardens and in that year the rate levied for the necessary relief of the poor (and other purposes) was 6d in the pound, quite a high level of local tax for that period. In 1847 Pett Village School was built as a double-storey building. The land was granted for use as a site for a school by Henry Thomas Pelham, Earl of Chichester, to the Rector, Churchwardens and Overseers of Pett on 1st May 1847. It was to be a mixed 'National School'. The Pett Methodist Church was built in 1848 as a result of the Bible Christians outgrowing their original place of worship in Barden's Forge. Pett was becoming more of a complete village.

The Vestry Meeting of the 28th February 1850 was held in the house of A.G. Thorpe, the assistant overseer, for the purpose of nominating Parish Constables. Other decisions made were, a rent to be imposed of 1½ d in the pound for repairs to the highways, and the pews to be altered to give more seats (these were the additional box pews in the chancel). Fred Hoad and A.G. Thorpe were Churchwardens and Richard Griffen, John Skinner and Robert Hills were noted as 'ratepayers present'.

In 1851 a Census of Religious Worship was taken throughout the land. All denominations were asked to give a return of the number of seats available in each place of worship. Returns were required asking for details of attendance at morning, afternoon or evening services on Sunday 30th March. This turned out to be very controversial, some clergy refusing to reply. On that day in March 7½ per cent of the population had not been to church or chapel and only 20 per cent had attended a Church of

England service. Even if they had wanted to do so, seating for only about 58 per cent of the population was available and in the great cities of London and Birmingham much less. Similar figures recorded today would show a dramatic decline in church attendance and the census of 1851 was never repeated.

It is interesting to compare the figures, available from the National Census and Clergy Lists, for the three sets of years, 1842, 1851 and 1861 for Pett, Guestling and Fairlight. Pett was the smallest of the three villages then, as it still is today.

Pett:
- 1842   Pop. 297
- 1851   Pop. 385 (364 in 71 households in the 1851 Census compiled by C.J. Barnes); Henry Wynch, Rector and Patron since 1823
- 1861   Pop. 363 (Clergy List); Incumbent, Frederick Young since 1857
  Valuation £460; Patron R. Thornton

Guestling:
- 1842   Pop. 768; Rector, J. Ashburnham since 1785
  Valuation £401; Patron, J. Ashburnham
- 1851   Pop. 803 (860 in 169 Households – C.J. Barnes)
  Rector and Patron, Sir John Ashburnham
  There is now a curate, H. Petley
- 1861   Pop. 860; Rector and Patron, J.M. Lukin
  Valuation £450

Fairlight:
- 1842   Pop. 533; Vicar, Hugh Totty since 1823; Patron, B. Pearse esq.
  Valuation £502; Curate, William Pearse
- 1851   Pop. 631 (625 in 117 Households – C.J. Barnes)
  Vicar, Hugh Totty; Curate, T. Hubbard; Patron, B. Pearse
- 1861   Pop 625; Vicar, Henry Stent since 1857; Patron, C. Young esq.
  Curate, C.J. Young; Valuation £502

Henry Wynch retired in 1852, the year his first grandchild was born. He and his wife moved to Tunbridge Wells, but had little difficulty in visiting their daughter, Florentia, and their grandchildren. By now the railway had been extended to Hastings and a first class single fare from Tunbridge Wells to Hastings cost five shillings and eight pence (28p) and the train journey took an hour and a quarter (in 2002 it still takes 44 minutes – if the train runs to time!). Henry died in 1868.

Photograph of the old St Mary and St Peter Church, Pett, taken some time between 1857 and 1864. The tall figure in the picture is the Rev. Frederick Young. The picture, with others, is of the stereoscopic type and was given to the Rev. F.C.A. Young on New Year's Day 1910 by Caroline H. Hale

The roads in and around Pett were still not good in the 1850s as the *Strangers Guide and Commercial Directory to Hastings and St. Leonard's for 1852* records. When mentioning Pett, the guide states that:

The road to this place forms a pretty ride, and branches off the Guestling road opposite the White Hart public house. The walk to it from Fairlight is its greatest recommendation, as the village is insignificant. It is called four miles from Hastings. There is a longer extent of ride by passing Fairlight, and taking the road to the left (Peter James Lane), but this is troublesome for carriages.

It is strange that so many visitors to Pett have thought it to be 'insignificant' or 'dull', when in reality this was not so and the true richness of the village could only be found by someone looking beyond the style of the buildings to study the villagers and their lives. It has always been the people of Pett that have given strength and character to the village; each household could tell a tale of its own and we can but scratch the surface in attempting to tell the story of Pett.

In 1837 a new Queen came to the throne and the Victorian age began. This was a time of great contrasts: pomp and splendour and appalling squalor, whimsical architectural romanticism and innovative feats of engineering. The desire to return to the principles of an earlier golden age were paralleled in the Church by the Oxford Movement, whose leaders tried to counter the spread of 'liberal theology' and to reassert the authority of the Anglican Church, which had become excessively susceptible to secular influence. Nearly two thousand new churches were consecrated in the first half of the nineteenth century and a further two thousand in the years 1851–1871. The present Pett church was one of these.

At the Vestry Meeting on the 29th March 1853, 'it was proposed by Mr S. Skinner and seconded by Mr A. G. Thorpe that the meeting be adjourned to the Royal Oak Inn. At the Oak, at 6 o'clock in the evening, it was proposed that Christopher Thorpe be nominated as Assistant Overseer of the Parish of Pett at a salary of £12 per annum'. His duties were, 'to consist of collecting all rates made in the Parish and to perform all other duties as "apputain" and are incident to the office of the Assistant Overseer of the Poor'. It was around this time that Robert West became the Rector of Pett, and at a Vestry Meeting two years later, on the 9th April 1855, the Rector proposed that Robert Hills stand as his Churchwarden and the previous Churchwardens (A.G. Thorpe and John Skinner) proposed and seconded that Thomas Hills be nominated as Churchwarden for the Parish. The practice of choosing a vicar's warden and a people's warden was commonplace and continued to the latter part of the 20th century. It is interesting to note that until recently, churchwardens' staffs (or wands) were to be found in most churches, next to the wardens' seats in the nave. The wooden staffs are usually surmounted by a brass or silver mitre – for the vicar's warden – and a crown – for the people's warden. The wardens' wands in Pett church are surmounted by a brass mitre and crown, respectively.

T.B. Brett in his *Manuscript History of Hastings & St. Leonard's, 1828–1864* tells a rather shameful story about Robert West. Brett says that West was a relative (possibly the son) of the Rev. J.J. West, for many years the Rector of Winchelsea. This gentleman was an avowed predestinarian and declared from his pulpit that 'Hell was paved with babes'. His eccentricities – to use a mild term – got him into disfavour with

The Old Rectory, Pett, pulled down in 1866

many of his parishioners, though he was a favourite preacher of many Hastings folk, who would walk eleven miles every Sunday to Winchelsea to hear him.

'The clergyman of Pett', so Brett says, 'caused the inhabitants to bear a record of a clerical scandal. On the 21st of December 1855, letters of request in the Arches Court (the Consistory Court of the Province of Canterbury, which at one time met at Bow Church, London) were brought from the Diocese of Chichester against the Rev. Robert West, Rector of Pett, for habitual drunkenness, and for brawling, smiting, using profane language and for other unclerical conduct. In the year 1853 the defendant had been inducted to that Rectory on the representation of Sir Richard Thornton of London, which Rectory had become vacant through the removal of the Rev. Henry Wynch, and he was charged with a series of acts of misconduct, commencing in May 1854. After that date he frequently exhibited himself in a state of intoxication, not only in his own parish, but also at Hastings and Rye. On the 24th June he went in his own private yacht to Folkestone and put up at the Hotel de Paris, where he and his crew got drunk. In the following September he sailed over in his yacht to Boulogne and made a stay of three days at the Hotel Bedford, during the greater part of which time he was in a state of inebriety. On the 2nd of August he gave a feast at the Rectory to the school children, and was then intoxicated. At the end of the same month he gave a party to his yachtsmen and some men of the preventive service at the "William the Conqueror" at Rye, when he again transgressed the bounds of sobriety. On Xmas Eve he was again drunk at the Rectory, and on that occasion he put his arms round the waist of his maidservant and endeavoured to induce her to dance with him. On the 1st of January 1855, he invited several parishioners to dine with him, when he was again drunk. On the 6th, while returning in his carriage from a neighbouring clergyman's, he had an altercation with a waggoner, whom he assaulted; and on the 3rd of the following month, he was fined by the Hastings Magistrates for violence. On another occasion he attempted to give a tradesman an order for "infernal" coals, but was unable to do so in consequence of his drunken condition; and on several occasions he was refused by the officers at the railway station to travel on the line. On the 10th of March he landed at Folkestone from a steam packet dressed as a sailor, and attended by a servant in livery. He went to the station, and being refused a ticket, he said, "I am Bob West, a captain in the Navy. I'll let you know who I am; damn you, I'll have the coat off your back." Shortly after, he went to the harbour-master and demanded of him, "Do you consider me beastly drunk?" The reply was in the affirmative, and he was advised to go to his hotel and keep quiet. On the 19th of the same month, he presented himself in a drunken condition before the school children. In the same month he visited a female parishioner, who lay dying, and even then he was intoxicated, and when he came downstairs he expressed himself in terms of levity and impropriety before the family. He offered to supply her with wine, and gave some money to one of her daughters for that purpose, but as she was going out he threw his arms around her and attempted to kiss her. Many other instances of impropriety were detailed, in answer to which the reverend gentleman put questions to the witnesses.

'The learned judge did not wish to press greatly on the counsel for Mr West, but thirty witnesses had been examined, all of whom had deposed to acts of drunkenness. He appeared, however to be a kind-hearted man, and had never been seen intoxicated in the church. The Court thought it would sufficiently discharge its duty by suspending him from the discharge of divine service for two years, at the end of which he must produce the usual certificate from three beneficed clergymen that he had conducted himself with greater propriety. He must also be condemned in the costs, and be deprived of the receipts of his benefice during the two years suspension. How the clergyman conducted himself after the loss of his annual income of £460 for two years I cannot say, but it appears that he was never reinstated; for at the end of his two years suspension (1857) the Rev. F. Young was inducted to the living of Pett on

St Mary and St Peter Church, Pett – photograph taken about 1875. The figures are Rev. Frederick Young (by the church), his younger brother, Charles Waring Young, and his son, Frederick Charles Ashburnham Young

the recommendation of the same patron, Sir Richard Thornton; nor can I learn that Mr West ever obtained another benefice.'

What a sad and difficult situation for the parish, and how tongues would have wagged in the houses of Pett and the neighbouring villages! The Rev. Robert West must have been a sick man, being an alcoholic, and would have had a greater opportunity for treatment if he had lived in the present times. His two-year period of suspension meant that the services in the church had to be conducted by clergy from other churches and put additional pressure on the Churchwardens.

T.B. Brett also mentions, in his *Manuscript History*, a blind postman. This man delivered letters in the parishes of Fairlight, Guestling and Pett. The post-clerk's practice was to read over to the blind postman the addresses of the letters in the order in which they were to be delivered. The postman would then place the letters in various pockets about his person and start on his round. There were a number of friendly folk on the round who would help him if he was in any doubt and, according to Brett, there was rarely an error made in the delivery of the post. What a remarkable man!

Among the School records at the East Sussex Records Office is a document which states that on 3rd July 1855, a 'piece of land with buildings in Pett, heretofore occupied by parish officers or paupers north of French Court Farm, south of road from Pett Church to Shellys Green, east land occupied by Robert Hills, west land formerly occupied by Thomas Ovary', was granted for use by the school. By this time the school was thriving and by 1862 Mr Phillip Turner was the Master and his wife Ann was the Mistress; of course, when, in 1870, school became compulsory for all children up to the age of eleven it would have been necessary to have more than one teacher.

Before we move on to the later years of the 19th century, more should be said about smuggling and transportation. With the end of the Napoleonic wars in 1815 there was a great revival of smuggling. Many unemployed ex-servicemen drifted into the profession. Unable to reduce duties, Lord Liverpool's administration determined at last to declare war on the smuggler and in 1817 established the blockade to give special protection to the coasts of Kent and Sussex. In addition the Navy provided ships and men for revenue duties.

The 'Blues', later known as the 'Aldington Gang', were the most desperate of the gangs that operated in this corner of England, terrorising the countryside in much the same way as the 'Hawkhurst Gang' had done almost a century before. Lesser gangs tended to work further west in Sussex, as the running of goods ashore in Kent and East Sussex became progressively more dangerous. In June 1829 a run of goods took place between Watch-House and Cliff End. Seventy or eighty men, each carrying two tubs, went through Winchelsea at about four in the morning. Smugglers appear to have received little in the way of reward, about 7/6 a run was the rate in the 19th century – but large syndicates of more wealthy men made big profits from the work their men did with the cargoes.

In 1831 the Coastguard took over the duties of the coast blockade and the Martello Towers were used as living accommodation. Later cottages were built for the Coastguard Officers and their families. There is a row of such cottages on Pett Level and the last two blocks were built at Toot Rock and at the Haddocks in 1900. Well armed and well disciplined, the Coastguards were prepared for trouble and numerous affrays took place in the area between Bexhill and Rye. The men of the Coastguards were hated and despised by all the local folk and the confrontations between the two groups were fierce and bloody in the years that followed. There are many local stories of smuggling, including the tragedy in the 1830s when men were drowned trying to cross the Military Canal while being pursued by the revenue men. On 13th April 1837, twenty or so local men were running a cargo at Cliff End when they were sur-

Watercolour sketch of Pett Church, c. 1900

prised and a fight ensued. The smugglers wrested some muskets from the coastguards, beat them with the butt ends and bayoneted one of them. The villains then retreated, leaving one man dead, and carried off their wounded. A man died while they were trying to escape and was left in the marsh, and another body was abandoned near Icklesham. The rest got away, though several were wounded, and one carried his friend all the way to Udimore. On 1st April 1838, an innocent man, a fiddler named Thomas Monk, was shot by coastguards near Camber Castle, and on another occasion in 1861 a revenue man was killed with an oar at Cliff End.

Perhaps the best-known smuggling tale is the one Zoe Vahey tells in her book *A History of Pett*; this tale has been told about other venues too, but it is good to feel that it could have taken place in Pett. It appears that one day (must have been between 1845 and 1855) a barrel of rum had just arrived at the Two Sawyers inn and was standing in the middle of the floor. To her horror, Mrs Catt, who was working there, saw a revenue officer coming up the path. With great presence of mind she snatched up a baby from its cradle, sat herself on the barrel so that her skirts hid it, and proceeded to feed the infant. The revenue man entered hardly a moment after she was ready and demanded to inspect the premises. 'All right,' she said, 'Carry on and go where you like, but I'm feeding the baby who's not well, poor mite, and you don't need me to show you around.' The man inspected the inn from top to bottom and then withdrew, apologising for his intrusion. Everyone had a good laugh later that night in the bar. However, it was not long before the Two Sawyers was caught red-handed and was closed down as an inn, not to sell liquor again until 1939, when it was opened as 'The Two Sawyers Country Club'. Much later it was reopened as a public house. Though there is still smuggling today, the nature of it has changed. The most important factor in the suppression of smuggling in the 19th century was the enormous reduction and abolition of most of the duties as part of the policy of Free Trade. With the wholesale reform of the Customs Service in 1853, which ensured a loyal and efficient force to deal with any bad cases of smuggling, the situation changed. Smuggling thereafter was relatively unimportant and declined.

From about 1790 to the 1850s those who committed crimes could expect to be transported to Australia. For crimes such as larceny, often quite minor; receiving stolen goods, often smuggled; fraud and embezzlement and false pretences; vagrancy, assault, poaching, killing or injuring animals and malicious damage, the perpetrator would have been dealt with at the Quarter Sessions (more serious cases were dealt with by the Assizes). In the Eastern Division of Sussex well over 800 people were sentenced to be transported, though not all these sentences were carried out. From 1790 to 1835 transportees from the County's Eastern Division were usually housed in Horsham Gaol until they could be forwarded to hulks in the Portsmouth harbour area for onward despatch. Hulks were not used after 1843, when Millbank Prison in London became the sole destination. From 1835 Lewes House of Correction superseded Horsham Gaol as the local place of detention prior to despatch. Those sent to Australia (some 16,000) were first sent to Jackson in New South Wales and later to Van Dieman's Land (Tasmania), which became the sole place of reception after 1840. The numbers sent for transportation became very small after 1853.

It was common practice in describing a prisoner to list him or her as 'late' of the place where the crime occurred, rather than of the true place of residence. The Quarter Sessions dealing with transportation and other sentences were originally held four times a year, at Epiphany, Easter, Midsummer and Michaelmas. From 1833 the number of occasions doubled to meet increasing demand, the additional courts being described as 'adjourned'. In this area there were several men, but no women, sentenced to be transported; they were:

Pett	1833	George Fowler	age 16	sentence 7 years	labourer
	1836	Robert Collier	age 31	sentence 7 years	labourer
	1837	George Sawyers	age 34	sentence 10 years	labourer
Fairlight	1829	William Edwards	age 22	sentence 7 years	labourer
	1834	John Lingham	age 27	sentence 7 years	labourer

There were none recorded for Guestling and four for Icklesham.

Over 80 per cent of the cases show the occupation of the prisoner to be that of 'labourer' and it is interesting to see that most sentences were for seven years (nearly two thirds of the total). About 59 per cent of those charged were under the age of 25 and 8 per cent under the age of 15, the youngest being a boy of nine. Only five were over the age of 61, the oldest being a man of 72. Australian records show that the average age of those who were actually transported was 26 and that 75 per cent of them were single.

We do know a little more about Robert Collier. He was prosecuted by Thomas Wilson for the crime of felony; the amount paid for the expenses of the criminal prosecution carried out at the Quarter Session, County of Sussex Eastern Division was £6 15s 0d. Robert Collier and four others under sentence of transportation in 1836 were conveyed from Lewes to Gosport at a cost of £10 14s 4d. It is most probable that Robert Collier was actually transported, but it is not known if the others quoted were, as many transportees served their time on the hulks or in prisons. Though three crimes occurred in Pett, there is no mention of the men concerned in the parish registers. It is possible that they lived locally and all three surnames are mentioned among families being in residence in Hastings or Ore.

The Rev. Frederick Young became Rector of Pett in 1857. This was his first and only incumbency, following his priesting in 1854, and curacy at St Leonard's, Bromley, Middlesex. When Frederick became Rector, the tithe rent was worth £508 and the population had grown. He was to be Rector for twenty-seven years and was the first member of the Young family that had such a great influence on the church in Pett. It was under his leadership and guidance that the present church of St Mary and St Peter was built.

8

The Building of a New Church and the Rest of the 19th Century

On 29th October 1863 a Vestry Meeting was held in the church, 'pursuant to notice duly given, for the purpose of giving the consent of the parish to the erection of a new Parish Church in the place of the old one standing and to hear a statement from the Rector as to the probable expenses. It was resolved that the consent of the parish be given to the said erection being so commenced as soon as the necessary funds should be found. Frederick Young, Chairman.'

This momentous decision was taken by: the Chairman; Mr R. Wickens and Mr John Skinner, Churchwardens; Messrs. Noakes, J. (or T.) Croke, G. Griffen, T. Davis and W. Wildish. No reason was given for such an important local event and the only clues we have are that some years earlier more pews had been added to cope with the increase in population and over the years the church had required many major repairs.

The architect chosen to draw up the plans for the new church was Benjamin Ferrey. This fine draughtsman was born on 1st April 1810, and was educated at the Grammar School at Wimborne, Dorset, where his genial disposition made him a great favourite with the headmaster and his schoolfellows. He showed an early interest in art and became one of the best architectural draughtsmen of his day. At a young age he was placed by his father with the elder Pugin. Augustin Pugin is remembered as a Gothic architect and he had a big influence on Benjamin Ferrey. Young Benjamin had a keen sense of humour and in his graphic manner could and did mimic, and play practical jokes on, the benevolent Mr Pugin. Though brought up in a Gothic school and known as one of the early workers in the Gothic revival, he was never bigoted as regards the Classic styles, with which his pencil was always familiar. In 1836 he married Ann, the daughter of William Lucas, of Stapleton Hall, Stroud Green, Hornsey. In 1841 he was appointed Hon. Diocesan Architect of Bath and Wells, a post that he held till his death. By 1845 Mr Ferrey was considered to be one of the rising church architects of the day and was commissioned to design one of his most important works, St Stephen's Church and Schools, Rochester Row, Westminster – a group of buildings in a late decorated style. He invented, around 1857, a mode of stamping or

The Rectory, Pett – c. 1869. Behind the Rectory was the Coach House, at one time the HQ of the Girl Guides

incising stucco surfaces while wet. This was a very cheap and effective way of decorating plaster and he used this process to good effect in the chancel of Pett Church. Benjamin Ferrey, with his pleasant manners, gained many clients, some of whom became personal friends. With young architects he was always very popular because of his good nature and willingness to help them. He was a skilful watercolour painter and was extremely fond of music, especially church music; he had a pleasing baritone voice. After his first wife died, he married Emily, daughter of William Hopkinson. By his first wife he had three children, a son and two daughters; his son Edmund Benjamin was an architect too, and worked with his father for about ten years. Drawings of Pett Church by Edmund Ferrey are held by the Royal Institute of British Architects. Benjamin Ferrey died in his 71st year on 22nd August 1880. He was responsible for designing many mansions, public buildings, schools, parsonages and churches, but the design of Pett Church has produced varying comments over the years.

On 18th February 1864 a Vestry Meeting was held to consider the plans and building estimates. Present at this meeting were the Rector, the Churchwardens, Mr

Noakes, Mr Wildish, William Drew Lucas-Shadwell esq., and R. Farenish Jr. The architect Mr Ferrey had estimated that the cost would be about £1600. In March the specification for building the church was prepared, and a transcript of this handwritten document can be seen in Table 7 in the Appendix. The building of the church was put out to tender and there were three estimates considered. On 7th April the three tenders were discussed at a Vestry Meeting held in the house of Churchwarden Wickens (the church being under repair). The tenders were presented by: Colegate – £2126, Porter – £1828, and Dove Brothers – £1795. Messrs Dove Brothers of Cloudesley Road, Islington won the contract and the work began.

The money was found as over the next eight months the new church was built. There must have been many mixed feelings in the village as people could see the old church, which they had known all their lives, being pulled down and a new edifice beginning to grow. Some people gained from the demolition, like the Barden family, who were able to use the tiles from the old church to roof the wheelwright's shop. History must record, then, that an ancient Sussex church suffered destruction at the hands of those who wanted something better. Today, it is difficult to know whether or not they succeeded; we can only guess after looking at the drawings and photographs of the old church. The new church's size was similar to the old one and there would not have been any more seats in it, but the state of repair of the old church in the 1860s had left much to be desired. One feature of the new church, which has frequently caused problems for the Parochial Church Council, is the tower with its high steeple. This is a landmark of the visible Christian Church for miles around and it rises nearly two hundred and fifty feet above sea level. Pett Church dominates the highest point in the village and in daytime guides the seafarer into the safety of Rye Bay. The building work was completed in good time, as on the 29th December 1864, the Rt. Rev. A.T. Gilbert, Lord Bishop of Chichester, dedicated the new church. A full description of the church can be found in Chapter 13.

At the first Vestry Meeting held in the new church it was resolved that 'an entry be made in the minute book of the seats appropriated to the several farms in the parish. The 3rd on the south side was appropriated to Carters Farm; the 4th, same side, to Gatehurst Farm; the 5th to Lunsford Farm; and the 6th to Elms Farm, counting from the pulpit'. This meeting was held on the 9th March 1865, and the other resolution made at it was that a rate of 2d in the pound was to be levied for the expenses of the church and general expenses connected with the same for the year.

Black's Guide to Sussex tells us that the naturalist would make some good finds in this vicinity:

Peppermint, catmint, calamint, wild cabbage, psamma arenaria, samphire, tamarisk, scorpion grass, henbane, wild celery and pellitory can be seen. The kestrel, tern, bee-eater, phalarope, landrail, hobby, snipe, plover and gull are met along this coast from Hastings to Rye.

Some of these plants are very rare in this area today, as are the phalarope, bee-eater and landrail (or corncrake). The guide goes on to say:

… from White Hart Hill, beyond the church, the view of the sea and land is broad, magnificent and constantly chequered with exquisite effects of light and shade.

At that time, before the new church was built, the guide also says '…. a church dedicated to Sts Mary and Peter is noticeable for its deformity'. This must have meant the buttresses that were necessary to support the south walls of the old church and squat tower. *Black's Guide* goes on:

…. At Cliff End, below Pett, commences to low marshy ground extending from the sandstone of the Hastings ridge to the chalk of the Folkestone heights. The Hastings sands stretch from this point over the whole valley of the Weald, bordered north and south by the chalk ranges. The forest ridge, alternating between sandstone and clay, includes Fairlight, Hastings and Bexhill, and gradually unites with the Wealden.

The *Kelly's Directory* of 1862 relates the names of some of the local people of the time. These were landowners, farmers, tradesmen and so on; some of them have already been mentioned. Others were: Mrs Griffin, Mrs Moyses and James Davis; Thomas & Spencer – graziers; William Gibbs – bricklayer; Samuel Hills – bricklayer; Thomas Hills – butcher; James Jury – grocer; George Martin – boot & shoe maker; Charles Thorpe – farrier; Ebenezer Ramsay – Two Sawyers; George Hills – Royal Oak and carrier to Hastings; James Foster – carrier; Henry Noakes – Elms Farm; George Griffin – Carters Farm; John Skinner – 'Lunsfort' Farm; Amos Wickens – Lunsford Farm, Abraham G. Thorpe – Gatehurst Farm; and Christopher Thorpe – Parish Clerk. It also gives the parish acreage as 1,945. In the *Post Office Directory* of 1878 Frederick Hammond was now a grocer and John Overy worked Elms Farm. In 1887, *Kelly's* tells us that Amos Barden was blacksmith, George Knight was a dairyman and Mrs Harriet Skinner now had 'Lunsfort' Farm.

In 1889 the church at Pett held a Certificate of Capital Value dated 20th March. This was associated with the Extraordinary Tithe Redemption Act of 1886 exchanging tithes for rents. This certificate shows the rents for four local farms as follows:

Lunsford	88¼ + 149¼ acres	Rent: £3 9s 7d
Carthouse (Carters)	130½ acres	Rent: £1 8s 10d
The Elms	122 acres	Rent: £1 1s 7d
Gatehurst	216¾ acres	Rent: £4 14s 5d

By 1895 *Kelly's Directory* gives still more information. The church living was in the gift of Charles E. Baring Young esq. and Francis Young esq. and had been held since 1882 by the Rev. John Moore Fincher. Robert Dunlop now had Lunsford Farm; James Marchant Rogers worked Elms Farm and Thomas Skinner ran the Post Office. The school catered for 56 children and the average attendance was 48. Mr Samuel Peters was the schoolmaster and his daughter Miss Grace Peters was the sewing mistress. The 1895 *Kelly's Directory* also mentions that Horace Screes ran the Temperance Hotel. Some of these folk have links in the village today.

The Temperance Hotel was, in fact the Royal Oak. Some time after her husband, William Drew Lucas-Shadwell, died in 1875 Florentia Lucas-Shadwell closed the Royal Oak public house. There are three stories about the reason for closing the inn:

- Zoe Vahey, in her book, says that James Barden (who died in 1989 aged 95) told her that the reason for taking the licence away was an incident in Mrs Lucas-Shadwell's childhood, in 1836. This was when a groom stopped one day for a drink at the Two Sawyers whilst in charge of her young brother and a pony. The pony shied, the boy was killed and the demon drink was held to blame. There is a memorial tablet to George Peter Baile Wynch (son of the Rector) in the present church, having been removed from the old building when it was being demolished.

- A second story is told that shows the men of Pett in a poor light. On receiving their pay on a Friday the men visited the Royal Oak before going home and by the time they did, the housekeeping money for their wives was somewhat depleted. The only way to stop them drinking their wages away was to close the public house by removing its licence.

- Rupert Taylor, in his *East Sussex Village Book*, says that drink cost the villagers their pub for a period of about seventy years. The Lucas-Shadwells had a very large estate that included the land on which the Royal Oak stands. Apparently, at one of the annual tenants' balls held at Fairlight Hall, the behaviour of some of the Pett tenants upset Florentia as they were having too much of a good time. It is probable that the men concerned had had a bit too much to drink before going to the ball, as it was unlikely that alcohol would have been served there. Anyway, the result was that Mrs

Lucas-Shadwell turned the pub into a temperance hotel and the sale of liquor was banned. Rupert Taylor says: 'Trade soon fell away but there was no relenting and the village stayed "dry" for a generation or more.'

I suspect that there is some truth in each of the stories and the revoking of the Royal Oak's licence was the result of a series of incidents that only added to Florentia's increasing interest in temperance.

Florentia's son William became MP for Hastings in 1895 and he held the seat for five years; Florentia herself died at the age of ninety in March 1921 after outliving her husband by forty-six years. A memorial to her is the lych-gate outside Fairlight Church.

John Moore Fincher had come to Pett as Rector from St John the Evangelist, Brighton. He was Rector from 1882 to 1909 and a lovely tale is told about him in a Parish Magazine dated 1946. In the magazine, T.P. Dunlop writes: 'He was an urbane and genial old gentleman, fond of music and a harmless joke. On one occasion at that time of the year (November 5th), it happened that a clerical friend was staying at the Rectory. The friend had never been to Canterbury, so they made an expedition thither. Mr Fincher was anxious that they should hear the choir singing, and was disappointed when they were told that there would be no afternoon service as the choirboys were out "Guying" (collecting or begging for money for fireworks, etc.). As the two friends came out of the Cathedral they met the choirboys returning. The boys, seeing them, struck up: "Remember, remember the 5th of November, Gunpowder, Treason and Plot ....", and prepared to take up a collection. Mr Fincher said, "Yes, I'll give you something if you'll give three hearty cheers for the Pope !" The boys agreed, and Mr Fincher, with his hat in his hand, led the cheering.'

During the Rev. John Moore Fincher's incumbency the custom of walking the Parish Boundaries was observed and this is recorded in the Vestry Book in April 1890 and in 1891. At that time the parish boundary stone on the sea coast was found to be missing and had to be replaced, and a note in the Vestry Book also records that the timber in the Church Steeple 'is decayed – need replaced'. The church had been built for not quite thirty years and yet the steeple was already giving problems, and as we shall see, continues to do so.

In a *Pett Directory* of 1894 (this being part of a larger *Post Office Directory*) we are told that the rebuilding of the church was in memory of Mrs Young, who died in 1862. She was the first wife of the Rector of 1864. It also states that the population of the village in 1891 was 282. The Post Office opened for business at 7 a.m. and there were two deliveries of letters per day, at 8.45 a.m. and at 12.15 p.m.; post was collected twice a day. It is worth mentioning here that an attractive Victorian Post Box can still be seen in a brick column outside the Royal Oak.

The Pett and Fairlight Friendly Benefit Society held monthly meetings in the Iron Room at Fairlight. This room was built by Florentia Lucas-Shadwell as a memorial to her husband. Tradesmen mentioned are: Thomas Barden – wheelwright; A.J. Colegate – dairyman and waggoner; Robert Ramsey – grocer and carrier; Abraham Barden – blacksmith; Frederick Cooke – grazier; W.H. Donavan – Pett Coastguard Station, chief boatman; C. Kellich – The Ship Inn; George Colegate (of Ivy Cottage) – builder. This little directory (1894) gives a short history of the village and lists all the householders along Pett Road.

The 1899 *Kelly's Directory* tells of more changes in the village. William Catt was acting Sexton; Thomas Skinner had expanded and not only ran the Post Office but a grocer's as well; Thomas Dunlop now ran 'Lumpsford' (Lunsford) Farm; Luke Moon – Elms Farm; Alfred Wickens – Gatehurst Farm; Alfred Harman – dairyman; James Hills – bricklayer; Edward Weston – carrier; Horace Screes now advertised as a Temperance Inn, picnics & other parties catered for, apartments. It would seem that whoever wrote the entries in *Kelly's Directory* was never sure how to spell 'Lunsford', as throughout the years there appears to be some considerable confusion.

It is interesting to look at the names of the fields in the parish at the end of the 19th century. Table 8 in the Appendix gives a list of the names as they were then and many of the field names remain the same today, though the ownership may have changed several times through the years. Names such as 'Godlins', 'Starve-Crow', 'Catstail' and 'Pilrags' can allow the imagination to conjure up some weird tales about origins; though the probable truth is that the farmers, being the practical people they were, named the fields after some event, shape or other feature of the land. Many of the field names describe themselves and all of the fields have provided a fragile livelihood for the men and women of Pett for many generations.

9

The First Part of the 20th Century – Including the First World War

By the end of the 19th century the church had a number of memorials on the walls of the chancel and also several stained glass windows. The churchyard was slowly but surely filling up and more ground was required for burials. In 1907 the churchyard was extended on the south side by land given by William Lucas-Shadwell (son of Florentia) and the Bishop consecrated the extension on the 13th March. The ancient extremities of the churchyard can be still seen as the old boundary wall ends are discernible at the east and west sides. It is worth mentioning here that in 1950 Mr Jones of Mill Cottage gave the land on the east side of the churchyard, known as the 'Twitten', for a further extension. Mill Cottage, across the road from the church, stands on the site of the old windmill, which was moved from Pett to Hog Hill in Icklesham in 1760.

In 1909 Frederick Charles Ashburnham Young was inducted as Rector of Pett. He was born on the 14th July 1867 and was the son of Frederick Young, Pett's Rector of that time. F.C.A. Young was educated at University College, Durham and was priested in 1896. Before coming to Pett he was curate in Lincolnshire (where he met his wife, Eva Mary), in Norfolk and at St John the Evangelist, Upper St Leonards. He was Rector at Pett until he retired in 1930, when he went to live at Hampton and then Bognor, where he died in 1938. His mother was Caroline, the second wife of Frederick and he had two elder sisters, Marion and Erica, a younger sister and two younger brothers, one of whom died at the age of just over one in 1870. A picture taken about 1874 shows young Frederick Charles with his mother, sister Erica aged about eight (on the pony), sister Ethel Flora, coming up two (in her father's arms) and the Rev. Frederick Young, his father. Frederick Charles Ashburnham Young was about seven when this photograph was taken outside the Rectory, which had been rebuilt after the old house had been pulled down in 1866.

One of F.C.A. Young's early letters to his father was written on 27th November 1877, when he was ten years old. The letter was written on the occasion of the Rector's birthday. It says:

Rev. Frederick Charles Ashburnham Young, Rector
of Pett 1909–1930

My Dear Papa,

I wish you many happy returns of the day and I hope you will like the little present I hope to get you and give you when we next meet. How are dear Mamma Rica Ethel and all at home. It was such a stormy night on Wednesday here. We went to Church on Sunday twice, in the morning and evening. I should like to see Auntie Mary, Arthur and Harcourt again for I have not seen them for a long time. I should like also to see our wagonette I am sure I shall like it very much indeed. At first we stayed in today as a shower seemed to be coming on, but it passed off. With best love to all and hoping you will have a very happy birthday. Believe me dear Papa.

Your loving son.

Fred. C. A. Young.

It is typical of many a letter sent by ten-year old boys to their fathers in the latter part of the century and was probably written while 'Fred' was at school in Hastings. The

Manor House

Hastings Nov 22 1877.

My dear Papa

I wish you many happy returns of the day and I hope you will like the little present I hope to get you and give you when we next meet. How are dear Mamma

Rica Ethel and all at home. It was such a stormy night on Wednesday here. We went to Church on Sunday twice, in the morning and again evening. I should like to see Auntie Mary, Arthur, and Harcourt again for I have not seen them for a long time. I should like also to see our

nice... I am sure I shall like it very much indeed. At first we stayed in today as a shower seemed to be coming on but it passed off. With best love to all and hoping you will have a very happy birthday.

Believe me dear Papa.

Your loving Son,

Fred. C. A. Young.

Letter from Frederick Charles Ashburnham Young to his father, The Rev. Frederick Young. The letter was written when 'Fred' was ten years old

Some of the Young family. Photograph taken outside the Rectory, c. 1874. From left to right: Frederick Charles Ashburnham Young, Caroline Maria Young, Erica Mary Young, Ethel Flora Young and Rev. Frederick Young

writing also is typical of the time (as we can see from the copy in this book) and the letter must have taken Fred a long time to complete.

The Young family have been the most generous benefactors to the church at Pett and are responsible for many of the fittings and items of furniture in the church. From the time when Henry Young was patron in 1860 until after 1962, when the most recent stained glass window was dedicated to the memory of the first Frederick Young, the family have had strong connections with the Church of St Mary and St Peter.

The early years of the century accounted for some dramatic storms along the coast and a cottage, under the cliff, belonging to Tom Collins, a fisherman, disappeared. In 1913 there was more serious flooding along the coast at Pett Level. People were rescued by boat from the old coastguard station and landed at the foot of Chick Hill. Several houses were damaged beyond repair and it was a very worrying time for the folk living on the Level.

However, Pett was a peaceful place when the First World War was declared and several events are worth recording from about that time. The first copies of a Pett

Rev. Frederick Charles Ashburnham Young, his wife Eve Mary (d. 22 February 1909) and their four children, Alan, Edie, Kathleen and Derek. Photograph taken in 1905

Parish Magazine were printed around 1910; if there were any earlier issues there seems to be no evidence of them. In 1915 Mrs Mabel Bircham was now the schoolmistress with Miss Grace Peters as her assistant; Joe Cooke farmed at Gatehurst; Charles H. Griffin at Carters Farm; Frank Foster was a private resident at Elms Farm and Mary Jane Cox was the shopkeeper at Pett Level. Thomas Dunlop still farmed at Lunsford and served on the Parish Council as he had done since the late 1890s.

On Wednesday 19th May 1915, the Rev. R.B. Jameson held the annual examination of 'Religious Instruction' at the school. He said:

The Religious work continues to be carefully taught in both Divisions (classes), the Rector taking a regular part. In the Upper Class the greater part of the syllabus has been covered, and the lessons from the Catechism and Holy Scripture have been reverently explained. Some answers were very thoughtfully given … . The younger children are kindly and successfully taught and trained. The Old Testament narratives were well known and a simple explanation has been given of the early portion of the Catechism. The written work was carefully done.

A very good report from the Diocesan Inspector; and note, children learned the Catechism 'by heart' in those days – and up to the time of the Second World war. As a result of this examination the following obtained certificates: Edith Beeching, Sylvia Beeney, Ivy Hills, Ada Butler, Olive Osborne, Winifred Cloke, Frank Bignall, Dulcie Hills, William Cloke and John Healey. Among the infants, certificates were received by: John Beeching, Marjorie Foster, Kathleen Cloke, Edwin Gates, Leonard Fleet and Marjorie Hills; and in the school reward cards were received by: Dorothy Beeching, Casper Knewstub, Gladys Cloke, Millie Osborne, John Harman, Robert Osborne and Grace Knewstub. On the following day in May, Mrs Lansdell presented prizes to children at the school for Regular Attendance, Good Conduct and Proficiency. Mrs Young, Mr and Mrs Dunlop and Mr Harman were present. Mr Dunlop wished to compliment the teachers on the success of the scholars, which was largely due to them, and he said that he was glad to testify to the good conduct of the children, outside the school – their behaviour in the village being so excellent. The families of many of the youngsters named still live in or have connections with the village.

On the last day of May in 1915 it is recorded that: 'We lost our squire, William Lucas-Shadwell, his death is a loss to the whole parish and we offer our sympathy to his aged Mother, his sisters and a widow, son and daughters, and feel that we have lost a friend, and another link in the chain of friendship has been broken.'

In the Parish Magazine for June 1915, the Rector writes:

On Wednesday in Rogation week we were able to revive the old church custom of 'The Perambulation of the Parish Bounds'. Before we started on our walk a short service was held in the Parish Church at which nearly all who perambulated were present, and we were glad to see others also able to attend. The service took place at 1 o'clock, and we started from the first Boundary Stone opposite the garden of Homestead at twenty past one, and did the round of the Parish with incidents but no accidents in 5 hours. It was 25 years since authority visited the confines of our Parish. The Rector, Messrs. G.H. Colegate, A. Harman (both churchwardens), F.C. Harman, T.P. Dunlop, R. Griffen (Chairman and Members of Parish Council), O. Baker, W.G. Colegate, James Dennett, Sydney Fleet, F. Glazier, Freddie and Charlie Harman and Jackie Harman represented the future generation.

This event proved to be very popular and was reported in the Local Press. On 20th May, *The Hastings & St. Leonards Pictorial Advertiser* filled the front page with four photographs, which included one of the Rector and Mr F. Harman 'bumping' one of

Tom Collins Cottage, Pett Level, washed away in a storm c. 1900

the schoolboys on a stone where the parishes of Pett and Fairlight meet, and one of the farmhouses at Low Winter farm, which stands in both parishes and through which the Rector and some of the party passed from back to front – after consulting the map.

All this seemed very far from the war that devastated the numbers of young men of Britain between 1914 and 1918. It is not until we read in the 1915 Parish Magazine that the Belgian Relief Fund stood at 17 shillings and six pence and that the Church-warden Mr Harman lost two of his grandsons, one of them killed in action, that the people in Pett fully recognised the fact that a war was going on around them. The Parish Council was taking the war very seriously in its discussions. In July 1915, a letter was read from J.A. Paton, secretary to the Central Organising Emergency Committee for Sussex, suggesting that Parish Councils should be asked to organise fire and salvage parties to act in case of air raids. And in January 1917 the East Sussex Agricultural Committee asked Parish Councils what steps they were taking to increase the growth of potatoes. Mr Dunlop read a letter to the Council from the Chairman of the East Sussex War Agricultural Committee relating to potato disease and the best way of preventing it, and at the same time increasing the crop by the use of sprayers. The kind of sprayer recommended as being the most suitable for small growers was the

Bucket Sprayer, which would cost £1. After a lot of discussion it was agreed that the Council purchase a Bucket Sprayer. Another letter was read, from Mr Davis, Chairman of the Hastings Rural National Service Committee, and leaflets about this were circulated at the meeting. It was decided that the Chairman would obtain a speaker to give an address on the subject of National Service. At that time the Rev. F.C.A. Young was Chairman of the Parish Council and members included Mr T.P. Dunlop (Vice Chairman), G. Colegate, R. Griffen, F. Harman and T. Gibbs; Mr Samuel Peters was the Parish Clerk.

Then the war came to Pett. On the night of the 16/17th March 1917, a Zeppelin dropped six bombs on the village. This was the date that the Germans carried out the first raid on England using their new 'height climbers', Zeppelins that had been specially lightened and equipped with oxygen supplies for their crews. They were designed to climb to an altitude of 20,000 feet, which was way above the ceiling of any contemporary fighter plane. Five Zeppelins took off from their base at Ahlhom on 16th March, but only four reached England, L35, L39, L40 and L41. Kapitanleutnant Robert Koch in L39 crossed the coast near Margate at 11.20 p.m. and moved southwest across Kent, going out to sea again at St Leonards. This route would have taken him directly over Pett, where he dropped his bombs and damaged two houses. On the trip home he ran into an unexpected 45 mph north-westerly wind and was driven way off course. It is thought that Koch suffered an engine failure, for at about 6.40 a.m. his Zeppelin appeared in the half-light of dawn over Compiegne and for a quarter of an hour drifted aimlessly over the town while the French anti-aircraft guns fired over a hundred shells at it. Finally, one managed a direct hit and the Zeppelin plunged to the ground in a ball of fire, taking her 17 crew members with her. There were no casualties at Pett and only £163 of damage was inflicted for the loss of one Zeppelin and its highly trained crew. The lightness of the damage did not deter large numbers of sight-seers who collected pieces of the bomb shrapnel as souvenirs from a field crater.

Pett was much alarmed by this air raid and at the Parish Council meeting in April, Mr Dunlop called attention to the searchlight apparatus 'in whose proximity to so many houses and buildings' and suggested that the searchlight be moved to some spot more distant from human habitation. A letter was sent to the War Office requesting that the searchlight be moved because the light could attract more bombing. The reply was read out at the July meeting from General Headquarters Home Forces, Horse Guards, London and stated that: 'The Search Light Station at Pett was sited in its present position for strong military reasons, and it is regretted that it cannot be moved.' And that was that! No more raids occurred at Pett and there was little more

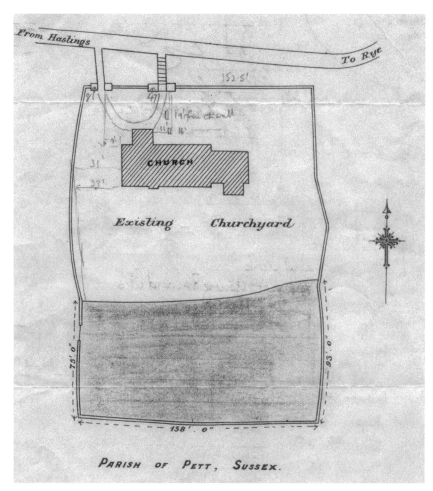

Plan of the Conveyance of land for the enlargement of the Churchyard of Pett,
dated 7 March 1907. The land was a gift from William Lucas Shadwell

mention of the war in the Parish Council minutes. One reference was made in September 1918 when a paper from Miss Rowe was read asking for members of the Council to sign a petition for the internment of all 'aliens' in the country. The clerk was directed to write to Miss Rowe and state that the Council was of the opinion that if she could obtain the signature of Major Curthope, MP for the Rye Division for such a petition, it would carry great weight! There is no mention of the nature of these aliens, possibly all those with German connections. Mr Samuel Peters was Parish Clerk as well as the schoolmaster from 1895 to 1918.

The First World War took its toll of the men of Pett just as it did in towns and villages all across the land. Their names live on in the memories of their families and on the Roll of Honour in the church and on the War Memorial in the churchyard facing

The water carrier by Sweetbriar Cottage, early 1900s

Pett Road. See Table 26 in the Appendix for the 1914–1918 fallen and for the names on the Muster Roll.

The Parish Councils, together with the Rural and District Councils, were set up in some 6,800 areas following an Act of Parliament of 1894. This Act created institutions having a civil origin, status and affiliations and transferred the civil functions of the older parish authorities to the new institutions. As a result the Church was excluded from formal participation in local government and the traditional functions of the parish, which had always had a 'Christian' connection, were to be administered by lay-men. In fact, in a place like Pett it made little difference, as the members of the Parish Council tended to be the members of the Parochial Church Council and the Rector was the Chairman. Until 1914 parish councils were locally opposed; nevertheless Parliament gradually saw fit to increase their functions. It was not until the end of the Second World War that real visible differences in the relationship between the Parish and Church Councils could be seen to be effective.

10

The 20th Century – the Years between the Wars

One event that took place in the latter years of the First World War, and yet seems very remote from it, was the sale of the outlying portions of the Fairlight Hall Estate. This took place on the 24th November 1917 at an auction by Messrs John D. Wood & Co. in the Castle Hotel, Hastings. The estate covered 3,680 acres, which included most of Pett. This was sold in 75 lots (some of the photographs accompanying the sales brochure are shown on pages 75 and 76). Table 9 in the Appendix shows entries for the Pett Grocery & General Store, Elms Farm, Gatehurst Farm, Lunsford Farm and Carters Farm.

When her son, William, inherited Fairlight Hall, Florentia Margaret Frances had a house built in Peter James Lane, known as 'Woodcote'. She lived there with her unmarried daughter, Florentia, until she died in 1921. It was after William died in 1915 that the decision was made to break up the estate into lots and sell it. Florentia's influence did not pass with her when she died as restrictions imposed by her, and then by her daughter, when parts of the estate were sold, are still in force today. The house my wife and I bought in 1985 has such a restriction in the form of a conveyance of land made in 1907. This states:

> … Neither the land nor any building to be erected thereon shall be used for carrying on any trade or business whatsoever… … nor a School Hospital or Public Institution or Charity nor for holding public meetings nor for Public Worship nor for the sale of Beer Spirits or any other intoxicating liquors for any purpose which shall or may be or grow to be in any way a nuisance damage or grievance or annoyance to the Vendor her heirs or assigns …

Note, no punctuation of any kind (as it is, after all, a legal document) – but the rules were clear! The influence of Florentia Margaret and her daughter Florentia Sarah Lucas-Shadwell lives on and the restrictive covenant remains in force. I wonder how many other properties in Pett have similar restrictions.

Another event that took place in 1917 was the foundation of the Women's Institute for Fairlight, Guestling and Pett. Later, as membership increased, each parish formed

Elms Farm. This and the following three pictures are taken from the catalogue for the sale of the outlying portions of the Fairlight Hall Estate on 24th November 1917

Gatehurst Farm (photograph from the Fairlight Hall Estate sale catalogue)

Lunsford Farm (photograph from the Fairlight Hall Estate sale catalogue)

At Cliff End (photograph from the Fairlight Hall Estate sale catalogue)

Mr Griffen driving a pony and cart past Sweetbriar Cottage, c. 1910

its own group. Then in 1918 women over the age of 30 obtained the vote and in 1928 both men and women over the age of 21 joined the electorate. Women were beginning to flex their muscles and show the world that they were just as intelligent, industrious and expert as the males who had dominated them for centuries. Equality, though, was a long time coming.

Before 1921 the only means of transport out of the village was by foot, horse or carriage. A milk cart went to Hastings twice daily and could take a few passengers. Some farmers had their own pony and trap, and a photograph showing Mr Griffen driving his pony along Pett Road near Sweetbriar Cottage makes a charming picture around 1910. Sometimes a taxi braved the poor roads in the village, but it was mainly horse-drawn vehicles that could be seen in Pett until the arrival of Pett's first Motor Bus. This was a converted van run by Mr Morris, of the Royal Oak, and driven by Mr Catt. There was no step up into the bus and a wooden box served as a portable one. The bus can be seen in the photograph of the Royal Oak on the next page. About 1931 the East Kent Bus Company started a proper bus service and Pett really became part of the twentieth century.

The 1927 *Kelly's Directory* gives a lot of information about the people of Pett. The

'Royal Oak Temperance Inn, Pett', c. 1925

area of the parish, it states, was now 1,898 acres of land, 10 acres of water and 157 acres of foreshore. The population in 1921 was 325. Principal landowners were: T.P. Dunlop, Robert Davis and Charles Henry Griffin; Mrs Pye was the Schoolmistress; William Gallop Colegate had the Post Office and was also a beer retailer; Percy Morris (as we have seen above) had the Temperance Hotel, was the motor-omnibus proprietor and a carrier; Mrs Mary Colegate – Stonedene Farm; A. Cook – Holford's Farm; Robert Davis – Gatehurst Farm; Thomas Parker Dunlop – Lunsford Farm; Charles Foster – Pannel Farm; Charles Henry Griffin – Carters Farm; Reginald Ernest Selmes – Farm Bailiff to F. W. Cooper esq. – Elms Farm; Reginald Cooke – Coastguard Officer, Thalassa, Pett Level; I.C.I. Elliott – Pett Garage; Robert Griffin – Boot Repairs; Owen Catt – carrier; Miss Violet Broad – Refreshments and Rooms at Pett Level; Sir Harry Bird J.P. – The Lookout; Charles Baker – Windy Ridge; Samuel Coxeter – High Cliff; Harold Eves – Chick Hill Cottage; Harry Rivers – The Hannays; Mrs Jenner – Bell Vue; Mrs Jones – Westcote; and Mrs O'Brien – Sans Souci.

The Village Hall was built in 1923 and was opened on 17th December by Lady Brassey. The monies to pay for it came from fetes and village entertainments held over two years and the site was presented to the village by Mr Dennett in memory of his son Preston, who was killed in action during the First World War.

VIEW FROM CHICK HILL PETT LEVEL.

View from Chick Hill, Pett Level

In 1927 the Parish Church was fitted with new heating. Originally a stove below floor level inside the church heated the building. This had been superseded by two slow-combustion stoves, which were now replaced by an installation of hot-water heating by pipes and radiators, with an external boiler house built against the south wall, next to and utilising the chimney shaft of the original system. The cost of the new heating was £194 17s 0d, Mr George Colegate of Pett was the builder and Messrs Upfield of Hastings were the heating engineers. Two years later, in 1929, electric light was installed in the church at a cost of £44 and was a gift of the Rector.

On 29th September 1930 the Rev. F.C.A. Young retired and two months later, on 14th November, 1930, the Rev. Herbert Ernest Moxon was inducted as Rector. He had been Vicar of Breedon-on-the-Hill with Staunton Harrold and Isley Walton in Leicestershire (near Burton-upon-Trent) between 1922 and 1930, and remained Rector of Pett for ten years before moving to St John's, St Leonards-on-Sea.

One of the parish highlights of the Rev. Moxon's incumbency was the dedication of St Nicholas Church in 1935. The building had been used by the Coastguards to house equipment, such as life-saving rocket apparatus, until it was purchased by the Parochial Church Council in conjunction with the Chichester Diocesan Fund and

The Wheelwrights' shop

Board of Finance in March 1935. On Sunday, 26th April 1935, the Bishop of Lewes, the Rt Rev. H.M. Hordern, dedicated the church to St Nicholas, the patron saint of sailors and of children. It was through the efforts of the Rector that a sufficient sum had been raised to purchase the building, and many people contributed to the furnishing of it so that it was soon converted into a really beautiful miniature place of worship, supplying a real need for residents and visitors. On 26th October 1935, the Bishop of Chichester affixed his seal to the Authorisation to hold Public Worship in the new Chapel of Ease to St Mary and St Peter, and in Mr Moxon's time there was an early celebration of Holy Communion there every week, and Evensong every other Sunday. As the Parish Magazine of 1946 says: 'The association with Life Saving is a very beautiful one and surely no mere coincidence.' The church was closed in June 1940, after the evacuation of all civilians from the area, and was reopened in August 1945.

It was also in 1935 that the relationship between the Winchelsea Beach folk and the Parish Church strengthened, with the start of services at Winchelsea Beach and the building of St Richard's Church at Dog's Hill Road. An insight into the finances of Pett Parish at that time show a record of the income and expenditure of the 'Living' for 1935 and a budget for 1936. These could be found in the Parish Magazine for April 1936, which has a heading for the 'Church of St. Mary & St. Peter, Pett with St. Nicholas Church, Pett Level and St. Richard's Church, Winchelsea Beach. Price 2d.' The complete magazine article is shown in Table 10 in the Appendix.

Because the Rector did not receive a stipend, the major part of his income was made up of Tithe Rents. The deductions from his income included taxes, pension contribution and the Queen Anne's Bounty collections (collection of Tithes etc.) The Tithe Act of 1936 finally ended this system and the parish clergy began to receive an annual stipend. The practice of giving the incumbent the total collections for Easter Day continued for many years and may still occur in some parishes today. The total budget figure for Pett in 1936 was £110 13s 0d; maintenance and insurance of the Church Fabric was only £20 and the Quota (payment to the Diocese) £14. How costs increase! In the budget for 2001, the Pett Quota is in excess of £7,500 (and that is less than a third of the Benefice total quota), and Pett's total budget figure stands at over £15,000. St Richard's Church, Winchelsea Beach, was part of the Parish of Pett until a change of Boundaries came into force on 11th November 1966. The lands east of the bend in the road by Winchelsea Caravan Park, which were in the parish of Pett, were added to the parish of Icklesham.

In May 1937 the Coronation of King George VI was a wonderful occasion for the village. A full programme of events was planned, and an appeal made for funds to support this met with a very good response. The May Parish Magazine states:

The Committee wish it to be as widely known as possible that they will welcome any who live in the neighbourhood of Pett and who care to make a donation towards the fund and join in our celebrations. The collectors are, Messrs L. Cooke, L. Coxeter, W.G. Colegate, J.F. Earle, Mrs W.G. Colegate, Mrs Harris and Miss Nuthall. There will, too, be a box at the Village Hall for contributions. Each child will receive a Coronation Mug and a Flag, this applies to children of subscribers too. It is almost certain that there will be a surplus which can be applied to the erection of some permanent memorial, probably public seats. The field opposite the church has been very kindly lent to us by Mr F. Dennett for the Sports. There will be a Refreshment Tent in the Field. A Cask of Beer has been provided from the Beach Club, Pett Level. To those who fear that this facility may lead to excess, and so mar the pleasure of others, the Committee wish it to be known that strict control will be exercised in its distribution. No

View from the church tower in 1911. The building in front is the village shop, now extended to include the upholsterer's. On the other side of the road the school house can be seen. The building on the far right is French Court Farm. The field opposite the church is where the sports were held as part of the 1937 Coronation celebrations

young people will be served unless by the expressed wish of their parents. We doubt if there are any who will regard "free beer" as an opportunity for immoderate indulgence, but in the unlikely event we may as well inform them that they are doomed to disappointment. We want all to enjoy themselves and all will agree that uncontrolled drinking would not make for that. I find it distasteful even to write these things. I believe it will be shown to be wholly unnecessary, but we do want to allay any fears there may be. For the sake of the children alone we are determined that there shall be no abuse.

The celebrations on 12th May started with a service in Church; then everyone was encouraged to go home and listen to the Coronation broadcast on the radio. The Sporting Events started at 2 p.m. and included races for all ages, the entrants for the 60 yards men's race having to produce their birth certificates. There were sack races, pick-a-back races, thread needle races for girls, high jump, throwing the cricket ball as

'Old Sussex Cottage' – in Pett Road in the early 20th century. The photograph of Gatehurst Cottage was taken before major structural change and additions were made

well as all sorts of running races. After the Sports, tea was served in relays in the Village Hall and at 8 p.m. there was an interval during which the King's speech (which was broadcast) was relayed into the Hall. At 9 p.m. there was a Grand Firework Finale, consisting of a Royal Salute of twenty-one giant rockets, with everyone joining in the National Anthem. It was a great time for everyone in the village and there appears to be no report of anyone abusing the gift of 'free beer'.

In April 1939 thanks were expressed to the two Churchwardens for their long and devoted service to the Church. Mr T.P. Gibbs had held office for 21 years and Mr W.G. Colegate for 20 years – and what stalwarts they had been. Then, on 10th September 1940, the Rector announced his resignation on his appointment to St John's, St Leonards-on-Sea. By March 1941 a new clergyman had arrived in the parish: he was the Rev. Victor Charles Roberts and had come from the Diocesan Church, Haywards Heath. Though he became Chairman of the Parish Council and lived for a short time in Mill Cottage, he did not live long enough to be inducted as Rector. Tragically, he died suddenly in May and so his name does not appear among the Rectors of Pett. By July of 1941 the Rev. Roland Clifford Wood had become Rector and remained in the parish until 1954.

Before moving on to the Second World War years, let us linger a little and take a look at Pett Level. Though this is very much a part of the parish, there have been times when the inhabitants of Pett and Pett Level have not been the greatest of friends. The folk at Pett Level sometimes felt that they were the 'forgotten people' and the Parish Council did not always serve their best interests. Pett Level is a wonderful place, with its many stories of the sea and the marsh. A somewhat mysterious place and a haven for wildlife. Pett Level has always suffered from strong gales and high seas, as has the whole length of the coastline in this part of England. In 1921 there had been a considerable storm that caused much damage along the Level. It was a result of storm damage that the old Ship Inn (which had been built about 1740) became unusable, and it was completely demolished in 1932. The owner, George Hickman, rebuilt the inn at Winchelsea Beach, using many of the old timbers and retaining the name 'Ship Inn'. The old Ship Inn had been very popular with artists and authors, and with the aviator Geoffrey de Haviland, who once telephoned an order from near London and, in order to consume it, landed his airplane on the beach, not far from the inn, thirty minutes later.

There had been an old earth sea wall some 200 yards behind the foreshore and this too was often damaged during gales and high tides. Between the wars there were few houses seaward of the Military Canal and some wooden shacks served as holiday houses for visitors. Later in this book is an article written by Mr Reg Cooke, a local man who was very well known and who loved Pett Level, the sea and the marsh. In this article Reg writes superbly about Pett Level and brings the area alive with his recollections. He could remember the building of another sea wall, built in the 1930s at a cost of £165,000. This wall was made of a double row of Oregon pine piles, boarded on both sides and filled with beach. It did much to hold back the sea until parts of the wall were breached when the army blew holes in it to flood the marsh early in the war. A railway ran along the top of this wall and was used to carry the shingle back to the beach at Pett Level after tidal movement had transferred it towards Rye Harbour.

In the 1930s, a Mr Seaton bought the land and houses around Pett Level, including the old Coastguard cottages. He upgraded and altered the cottages by adding a first floor to them, but met his match with Mrs Crampton, who refused to let workmen into her cottage and would not let any such alterations be made to her house. 'Granny's Cottage' is still to be seen with a lower roof than the rest of the dwellings in the row. Mr Seaton also built a golf course and a tennis court on the Level and then, after selling off all his acquired property, built his own castle-like dwelling under the cliff at Cliff End.

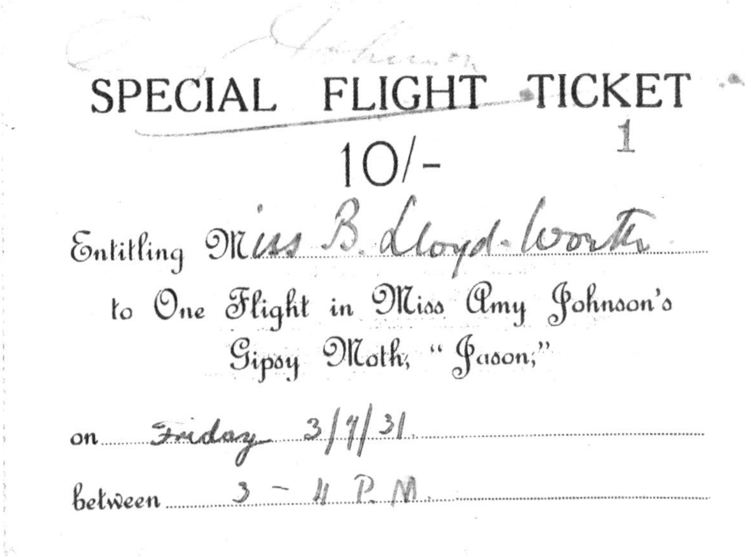

SPECIAL FLIGHT TICKET

10/-

1

Entitling *Miss B. Lloyd-Worth*

to One Flight in Miss Amy Johnson's

Gipsy Moth, "Jason,"

on *Friday 3/7/31*

between *3 – 4 P.M.*

A ticket for a flight with Amy Johnson

A 'Great' day occurred during the July of 1931, when Amy Johnson brought her Gipsy Moth aeroplane, Jason, to the locality. The plane landed in a field belonging to the Milward-Sayers near Fairlight Hall and then took passengers up in the sky for a trip.

Pett resident Barbara Lloyd-Worth can well remember her flight, which took her over the lovely countryside, giving splendid views of the sea. Her special flight ticket is shown above, together with Amy Johnson's autograph.

Liability was an important issue, even in the 1930s, and the reverse of the ticket stated:

CONDITIONS OF ISSUE. Although every possible precaution is taken in the avoidance of accidents it is understood that the Owner and Pilot of this machine accept no responsibility, and the passenger by the acceptance of this ticket accepts and takes upon himself all the risks and dangers of the conveyance however arising.

Barbara, however, landed safely after a thrilling and exhilirating flight.

Pett and Pett Level were very rural in the 1930s and the numbers of visitors to the beach and the countryside were still quite small. The doubts about the possibility of another war seemed far away from the parish and yet it was not long before life in the village changed dramatically.

11

The Second World War

In 1939, at the beginning of the Second World War, Pett was considered to be a safe area and children from Camberwell were evacuated to it. There was a committee of billeting officers under the leadership of the Rev. H.E. Moxon whose job it was to get the children settled, and they took over the Village Hall for a schoolroom. The Rev. H.E. Moxon was a great favourite with the children and they would ride in his car and trailer – or anywhere where there was room for them to climb aboard. However, after the fall of Dunkirk, Pett became a threatened area and the evacuee children were moved on to Wales.

A period of defence measures followed. Pett Level, south of the canal, was evacuated and filled with troops. Roadblocks were constructed of old timbers and manned by the newly formed Home Guard armed with shot guns. Possible airfields were blocked with old carts, and barbed wire sprang up everywhere. Every available man worked hard to construct tank traps and other obstacles; Pett was preparing for war and the possibility of invasion. Once again the marshes and the foreshore were extensively mined, the sea wall was blown up in three places and the marsh flooded as far as the Royal Military Canal. All who had no business in the neighbourhood left and the community shrank in size. Military rules were very strict: to enter Pett or to go down to Pett Level required a permit. The village was almost a closed area for the rest of the war.

It was during the summer of 1940 that the marsh at Pett Level was flooded. This covered an area of about 1,000 acres and returned the marshlands to the conditions that prevailed in this low-lying area before man's attempts to reclaim it. The flooding had a big effect on the bird population. Many of the marsh and shore birds that had, in normal times, been visitors, now came to the area to breed. There was great excitement when the black tern bred here in some numbers in 1941–1942. Oyster-catchers and wigeon nested and reared young too, for the first time in living memory. The flooding of the marshes was, in most people's minds, a deplorable necessity, but it was also an event of exceptional interest and a 'duck paradise'.

To complete the defences at Pett Level two six-inch Royal Naval guns were emplaced on Toot Rock and anti-aircraft guns were also sited and ready for any enemy airplanes. The bridges over the Canal were blown up, the Rectory was taken over by the Army, who put an anti-aircraft gun on the roof, and Pett was ready for war.

East Sussex played a notable part in the war and received its full share of bombing by the Luftwaffe and by flying-bombs. In all there were some 4,000 air-raids in the county and some of these were in Pett. The ARP (Air Raid Precautions) did a valuable job as part of the Civil Defence and manned their posts with vigilance and enthusiasm. Blackout, rationing and all sorts of restrictions were dealt with by people as necessary intrusions into their lives, and some children living in this area were evacuated to places that were considered to be safer. The RAF had personnel operating observation posts on Gatehurst Farm land; these plotted the course of enemy planes and this information was passed to the headquarters and then on to RAF airfields and relevant gun sites. The anti-aircraft units put up heavy barrages during the Battle of Britain and were greatly reinforced during the flying-bomb period. Flying bombs falling in East Sussex numbered 775, with many hundreds more in the sea around the coast, some of them close enough to the shore to do damage to property inland. Battle Rural District, of which Pett was a part, bore the brunt of this campaign, with a total of 374. In the Battle District there were 105 properties totally destroyed by explosion, a further 153 capable of repair and 5,575 with some slight damage. The personnel of the Civil Defence General Services in the district totalled 1,400 and the Fire Guard Service 3,500, all of whom were part-time workers. If we take a look at the air raid statistics for the parishes in the Guestling Hundred we find:

Result of Air Raid	Pett	Guestling	Fairlight	Icklesham
Flying bombs on the ground in parish	4	8	1	14
Flying bombs in sea or close to land	9	–	16	11
Unexploded anti-aircraft shells	3	1	3	3
Anti-aircraft shells and petrol tanks	–	3	1	1
High explosive bombs	54	99	26 + 20 in sea	28
Unexploded high explosive bombs	10	6	2	6
Incendiary bombs	–	1295	30	80
Oil and phosphorus bombs	–	6	–	–
Machine gun & cannon fire attacks	3	6	5	4
Civilians killed	–	3	–	–
Civilians injured	–	17	9	4

Mrs Elliott, one of the early Presidents of the Women's Institute, was killed when her house (in Guestling) was destroyed by a German bomb at 8.45 a.m. on 9th January 1943. The machine gun attacks were frightening when the hit-and-run raiders flew in extremely low, almost touching the ground, so that the anti-aircraft guns could not depress sufficiently to fire at the planes to bring them down. The gun on the Rectory was used for this purpose, but to little effect as there was no warning of an attack and anyone about at that time took cover anywhere they could. During the period when the flying bombs were being sent towards London, the noise of the guns attempting to shoot them down was deafening. Someone said that it didn't seem possible that so many guns could be firing in such a small area and making so much noise. Day and night they fired into the sky causing pandemonium. Tin-hatted service personnel, both men and women, were forever running to and from their billets (or from their tents if sleeping under canvas) to their stations. More than half the number of flying bombs crossing the coast did not reach London.

One other problem that faced Pett was that of sea mines. Both English and enemy mines occasionally got shaken loose from their moorings by the action of the sea and drifted in to the coastline. One or two of these reached the beach at Pett Level. A mine hit the wooden slipway and blew up causing some damage, including blowing some timbers on to the land. One piece of timber was blown a considerable way inshore, landing in a field belonging to Lunsford Farm.

Eventually the air attacks and any threat of invasion passed. The theatre of war was passing away from Britain to other areas. The first Italian prisoner of war appeared in the district, to be followed by others (Italian and German), who worked on the land. Finally, in 1945 it was all over. The war ended and Pett mourned the men of the village who lost their lives in the conflict. See Table 26 in the Appendix for the names on the 1939–1945 Roll of Honour.

There are one or two entries in the Parish Council Minute Book and the Minutes of the Parochial Church Council that add to the information about Pett's role in the war. Before it even started, in January 1939, the Parish Council met to consider a request from the Ministry of Health via the Battle R.D.C. that the Council should arrange for, and undertake a complete house survey in the parish with the 'object of obtaining information as to the capacity to absorb refugees from London and the suburbs in the event of the start of hostilities'. The Council appointed the Rev. H.E. Moxon as chief billeting officer for the parish and suggested to the parishes of Fairlight and Guestling that it would be advisable to use the existing ARP boundaries for evacuation purposes. The Parish Council was very much involved with giving advice to people wishing to enrol for National Service and set up a panel consisting of: 'Mr

Morris, The Old Lodge (whom failing Mr J. Earle); Mr Wright, Sunset; Mrs Hake, Hill House (whom failing Mrs Giles)'. In August and September 1940 the Council received complaints from residents about the way work was being done on defence preparations at Pett Level:

> The schedule was unsuitable, men – physically unfit and badly experienced. There is a lack of proper supervision and much inefficiency. The Parish Council is in contact with the officer commanding troops at Pett with regard to the number of accidents which had occurred in the parish. The Council moved to write to the Hastings Borough Council and two MPs serving on the Select Committee in the House of Commons.

In 1941 liaison was set up with a Battle War Weapons Committee and Mr Earle was now the Parish Billeting Officer. In May 1941 a girl was injured by a motorcycle despatch rider while walking in one of the parish lanes.

In July 1941 the Rev. R.C. Wood was welcomed to the parish and at the PCC meeting of that month it was reported that bomb damage repair to Pett Church had been carried out by the Battle Urban District Council and that the fabric of the church was now in good order. It was also agreed to restart the Parish Magazine in the September of that year. On 18th October 1943 the Archdeacon visited the parish and met with the Rector and the two Churchwardens to discuss the Winchelsea Mission Church, St Richard's. It had been damaged by bombs and was temporarily closed with its furniture put in store. Discussions also took place on the Parish Boundaries, which needed to be reconsidered in the near future (changes did not occur till 1966), and on the Pett Rectory, which was being let to the Military for £75 per annum. By February 1945 a war-damage claim had been forwarded in connection with St Richard's Church, which was still in the hands of the Military. It was not until the 1950s that some services were transferred to Winchelsea and a new St Richard's was built in 1962. In 1945 a full-sized Parish magazine was published; 100 copies were printed and all were sold.

12

The Years after the Second World War

During 1946 and 1947 a new sea wall was built. This extended from Cliff End, by the Beach Club, where it joins the old wall, to Winchelsea Beach. Much of the clay used in the sea defences was dug out from what became the Colonel Body Memorial Lakes, four pools surrounded by reed beds and grazing marsh that are now all part of an area of international importance for wildlife. During the winter the pools are home to many water birds, including wigeon and pochard. Curlews, lapwings and winter visitors flock to the marsh to feed on the damp pasture. In most years, the Sussex Ornithological Society lowers the water level in the pool nearest the road to expose large areas of mud. This attracts huge numbers of migrating wading birds that stop here to feed as they travel from their Arctic breeding grounds towards Africa.

The new sea wall had a walkway along the top and steps at intervals along its length; it looked solid and permanent. But by the end of 1951 there was a storm in which very strong winds coincided with extremely high tides and severely damaged the wall. Some of the walkway disappeared, some of the steps were thrown aside, and water swirling over the top of the wall washed away much of it, the clay and dirt falling into the road below. The damage was repaired, wave screens and groynes were strengthened and erected, and over the years further work has been done in the attempt to beat the fury of the wind and sea. More visitors came to the area, caravan sites appeared at each end of the long stretch of beach and life began to get back to normal.

By late 1946 the Rector, who had moved out of the Rectory when the Military took it over, was back in his house. However, he was not very pleased about the way he had been treated by the War Office, as these two extracts from the Parish Magazine of the time show. In his letter of November 1946, the Rector, the Rev. R.C. Wood, writes:

> We are very happy in the Rectory and like it very much indeed. The condition in which the house and grounds were left by the Military reflects little credit on the troops who occupied it, and still less on the officers who were supposed to be in charge of them. I should like to record my deep dissatisfaction with the

way in which I have been treated. For over a year after my arrival no rent was paid, and at the time of writing no compensation has yet been paid on the house and outbuildings. There also seems no adequate machinery to safeguard the interest of the Clergy. As far as I can judge the Military Authorities have a free hand to requisition land and buildings at their own price, to pay rent when they think they will, and fix both the amount of compensation and the time when it will be paid. No one seems to be able to bring them to book. This is a thoroughly undemocratic situation which should not be tolerated.

It was not until February 1947 that the Rev. Wood was able to report in the magazine:

I am glad to say that the compensation on the Rectory has at last been paid after persistent pressure from all sides. I should like to take this opportunity of thanking Mr Jim Barden for all his help and patience in this matter. I am most grateful.

Once all signs of war had been removed and people were getting used to 'peace', life gradually got back to normal. This took a year or two and there are still some relics of the war left; the occasional 'pill box' can be found hidden away in a field or at the bend of a lane, the gun emplacement at Toot Rock commands a good view across the landscape and the remains of the observation posts can still be seen in the fields of Gatehurst Farm.

In the 1950s there was a lot of correspondence about the closure of the school in Pett and the eventual sale of the school building. In 1953 Mrs Watson had retired and Mrs Bright had been appointed head teacher. The school was finally closed in 1957 and the children were all accommodated in the remodelled Guestling Bradshaw Church of England School.

On 11th September 1954 the Rev. Ernest Algernon Parkins was inducted as Rector and he stayed in the parish until his retirement in 1971. It was the Rector's son, Richard, who wrote the first leaflet on the history of St Mary and St Peter Church in 1959. It was priced 3d when the leaflet was first produced but by 1967 it was updated and reprinted at 6d each. In eight years more than 400 of the leaflets had been sold. In July 1957, the Rector reported in the Parish Magazine that six churches could be seen from the Rectory roof on a clear day. These were Guestling, Icklesham, Rye Harbour, Fairlight, Lydd and, of course, Pett. Seven years later, Richard Parkins wrote that on an even clearer day they had managed to spot Rye and Playden churches, bringing the score to eight – and he wished to add a lighthouse (Dungeness), a castle (Camber) and a nuclear power station to the sights seen.

Sunnyside, Pett Level (on the corner at the bottom of Chick Hill)

It was in the early 1960s that the Rectory was demolished and a new house built further down Pett Road with the most stunning view across the fields and marshes towards Folkestone. The site of the old Rectory was sold and became Rectory Park with nine attractive detached houses built on the site. The new Rectory was the home for six incumbents and their families until it was sold in 2002, when a new Rectory was built in Fairlight, the Rev. Bernard Crosby and his wife Carol being its first occupants.

In November 1966 the Parish Boundaries were changed. There had been little or no change in the boundaries since medieval times and yet there were to be two alterations within twenty years. The 1966 change reduced Pett Parish in size to pass St Richard's and the land east of the bend in the sea road by Winchelsea Caravan Park to Icklesham parish. Then in July 1980 a further change took place that transferred land from Fairlight parish to Pett. The strip of land added to the parish of Pett is a stretch embracing Roughter's Wood, Fairlight Wood, Pett Wood, Burnt Wood and Pannel Wood that used to link Fairlight to Icklesham. The shape is rather like that of a saucepan handle coming out of the remainder of Fairlight parish. The value of the land in the Middle Ages would have been considerable, which is probably why Fairlight held on to it, but from an ecclesiastical and parochial point of view it makes more sense to include this strip in Pett. The story of changes does not end here as in 1968 (again in

July), the benefice of Pett and the benefice of Guestling were given to the Rev. Ernest Parkins to hold in plurality. Later, on 31st May 1978 the parishes of Guestling and Pett became a United Benefice. This was not long after the dissolving of the Archdeaconry of Hastings and the creation of the new Archdeaconry of Lewes and Hastings. Finally on 8th September 1994 the United Benefice of Fairlight, Guestling and Pett was formed with John Robin Balch as Rector.

Between the Rev. Ernest Parkins and the Rev. Robin Balch Pett had four Rectors: George William Egan Manners, from 1971 to 1978; John Hanson Read, from 1978 to 1984; Michael Butler, from 1984 to 1988 and Norman John Charles Greenfield, from 1988 to 1994. Each of these clergymen brought his own special contribution to the life of the Church in Pett and Guestling, and in latter years to Fairlight as well. Robin Balch retired at the end of September 2001 and on 7th June 2002 Bernard Edward Crosby was inducted as Rector of the United Benefice.

During the second half of the 20th century the social life in the village increased. Various clubs were set up, in addition to organisations such as the Women's Institute, which continued to flourish. The Pett Sports Association started in 1963 and uses the recreation field for cricket, stoolball, bowls and tennis; each having their own club. The Pett Level Naturalists' Society was formed in 1972 with Fred Bottrill-Smith as its first President and by the following year had over 150 members. The Pett Level Preservation Trust grew out of the love of the area and the nature of the environment, and in 1973 land was purchased by the Trust. These and other organisations began to make their mark on the life of the people of Pett as they grew in size and influence. The clubs and societies continue to meet regularly but membership is somewhat less these days than in the last quarter of the last century, as a result of factors such as an increase in the television viewing habits of the population and the ease of travel by car etc. to leisure activities outside the village. How much this may change with the building of a new Village Hall, completed in 2002, remains to be seen, but the community spirit in the village is as strong now as it ever was.

The great storm of 1987 is recent enough to remind us of the immense strength of the natural forces that are all around us. This part of the country has always suffered from storms: the wind and the tide together with the rain have created havoc along the coast in this area for as long as man can remember. Yet on the night of 16th October, or rather, in the early morning of 17th October 1987 hurricane winds of up to 108 m.p.h. were recorded in East Sussex. The barometric pressure dropped to 958 millibars, the lowest since records were kept. Within four hours 15 million trees were lost, lorries overturned, church steeples crashed to the ground, cars were crushed and houses lost their roofs. Power supplies failed and 3,000 miles of telephone lines came

The New Pett Village Hall

down. It was a terrifying night that left devastation behind the tremendous storm. Pett church was damaged, the roof losing many of its tiles, but the tower survived. Damage to property in the village was severe and many trees were lost in this area. Fortunately no one was killed in and around the village.

Since 1864 when the church was built, the roof and the tower have been repaired on a number of occasions. Not only is that part of the church very susceptible to the prevailing winds, being the highest point in the village, but it appears that the west end of the church and the tower were not built as well as some other parts. It has been said that the money ran out when the church was built and the west end and tower suffered. Certainly, there have been many maintenance problems with that end of the church. In 1890 the Vestry Book records that the timber in the church steeple was decayed and needed repair. In 1911 the steeple was repaired and the cost to parishioners was reduced by a grant from the Bishop of Chichester's Fund. A strong gale on 29th July 1956 caused the roof of the church to undergo considerable repairs. By 1970 the entire steeple needed 're-shingling', two of the eight sides being in a very

Set of six porcelain plates – part of the Canterbury Collection. Top left: The Church from Pett Road; Top right The Village Hall (built in 1923 and pulled down in 2002; New Village Hall opened in March 2002 near the Two Sawyers); Centre left Methodist Church (original church – now the hall – built in 1848; new church – on the left – opened August 1956); Centre right Sports Pavilion in the Recreation Field (used by cricket, stoolball, bowls and tennis clubs); Bottom left The Two Sawyers Inn and Pett Brewery (formerly the wheelwright shop and forge); Bottom right The Country Stores and the Butcher's Shop (just beyond the parish boundary in Guestling)

Pett Level Road in the early 1950s. On the right of the picture is the old Beach Club, now The Smuggler
public house. Beyond the Beach Club are the old Coastguard Cottages and some holiday homes. More
permanent homes and the New Beach Club are built along the coast road now. Between the Beach Club
and the Coastguard Cottages is St Nicholas Church and the Pett Life Boat

bad condition and many shingles on the remaining six sides requiring replacement.
The work was carried out in 1971 at a cost of £1,100.

One of the major repairs took place in 1975, during the incumbency of the Rev.
G.W.E. Manners. An article in the *Sussex Express and County Herald* of 17th January
1975 states that the cause of the problem with the church building went back to the
time when the church was built. The article, on the front page of the newspaper, says
that after the decision had been made to build a bigger church there was a cash short-
age when it actually came to the building. Corners had been cut to bring the plans in
reach of the parish pocket. An inspection made in 1973 showed that some of the
stonework was a 'cement rendering'; rain gutters had not been levelled off properly in
places with the result that the spire stood in a small trough of water and damp. Similar problems made some of the chimneys unsafe, and the parapet around the tower
below the spire was, in one place, resting on only one inch of support. A new roof
was needed on the north side and all the chimneys had to be taken down and the one
still in use had to be rebuilt. The inspection by the architect gave the Church Council
a severe shock and all kinds of events took place to raise the monies required to put

in hand these major repairs. The work was carried out between August and October 1974 at a cost of around £3,000. After the work was completed the Rector, the Rev. G.W.E. Manners, planned a number of events to celebrate the church's 111th anniversary. 'Somehow the 100th passed without celebration,' he said. The Church Council felt that the next appropriate date would be the 111th. A Flower Festival was planned in the April of 1975, a Patronal Festival arranged for St Peter's Day in June, and a service to mark the anniversary of the building's consecration on the 28th December (1864) was also programmed. The guest preacher at the St Peter's Day service was the Rev. Alan Young, grandson of the Rev. Frederick Young, the Rector when the church was rebuilt in 1864.

Severe winds have often caused tiles to move and sometimes fall, and this in turn has meant more repairs to the roof and spire. As we have seen, the hurricane winds of October 1987 were no exception and extensive repairs took place after that terrifying event. The latest chapter in the saga of the 'West End' is an appeal made to the parish and friends of the church in January 2000. This followed a Quinquennial Inspection by the Architect, which revealed much deterioration in the stonework at the west end of the church and around the west window, defective guttering and drains around the tower, major repairs required to the stonework and timbers of the tower, and considerable redecoration needed inside and outside the church building. The total cost of the repairs would be in excess of £150,000 (compare this with £1,700 approximate cost of building the church). A sum of money this size is far beyond the means of a parish like Pett, and the absolutely essential work was costed at around £40,000, the remainder being major but not necessary to prevent the building falling down. It is mainly because of the generosity of the villagers of Pett and friends from past times that much of the £40,000 was raised fairly quickly, and this with grants and monies from a Fabric Repair Fund allowed the first stage of the repairs to be carried out before the end of the year.

During 2000 and the early part of 2001 Mrs Eileen Balch, wife of the Rector, the Rev. Robin Balch, did much to enable the creation of a Memorial Garden in the churchyard. The Archdeacon of Lewes, the Venerable Nicholas Reade, dedicated the Memorial Garden and the repairs to the west window and the end of the church on Sunday 6th May 2001.

There is still more than £100,000 needed to complete the repairs and decorations to the church, and this places a very heavy burden on the Parochial Church Council and dwindling congregations. How the money will be raised and what the future will be no one knows, but a Christian presence in the village is still felt, by most people, to be essential and the village church is still a focal point in many people's lives.

13

St Mary & St Peter Church – Description of the Church and Memorials, etc.

The parish church of Pett has been described in various ways by different authors. V.J. Torr in his *Pett Records* says that it was 'rebuilt in a rather mediocre fashion'. Some have described it as 'dark and dull' and being a typical Victorian church. W.S. Mitchell in his *East Sussex Shell Guide* calls it, 'a rather perky successor to an older church on the same site' and the *Post Office Directory* of 1878 calls it 'a handsome structure'. To anyone who looks at the church closely, the beauty of it will become apparent the longer they study the design and the features it displays.

The church stands at the highest point in the village and can be seen from most houses along the ridge of Pett Road. The building is in the Early English Decorated style and is made of brick and stone. The church consists of a nave, some 53 feet in length and 23 feet wide (internally), and a chancel 24 feet by 16 feet with a vestry on the south side. There is a tower with spire more than 75 feet high on the north side of the nave at the west end of the church. This makes the top of the tower nearly 250 feet above sea level and allows it to be used by local fishermen and other sailors as a navigation point when approaching Rye Bay and Rye Harbour. The walls of the church are faced with local bluestone, quarried from the Marsham slope of Pett ridge, with Bath-stone quoins (dressed angle stones) and string course (a continuous project-ing horizontal band in the surface of the wall).

If one looks at the church from the outside, the chancel has a three-light east window with three decorated circular motifs, one above each light. On the north side of the chancel are two lancet windows, and on the south side the vestry is lit by three windows: a small stained glass rectangular window on the east wall, a two-light window (rectangular on the inside) on the south wall and a rectangular window on the western wall of the vestry. There is a recessed door to the vestry from the outside of the church, the entrance to which is at the east end. On the south side of the nave there are four windows and on the north side three; all windows are of two lights with a trefoil in the upper part of each. At the west end of the nave is a three-light window with a quatrefoil and six small circular window panes above. The

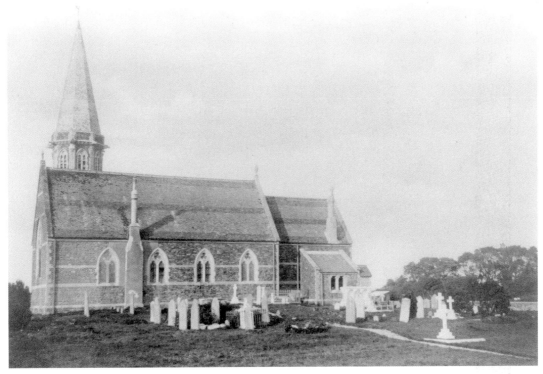

St Mary and St Peter Church, Pett – photograph taken about 1920

small tower is about nine feet square internally and forms an entrance porch to the church on the ground floor. In the upper square part of the tower are three single lancet windows on the north side and one on each of the east and west sides, above which is a trefoil. Above the three lancet windows on the north side of the tower is a gilded clock face. The upper part of the tower assumes an octagonal form in which there are eight belfry louvre openings, and this terminates in an eight-sided spire surmounted by a weather vane in the shape of a cockerel. There are eight griffin-type gargoyles and a decorated motif round the top of the tower, and eight decorated columns, one at each corner, of the top part of the tower – below the gargoyles. The outer entrance to the porch is under a pointed moulded arch above jambs with marble nook-shafts. On top of the roof were three wheel-headed crosses, one above each end of the nave and one at the east end of the chancel. The 1987 gales brought down the cross at the east end of the chancel and it has not been replaced. Two remain!

On the south side of the church is the entrance to the boiler house. The church was originally heated by a stove inside the building and below floor level, with hot air

St Mary and St Peter Church, Pett – photograph taken in 2001

ducts and gratings at the west end. This system was superseded by slow-combustion stoves, and later in 1927 these were replaced by an installation of hot water pipes and radiators. There are radiators at the ends of alternate pews as well as others in the church and vestry. It was in 1927 that the boiler house was built against the south wall and the boiler utilised one of the chimney shafts of the original system. The chimney was rebuilt in 1974, and other chimneys were removed during the major repairs carried out at that time. The engineers installing the boiler and heating system in 1927 were Messrs Upfield of Hastings, and the builder was Mr George Colegate of Pett; the cost of installation being £194 17s 0d. There have been various updates of the heating system since the 1930s and the boiler was replaced in 1987, but the boiler house is still in use and the system continues to provide warmth in the church during the cold spells. The original iron gratings can still be seen in the west end of the church, though some are covered by carpet.

St Mary and St Peter Church: the nave in the 1870s. Church lit by oil lamps

The original door to the vestry was built in 1910. The architect was V.E. Young esq. and the builder was G.H. Colegate; the cost was £40 5s 0d. The vestry itself was enlarged later.

If one enters the church through the door of the porch (on the north side) several items of interest can be seen. There are wooden benches on each side of the porch, a sturdy ladder going up to the tower, a bell rope for the single bell, notice boards and two oak tablets. These tablets record the repairs to the steeple in 1911 and in 1971. The top tablet states:

The steeple of this church was repaired in A.D. 1911 by the generosity of parishioners and friends and helped by a grant from the Bishop of Chichester's Fund. F.C.A. Young – Rector A. Harman G.H. Colegate – Churchwardens.

A grant of £25 was received from the Bishop's Fund. The lower tablet recalls that:

Further repairs were made in 1971 towards which a donation was given as a thank offering for the ministry of Frederick C.A. Young Rector 1909–1930.

St Mary and St Peter Church: the nave in the 1950s. Note the position of the organ. Mrs Parkins, the Rector's wife, is one of the ladies in the front pew

A pitch-pine door separates the porch from the nave. It is interesting to note that in many churches the porch can be quite large: the porch was almost certainly the predecessor of the village hall. It was used as a meeting place where the issues of the day were discussed and decisions taken. Oaths were witnessed by the priest in the porch and, until the Reformation, both baptism and marriage began with a ceremony at the church door or porch.

On entering the church the first thing that catches the eye is the font. This is not surprising when one considers the ancient practice of baptising infants soon after the

View of the Church from the Churchyard (south)

birth; until a baby had been cleansed of all sin he or she could not enter the body of the church, and as has been mentioned the baptism service used to begin at the church door. Fonts in many churches are close to the door and it is a short walk from the door of Pett Church to the font in the centre of the nave at the west end.

The font at St Mary & St Peter Church has had a chequered history. It was given to the church by the Rev. Augustin Diones Geere in 1753, while he was Rector of Pett, and remained in the old church for at least a hundred years. Between 1848 and 1852 considerable repairs were carried out in Icklesham Church under Canon the Rev. H.B.W. Churton. A new font was placed in All Saints at Icklesham and the Rev. Churton gave the old font to Pett. The reason for this was that the Geere font was by this time damaged and in a state of disrepair. So the old font from Icklesham was placed in the church at Pett and the damaged Georgian font preserved under cover in the churchyard. Then in 1953 the Georgian font was restored thanks to the generosity of Mr Vincent Lines, a striking looking man, over six feet tall with very red hair; he was

Octagonal Georgian font on a fluted balaster stem, presented to the Church in 1753 by the Rector, the Rev. Augustin Diones Geere, and restored in 1953 as a memorial to Agnes Rose Lines

an artist and a teacher and lived with his parents at No. 1 Coastguard Cottages, Pett Level. He paid for the restoration of the font in memory of his mother Agnes Rose Lines. Vincent, Agnes and her husband Benjamin are all buried in the churchyard.

The Georgian font is octagonal on a fluted baluster stem. An octagonal font was sometimes known as a Seven Sacraments font, seven sides representing the seven sacraments – baptism, confirmation, mass, penance, extreme unction, ordination, and matrimony, with the eighth side representing the Crucifixion or Baptism of Christ. The number eight as a Christian symbol also represented the Resurrection and New Life. Around the outer sides of the bowl of the font the following inscription is carved: 'Ex Dono Dionysii Geere hujus Ecclesiae Rectoris May 20, A.D. 1753' – translated from the Latin reads: 'Given by Diones Geere of this very church Rector May 20, A.D. 1753'. At the base of the fluted stem, just above the bottom step and facing towards the east, is a plate inscribed: 'This font dated 1753 was restored in

1953 to the memory of Agnes Rose Lines'. The font has an oak cover surmounted by a brass cross. It was fitting that the restoration should be carried out in the bi-centenary anniversary of the font's presentation to the church, and it was also the Coronation year of Queen Elizabeth II. It is good that the old Bath-stone font of 1753 is back in its rightful place; and what of the ugly early Victorian font given to Pett by Canon Churton? Well, it now resides in the churchyard looking somewhat like a sad bird bath, not far from the main door to the church and slowly being eroded by the weather.

The interior of the church today is more like the inspirational design of Benjamin Ferrey than the inside of the building during the late Victorian period. Now the walls of the chancel and nave are clear of boards depicting the Ten Commandments, Lord's Prayer and Creed, as well as hangings around the altar. Some of the moulding that was coloured has had the paint removed and the church looks neat and light. Originally the church was lit by oil lamps, causing the interior to look dim for much of the time. The electric light was installed in 1929 as a gift of the Rector and others at a cost of £44. The plan for this lighting was by F.T. Wordley, Electrical Engineer, St Leonards. In 1981 the light fittings were replaced and the lighting system updated. The effect of this was to lighten still further the interior of the church and to highlight some of the furniture and fittings that were previously somewhat hidden.

The church is based on the Pugin style of Gothic revival, insomuch that Ferrey was one of Pugin's pupils, and his influence can be seen in some of the decorative features. There is a collar beam roof in the nave consisting of four bays, formed by three arched braces supporting it. The chancel arch is elaborately moulded, springing from square capitals each carved with foliage and four corbel heads. There are two polished marble columns on each side of the chancel arch similar to the nook shafts on the outside door to the church. Supporting the braces on each side of the nave are more moulded capitals, four of which have a corbel head. Altogether there are 12 heads, each of which is slightly different, and it has been suggested that they could represent the twelve Apostles. The roof of the chancel is also of the collar beam type with four bays, though the bay at the east end is very small. The roof is painted and varnished in a pleasant orange–brown colour and, like the nave, is supported by three arches. Where they meet the walls of the chancel, the ends of the arches are decorated with wooden shields. On the north side – from west to east – are: St Matthew, an angel; St Mark, a winged lion; and a Lamb (Paschal), Passover. On the south side – from west to east – are: St John, an eagle; St Luke, a winged ox; and a Dove, representing the Holy Spirit. John Rootes painted the shields at the end of 1957 when the chancel was reconstructed.

The chancel in 1959 after the reconstruction and redecoration of 1957

At the end of the 19th century the chancel did not look as it does today. The decorated stamping in the plaster was painted a deep red, boards with the Lord's Prayer and the Apostles Creed stood one on each side of the altar on the east wall, and the Ten Commandments were painted on two boards, one on each side of the chancel arch facing the nave. There was a harmonium on the south side and there was one row of choir stalls on each side of the chancel. Between 1957 and 1959 the chancel was reconstructed in order to resite the organ and add new choir stalls and an additional priest's stall. During this time the boards on each side of the altar and the chancel arch were removed and a curtain was hung across the east wall of the chancel behind the altar. When the church was decorated again, the curtain was removed and

Decorated stamping on the east wall behind the altar. This method of incising stucco surfaces while wet was an invention of Benjamin Ferrey, architect of St Mary and St Peter Church

the decorated stamping in the plaster was whitened, leaving the chancel looking much as it is now.

Benjamin Ferrey's invention of incising the stucco surfaces of church walls while wet was used to good effect in the chancel of St Mary & St Peter Church. There are decorated surfaces behind the altar on the east wall with a fleuretty type wheel cross each side of the east window, and above the east window is a monogram with the letters 'IHS' in the centre of a circle from which radiate eight fleur-de-lis. The letters are the first three letters for the name of Jesus, and the number eight signifies regeneration. The stylised lily is generally believed to represent the Madonna Lily and is a symbol of purity. The decorated surface behind the altar is in the form of a large area of patterned diamonds in diagonal rows, each alternate row containing either a fleur-de-lis or a five-petalled flower in each diamond. Decorated stamping in strip form surrounds the patterned area and continues to both sides of the east wall, along the north wall of the chancel, running over and under the two lancet windows, and also along the south wall at two levels. The effect of this is most pleasing to the eye and enhances the beauty of the sanctuary.

The floor of the chancel is tiled in square patterns. The pattern in the sanctuary is slightly different from that in the body of the chancel, where it would appear that one or two large squares are different from the rest. There is one step from the nave to the chancel and two steps from the chancel to the sanctuary. On the top step to the sanctuary are three long embroidered kneelers designed and made by Mrs Joan Zeepvat. These lovely Communion kneelers were made in memory of Mrs Janet Jury, who left money for the materials, and they took two years to complete (1986–1988). Crafted in exquisitely worked stitches, their theme is the Bread and Wine. The whole set of kneelers is 15 feet long and 10 inches wide. The left-hand section comprises pictures of the parables of the 'sower' and the 'loaves and fishes', one on each side of a hand holding a Communion wafer. Wine is the subject of the right-hand section; with representations of the 'wedding at Cana', water pots and the Communion Chalice, surrounded by grapes and the vinedresser. The centrepiece is the figure of Christ with His 'I AM' sayings – the gate of the sheepfold, the Good Shepherd, the Way, the Truth and the Life, the Light and the Resurrection. Worked into the whole are many local features – sheep, cattle, the fox, badger, blackbird and rabbit, and wild flowers and insects. Pett Church is also included in this superb piece of embroidery, which does much to make the church attractive and complements the design of its architect.

The altar table is of pine faced with oak and with a carved oak frontal. In the front there has been set an elegant 17th century carved panel with two cherub's heads in the centre. There is considerable intricate floral carving around the heads and four narrow panels, two on either side of the central carving. It is thought that some of the carvings are of a later date than the central panel, which may have originated from another piece of furniture, or even from another church. There are no records of where it came from or what it was.

The organ was built by W. Richardson, organ builders of London, and replaced a harmonium. It is a pipe organ, probably built from second-hand parts before 1870. It has two manuals and a mechanical action with a pneumatic pedal board. When it was first placed in the church, in the 1870s, it stuck out some way from the south wall and partially obscured the view of the chancel from the nave. The Rev. F. Young and others raised the money for it.

The organ was resited in 1958 when the chancel was reconstructed. The vestry was enlarged and a recess built to accommodate the organ. Part of the south wall of the chancel was removed so that the organ pipes stand just proud of the organ recess. The old choir stalls were discarded and new oak stalls provided. The generosity of one parishioner enabled a replica of the existing priest's stall to be made, and this was placed on the south side of the chancel. The work of the restoration amounted to £1,600, nearly the total cost of the building of the church one hundred years earlier.

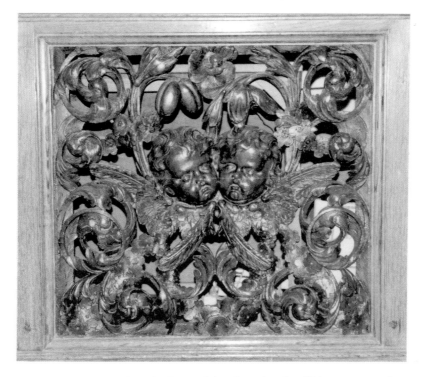

The centre oak panel on the front of the altar, showing 17th century carving

On the north side of the chancel is a wooden plaque commemorating the work done at this time, which states:

Pett Parish Church
The additional church vestry, the resiting of the organ and its reconstruction, an additional priest stall and new choir stalls, and the re-decoration of the church were carried out in the years 1957–1959 at a cost of £1,600 provided by the generosity of the parishioners and friends, including a grant of £50 by the Diocesan Board of Finance. E.A. Parkins, Rector; N.M. MacLeod, Treasurer; H.C. Pratt, Secretary; T. Hyde Ebbutt *(who gave the plaque to the church)* and C. Barden (Churchwardens); A.C.S. Hickes, Architect; H.A. Jury (decd. Churchwarden).

There is a Withers safe in the vestry, purchased in 1928, which replaced the Chest that was broken to pieces in 1927 by burglars.

The credence table in the sanctuary is made of oak and stands on the south side of the altar. The altar rails are made of oak with wrought-iron supports, each with a six-petalled flower. As in many churches, a light glimmering in the vicinity of the altar is a familiar and welcome presence for visitors and parishioners. It means that the Sacra-

The aumbry door, showing 1983 carving of fig leaves, wheatsheaf and grapes by Michael Renton of Icklesham

ment of Holy Communion is reserved, usually for the sick and housebound, and it is kept in the aumbry.

In 1982 the Parochial Church Council proposed that an aumbry (a closed recess in the wall of the church) be installed in the chancel. Regulations require that an aumbry must have a metal lining and a four-lever lock. The Rev. John Read, Rector of Pett at the time, had an interesting talk with Mr Tom Driver, blacksmith of the forge at Guestling Thorn. Mr Driver did have a suitable piece of metal – as used to repair farm implements. He also had a brass lock and key. Tom was delighted to make up the metal lining and did so without charge. The remainder of the piece of metal used for the lining finished up as a repair job for a 'dung-spreader'. The lovely door to the aumbry is of oak. John Read happened to be a duty clergyman at Westminster Abbey at this time and he contacted the Dean who willingly arranged that the Clerk of Works provide wood from one of the old oak timbers that had been removed from the Abbey roof. After struggling to get the timber back to Pett, John Read put it in the hands of Leslie Barden, who made a door and its surround. The door was then given to Michael Renton of Icklesham who carved the decoration of four fig leaves, a wheat-sheaf and two bunches of grapes. The finished aumbry was fitted in 1983. The light above it was designed and constructed at the forge in Appledore (Kent), the cost borne by Miss Peggy Daly in memory of her sister Sheila Brentnall MBE, who died in 1981. The reserved Sacrament is kept in a small container (pyx), which was given in memory of Mrs Davidson. The aumbry is a beautiful addition to the furnishings, a truly local endeavour and a good illustration of the generosity of local people and the love they have for their church.

The nave is tiled with black and red squares and has pitch-pine pews. Originally there were twelve pews on the north side of the church and fourteen on the south side. Over the years some of these have been removed to give more space in the body of the church. In the front of the nave, nearest the chancel, two pews were removed on the north side to give space for a piano and a table. On the south side first one pew, nearest the pulpit, was removed while recently two pews at the back of the church have been removed to give more space to display a cabinet for the Memorial Garden Book of Remembrance and to enable refreshments to be served after some services. At the end of alternate pews there are brass umbrella stands with enamelled troughs, and radiators at the ends of the others. Two Churchwarden wands (or staffs) are positioned, one on each side of the aisle, halfway down the nave.

The pulpit on the south side of the nave is made of stone and marble, the marble columns being similar in style to those on the chancel arch. There are also two circular designs with marble inlay on the sides of the pulpit. The pulpit book-rest and a set of antependia (or embroidered frontals) were given to the church by Miss G.E. Young in 1911. The lectern is of oak and was given to the church by F. Young esq.; it is in the form of an eagle. The eagle is a symbol of victory, and became so because of its powerful upward flight towards the sun – representing the Ascension. It was also the symbol of St John, emphasising the light of Revelation. The eagle with its out-stretched wings stands on a sphere supported by a baluster stem and circular base. This in turn is an integral part of the foot, which is in the form of a stylised cross. The lectern replaced a simple tall bookstand that was used in the early days of the 1864 church.

At the west end of the church are two pews that have been converted to a table supporting hymn books, notices, visitors' book, etc., and behind this and running along the west wall is a bench that also continues a short way along the south wall. There are various cupboards and portable notice boards at the back of the church and above the bench on the south wall is a war memorial commemorating the men of the village who were killed in action during the two World Wars. At one time this was sit-uated on the north side of the east wall of the chancel arch (facing the nave), but was

The clock constructed in 1829 by John Moore and Sons, Clerkenwell, London and placed in the Church tower in 1865. It is a turret clock with a cast-iron frame and brass gears and bearings

moved following the decorations of 1959.

Two other features of the church are in the tower. They are the clock and the bell. The clock was placed in the tower in 1865 from Denbies, Dorking. It is a turret clock with a cast iron frame, brass gears and bearings, and a moderate pendulum of seven feet. Basically the design is similar to that of 'Big Ben', but on a much smaller scale. It was constructed by John Moore and Sons, Clerkenwell, London for W. Denison esq. in 1829. This was the year when George Stephenson was testing his steam railway locomotive, the 'Rocket'; George IV was king; and the Duke of Wellington was Prime Minister. The clock was second-hand when it came to Pett. Its pointer shaft was fitted through an existing and convenient window in the north side of the tower and motive power is derived from gravity weights suspended by high-tensile steel cables wound round the driving drum. The clock weight is about 500 lb and the weight of the hourly chime about 65 lb. Both these iron weights have to be raised by hand cranking some 20 feet to achieve 7 days (maximum 8 days) running time. It takes a strong man to wind up the main weight single-handed: the 18-inch cranking handle is designed for a two-man operation. This is an arduous weekly task, as the winder has first to ascend some 20 feet to the clock platform by near-vertical ladders. The village owes a debt of gratitude to Vic Goodsell, who has regularly wound the clock for many years. The exterior of the clock face has no backing (or face) and both it and the clock hands are gilded.

When the old Sussex church was pulled down, the most ancient treasure from it, the bell, was placed in the 1864 church. The bell – 'music's laughter' as the poet Hood called it – is dated 1641. It carries the inscription: 'Robert Foster gave XVL (£15) towards me in 1641'. The single bronze bell is about 2 feet 6 inches in diameter and weighs about 6 cwt. (the hour bell of Big Ben is 9 feet in diameter and weighs 13½ tons). Originally it was designed as a normal tolling church bell with a free clapper, but since 1865 it has also served as an hourly chime for the clock, with a clock hammer striking the outside rim and the tolling clapper the inside rim. From the considerable indentations made round the inside rim by the clapper over many years, it is clear that the bell has been rotated several times in its lifespan of over 360 years and millions of blows from the clapper. Nevertheless, the bell produces a clear ringing tone, and is still free from cracks, which is more than can be said for 'Big Ben'! It can cause embarrassment if the bell is tolled at the same time, or close to the moment when the clock strikes the hour, and care is taken to avoid this. In 1967 an inspection found the bell-clapper to be beyond repair. It was striking in such a low position that on some occasions the clapper rested on the bell itself, giving the effect that the bell was cracked. A new clapper and bearing were fitted at a cost of over £100. The sound of the bell chiming the hours and tolling before services is a familiar feature of Pett village life, and when the clock is silent due to maintenance or repairs the village folk 'fret' until the sound is restored.

The windows and memorials in the church, together with some of the furnishings, are a legacy of the love and generosity of parishioners from every age. Earlier, in Chapter 4, George Theobald is mentioned, and a record of his gift can be seen in the oldest memorial in the church. Just inside the door, behind it on the north wall is a brass plate. This brass was taken out of the old church and fixed centrally in the riser of the step from the nave to the chancel. It was later moved to a position in the west face of the north side of the chancel arch. Still later it was moved to its present position, where it proclaims to the world:

Aedibus his moriens Campanam sponte dedisti Laudes pulsandae sunt Theobalde tuae. Here lies George Theobald a lover of bells and of this howse, as that epitaph tells. He gave a bell freely to grace the new steeple. Ring out his Prayse therefore ye good people. Obit 10 die Martii 1641

There is no mention of George on the bell that currently hangs in the steeple, and it is possible Robert Foster gave his £15 towards the cost, or recasting, of the bell that George Theobald 'freely gave'.

There are eight stained glass windows in the church, three in the chancel, one in the vestry and four in the nave. The other four windows in the nave are made up of clear diamond-shaped pieces, and those in the vestry are of the sash type. The quality of the stained glass varies from window to window but they all tend to blend into the beauty of the building. All except one of the windows are in memory of various members of the Young family, who over many years have been great benefactors of the church. Table 11 in the Appendix lists members of the Young family who had connections with Pett Church.

The east window in the chancel was the first to be placed in the church. It is a three-light window with stained glass pictures in the middle of each light. Above and below each picture are diamond patterns, each with entwined 'IHS', surrounded by a coloured strip motif. In the northern-most light St John, the Evangelist, is shown holding a chalice from which is emerging a dragon's head. St Peter, holding keys and a book, is shown on the southern-most light, and Christ with two kneeling children is shown in the centre light, under which is the quotation: 'Suffer little children to come unto me'. Beneath the window, in glass, it states:

> This window is erected by some of her friends in memory of Anne wife of Rev. F. Young Rector of this Church. Elder daughter of Ven. W.H. Hale, Archdeacon of London. She died Oct. 29th 1862.

Inscribed on the bottom right-hand corner of the window in one of the diamond panes is Chas. A. Gibbs. Charles Alexander Gibbs of London, 1825–1877, was a well-known designer of stained glass windows. The Ven. William Hale (1795–1870) was also master of Charterhouse from 1842 to 1870 and his daughter Anne was the first wife of the Rev. F. Young, Rector when the church was built.

The two lancet windows on the north wall of the chancel are similar and were designed by the same stained glass maker. The motifs on both windows are alike with the exception of the design at the top. On the eastern window the Greek letters alpha and omega are entwined and on the other window the letters 'IHS' are depicted. The north-eastern window is dedicated to James Forbes Waring Young, born 2nd September 1867, died 28th April 1869. James was the 4th son of Charles Waring Young (brother of the Rev. F. Young) and Augusta Emma and was just 18 months old when he died. The north-western window is dedicated to Henry Arthur Byron Young, born 8th September 1868, died 6th January 1870. Henry Arthur was the son of the Rev.

East window in the chancel, given in memory of Anne, first wife of
the Rev. Frederick Young, Rector of Pett 1857–1882

Frederick Young and his second wife Caroline Maria, and again this young boy died
when he was only 18 months old.

The small rectangular stained glass window in the vestry was given in memory of
Eva Mary Young, wife of the Rev. F.C.A. Young. It shows the Virgin Mary with the
infant Jesus in her arms and has A.D. D.G. inscribed at the bottom together with: 'In
Loving Memory, Eva Mary Young'. Eva was born in November 1870 and died on the
22nd February, 1909; she is buried in the churchyard.

The most recent window is that on the eastern end of the north wall of the
nave. It is dedicated to the memory of the Rev. Frederick Young M.A., Rector of
Pett 1857–1882. The window represents St Nicholas with a lifeboatman on the
shore. In the background there is a somewhat abstracted lightship, which is symbolic
of the Church Universal. St Nicholas is holding a model of the building that was

St Nicholas window on the NE wall of the nave, dedicated to the memory of the Rev. Frederick Young MA

formerly a Rocket House but is now used as the church of St Nicholas, Pett Level. The artist is Lawrence Lee ARCA of New Malden, Surrey, who was one of the artists responsible for the stained glass windows in Coventry Cathedral. The window was dedicated by the Rev. E.A. Parkins at a service, at which members of the Young family were present, on 1st April 1962, 80 years after the death of the Rev. F. Young.

The window on the west end of the nave, on the south wall, is of the patterned two-light style with a trefoil window above. In the left light, looking from the nave, Christ is shown raising the daughter of Jairus whilst her parents look on, and in the right light Jesus is being attended by Mary and Martha. In the trefoil above are the head and shoulders of an angel. A brass under the window reads: 'To the Glory of God in memory of Jane Maria Young who died the 13th October 1871, age 45.

Window on the SW wall of the nave: The raising of Jairus' daughter and Martha and Mary – in memory of Jane Maria Young, d. 13 October 1871

Erected by her brothers'. Jane Maria was the daughter of Henry Young and his wife Maria and her brothers were the Rev. Frederick and Charles Waring Young.

The large window on the west wall of the nave is probably the finest in the church. The designers were very well known as makers of stained glass windows, and their names, Lavers, Barraud and Westlake, appear on the bottom right panel of the window. Nathaniel Wood Lavers (1828–1911) and Francis Phillip Barraud (1824–1900) set up partnership in 1858 and worked in a conventional Gothic Revival manner. When Nathaniel Westlake (1833–1921), a protégé of architect William Burges, began to design for Lavers and Barraud in 1858, he brought a more distinctive style to the firm. Westlake became a partner in 1868 and retained the name of the firm when he became the sole partner in 1880. It was Westlake's knowledge of medieval art, Pre-Raphaelite style and simplification of previously over-elaborate drawing that brought the firm fame and success in the 1860s. From the 1870s to the end of the century the

West window in the nave, given in memory
of Henry Young, 1797–1869

windows were technically excellent, but lacked some of the earlier creative originality. The firm closed in 1921.

Above this three-light window are six eyelet windows, four of which are smaller than the other two. Each of these has a pattern incorporating a cross, and in the centre of them is a larger quatrefoil window. In this Mary is shown, with the dove of the Holy Spirit descending towards her head, surrounded by four figures representing the four Gospel writers. The three-light window below contains two Biblical scenes going across the three lights. The top scene shows the Sermon on the Mount (Matthew Ch. 5–Ch. 7) with Christ in the centre with his arms outstretched as he talks to an enthralled crowd who watch Him closely. The bottom half of the window shows Moses, in the centre, after coming down from the mountain and carrying two tablets containing the Ten Commandments. On each side of Moses are crowds of Jews listen-

The Medley window on the SE wall of the nave, given in memory of the Medley family and the 3rd Earl of Liverpool – erected in 1899

ing carefully to his words; some are kneeling, some are holding their hands up to their faces, and Aaron can be seen with his staff (Exodus Ch. 34 v. 29–35). The window is full of characters and colour, and the effect of the restoration of it in 2000 will continue to give pleasure for many years to the visitors and locals who look at it. Under the window is a brass plate, which reads: 'To the Glory of God, in memory of Henry Young, who died 1st of December 1869, age 71, erected by his widow'. Henry Young, father of the Rev. Frederick Young, was also formerly Patron of the living and did much to raise money for the building of the church.

The only stained glass window in the church that is not in memory of the Young family is that at the eastern end of the south wall of the nave, near the pulpit. This fine window has St Mary in the left light and St Peter, holding a staff in the shape of a shepherd's crook in the right light. At the bottom of the window and inscribed on the glass and on a brass plate are the words: 'This window is erected by Cecil Lord Hawkesbury to the Glory of God and' (on the brass plate beneath the window) 'in memory of his ancestors of the Medley Family, formerly Lords of this Manor, also his Grandfather (their successors here) C.C.C. 3rd Earl of Liverpool G.C.B. erected 1899'.

There are a number of shields depicted, on the glass and one on the brass, bearing the coats of arms of the many families associated with this window. The families are: Medley of Buxted, Medley of Warwickshire, Earl of Liverpool, Evelyn, Shuckburgh, Howard, Cavendish, Foljambe, Partridge, Reynes and Dashwood. For anyone interested in Heraldry a complete list of the coats of arms in the Medley window, and their contents, can be found in the *Sussex Arc. Society* Volume No. 68, pages 230 and 231. The links between these families are complicated, but below is an attempt to show the relationship between some of them.

Charles Cecil Cope Jenkinson came from a most distinguished family. His father Sir Charles, 1st Earl of Liverpool and Baron Hawkesbury (in the county of Gloucestershire) was a great statesman, and his half-brother, Robert Banks, was not only the 2nd Earl, but also Prime Minister between 1812 and 1827, succeeding Robert Percival after his assassination. The 3rd Earl and his wife Julia Evelyn Medley had three daughters, the second of whom married twice. Her name was Selina Charlotte and she married first William Charles Viscount Milton (who died in 1835) and second George Savile Foljambe. They had seven children, the eldest being Cecil George Savile Foljambe, who was created Baron Hawkesbury in 1893 and was Lord in Waiting to Queen Victoria until 1895. It was this Baron Hawkesbury, created a new Earl of Liverpool in 1905, who erected the window in Pett Church. So the 1st Earl of Liverpool was the grandson of the 3rd Earl of Liverpool, though when the window was placed in the church at Pett in 1899 he was still just Lord Hawkesbury. Cecil George Savile Foljambe's first wife was Louisa Blanche Howard (died 1871); they had two children, and his second wife was Susan Louisa Cavendish, who bore Cecil five sons and six daughters. The Dashwood connection is through the mother of Sir Charles, 1st Earl of Liverpool. The 3rd Earl is buried at Buxted, Sussex, and a number of monuments and memorials to the Jenkinson family and their descendants are in the Hawkesbury Church in Gloucestershire. There are at least 31 churches in different parts of the country where Cecil Foljambe inserted windows or brass plaques, most of them commemorating Louisa Blanche by name. These churches were all connected with his family, either on the Foljambe or Jenkinson side and in Sussex the churches are Westham, Buxted, Barcombe, Tarring Neville and, of course, Pett. The family story is made more complicated by the fact that four of the people mentioned above married twice.

There are several memorials in the church in the form of tablets on the walls. The oldest of these is the lovely memorial to Cordelia Sayer which is above the vestry door on the south side of the chancel. The memorial itself is in the form of a sickle and a sheaf of corn above a marble tablet. It has been attributed to Sir Richard Westmacott

(1775–1856), who was trained as a sculptor under Canova in Rome. His works include Addison, Pitt and Fox in Westminster Abbey; Collingwood, Abercromby and Captain Cook in St Paul's Cathedral; and the bronze Achilles in Hyde Park. Though Cordelia cannot claim the fame of these gentlemen, it is pleasant to think that her family was able to commission a memorial sculpted by such an eminent artist. The words on the stone tablet are as follows:

> Sacred to the memory of Cordelia Sayer, who was born on the 18th April 1776 Died at Hastings Jan. 1820, and was at her own desire buried here. She was the daughter of Henry and Sarah Sayer of London and the granddaughter of John and Mary Collier of Hastings

And, underneath this:

> *Farewell, Cordelia. Sweet object of a mother's love. Dear as the name of daughter e'er could prove*

Why did someone, aged nearly 54 when she died, who certainly did not live in the parish and who had many connections with Hastings, wish to be buried at Pett? Well, there are links with the area and with this church. Cordelia may have spent some time in the village during her life. She came from a very well-known Hastings family, the Colliers. Her grandfather, John Collier came to Hastings early in the 18th century and played a very important role in the history of the town. He was, at least, four times Mayor of Hastings, was appointed solicitor to the Cinque Ports in 1714 and 1727, and also held the position of Town Clerk. He had the honour to be one of the canopy bearers at the coronation of King George II and Queen Caroline, and he was an able magistrate. He married twice and had 18 children, four by his first wife Elizabeth and 14 by his second wife Mary Cranston, whom he married in 1717. Mary's father, the Rev. James Cranston, would, at that time, have been Rector of the United Parishes of St Clement's and All Saints in Hastings for 27 years. He continued to be Rector there for another nine years. On the 17th December 1702 he had also been inducted as Rector of Pett. James Cranston's daughter Mary was Cordelia's grandmother, and it was this Mary who must have instilled a love of Pett into her daughter Sarah, both of them passing this on to Cordelia.

A number of the 14 children born to John and Mary Collier died at a tender age, and some names occur more than once: there were two Janes, two Thomases and two Williams. Another Mary, a sister to Cordelia's mother Sarah, married Edward Milward, who for fifty years was Mayor and Deputy Mayor of Hastings. The Milwards lived at Fairlight Place and Cordelia must often have stayed in the house of her uncle, aunt and cousin Edward. Cordelia's father, Henry Sayer, was of Carey Street in London and his marriage to Sarah took place at the Church of St Dunstan in the West in 1763. The couplet on Cordelia's memorial tablet would seem to suggest that her mother survived the death of her daughter; if this is so she would, at that time, have been in her 81st year. The family were very much involved with St Clement's Church in Hastings and there are memorials to them there.

Of Cordelia herself we know little. How did she travel to Pett and how often did she make the journey? The roads at that time were little more than tracks once you turned off the turnpike road between Hastings and Rye. Whom did she visit here? The Lucas-Shadwells were friends of the Colliers and Sayers; perhaps this was another link!

Also on the south side of the chancel, there is another memorial tablet. This is partially hidden in the recess for the organ, and was placed in its present position on the eastern side of the chancel arch wall when the reconstruction took place in the late fifties. The memorial is to Frances Ursula Pellew, and at the top of the tablet there is a cross on the left side and an anchor on the right side. Inscribed on the memorial are the words:

> Sacred to the memory of Frances Ursula Pellew. The eldest child of the Hon. George Pellew D.D. Dean of Norwich and Frances his wife. She was born March 10th 1821. Died at Hastings February 17th 1840 and is buried in the aisle of this church. *"We sorrow not as those without hope, humbly trusting that to her might be applied those beloved words of Christ: 'Daughter be of good comfort: thy faith hath made thee whole: go in Peace'"*.

There is also a small stone slab about midway up the nave in the centre of the floor, inscribed 'F.U.P. Feb. 17 1840'.

We know little about Frances Ursula Pellew; she was not quite 19 when she died in Hastings. She would have been buried in the old church in the time of Henry Wynch, but the reason for this is lost in time as there are no church records available to enlighten us. Frances was descended from a family which originally came from Normandy, France, but for many centuries had been settled in the west of Cornwall and finally Devon. Her grandfather was Sir Edward Pellew, 1st Viscount Exmouth, who at the age of 57 had risen to the rank of Admiral in the Royal Navy, having been famed for his seamanship and fighting ability. He died in 1833 having had five boys and two girls. George Pellew was the third son (1793–1866) and was born in Flushing, Cornwall. He was educated at Eton and Oxford, and was ordained in 1817. He was Dean of Norwich and Rector of Great Chart, Kent, from 1828 till his death. In 1820 he married Frances, second daughter of Henry Addington – Prime Minister (1801– 1804) and First Viscount Sidmouth. They had one son and five daughters, of whom Frances was the eldest. George printed many sermons and tracts and also *The Life and Correspondence of Addington, First Viscount Sidmouth*. The only clues we have about Frances Ursula are in the words of Christ on her memorial tablet. The fact that 'Faith hath made thee whole' may indicate that Frances was not a well person and may have been poorly for much of her short life. In her passing, her 'Faith' may well have given her 'Peace'. The anchor and cross on her memorial would surely represent her naval and ecclesiastical associations.

There are two memorial tablets on the north wall of the chancel. The eastern-most tablet is situated between the two lancet windows and is a memorial to George Peter Baile Wynch. Words inscribed on the tablet read:

> Sacred to the memory of George Peter Baile Wynch, only son of the Rev. Henry Wynch Rector of this Parish and Charlotte his wife, who was born June 27th MDCCCXXVIII (1828) and whose pure spirit was recalled by his Heavenly Father on the 19th April MDCCCXXXVI (1836). His earthly remains are deposited in a vault in this chancel. '*Of such is the Kingdom of heaven. Therefore we sorrow not even as others which have no hope, for if we believe that Jesus died and rose again – even so them which sleep in Jesus will God bring with Him*'

On the top of the memorial there are a butterfly and a sheaf of two lilies carved into the marble; there is an amphora on each side of the inscription and underneath this, below the words, is a decorative ivy branch. At the very base of the tablet is a floral patterned decoration. It was this George who was killed when a pony shied outside the Two Sawyers inn.

The other memorial tablet is at the western end of the north wall of the chancel. It is a fairly plain marble tablet with words that are very difficult to read as the black colouring has faded. The memorial states that it is:

> A tribute of Filial Affection. Sacred to the memory of George Wynch esq. who died May 5th MDCCCXXVIII (1828) in the LXXIII (73rd) year of his age and whose body was interred in Winchelsea Church, and of Mary his widow who departed this life October 30th MDCCCXXXVIII (1838) in the LXXXI (81st) year of her age. Her mortal remains repose in this chancel. '*Blessed are the dead which lie in the Lord – for they rest from their labours and their works do follow them*'

George Wynch held the advowson for Pett when his son Henry became Rector. There is an interesting error in the carving of the first date on this tablet. The figure 'V' appears to have a vertical line carved through it, rather like an 'I'. Now the black colouring has worn the 'I' can clearly be seen. Perhaps the engraver got the date wrong and it had to be corrected, though there is no crowding of letters – so if there was an error it occurred when the date was first carved.

There are two further memorials in the nave, on the south wall. The one nearest the pulpit (at the eastern end of the wall) is made of two different types of marble. Unfortunately it has lost the canopy that originally lay on the top. The memorial has two short columns either side of a shaped tablet. There is a quatrefoil design at the apex of the tablet, below which are the words: 'In affectionate memory of Frank Wickens of Gatehurst, Pett, Sussex, who died Feb. 3rd 1875, aged 18 years. *His end was peace*'. There have been members of the Wickens family associated with Pett since before 1695, a number of them being baptised and buried in the village. Amos Wickens, Frank's father, farmed at Lunsford and also at Gatehurst. Both Amos and his wife Sarah are buried in the churchyard as is their son Frank; on whose grave are the words: *'Come with me for I was wearied sore and have found a mighty arm which holds me ever-more'*.

The western memorial on the south wall consists of a white tablet affixed to a black one, both marble. It reads:

Sacred to the memory of Lieut. Choyce William Moyses R.N. who died at Pett Oct. XV, MDCCCLIII (1853) aged 65 years. Also in beloved memory of Elizabeth Ann Moyses, widow of the above, who died Nov. XII, MDCCCLXXXV (1885). Universally respected

Choyce Moyses was not a Sussex man, but came from Tooting in Surrey. He was the son of William and Sarah Moyses and owed his unusual Christian name to his mother, who was born Sarah Choyce. He entered the Navy when young, and at 16 he was already a Midshipman on the 64-gun *Utrecht*. Later, while on the *Blanche* he was wrecked off the island of Ushant and taken prisoner by the French. He was kept prisoner until the end of the Napoleonic war and was released in 1815. Choyce was promoted to lieutenant and after 11 years on full pay he was to spend nearly 40 years on half-pay. Many officers were made lieutenants at this time, largely as a reward for war services; the five shillings (25p) a day he received on half-pay gave Moyses some independent means for the rest of his life. Nothing is known of his life after the war until 1828, when he was described as a 'keeper of a Receptacle for Lunatics' at Tooting Graveney. He was brought before justices at Wandsworth for being the father of an illegitimate child. The three-month old baby, William, was a charge on the Parish and Moyses was ordered to pay the Churchwardens and Overseer of the Poor of All

Saints, Wandsworth, four shillings and six-pence (22½p) weekly towards the child's maintenance. The mother, Sarah Peters, a single woman, had to contribute sixpence a week.

When Choyce Moyses married in 1845 at St Luke's, Chelsea, his address was in Westminster. Elizabeth was the widow of John Phillips, by whom she had two daughters. Choyce and Elizabeth came to Pett soon after their marriage, but their time together was short as Moyses died in 1853. Elizabeth spent the next 30 years as a widow in Pett, living with her servant Cecilia Bartholomew (of Battle) at Pett Lodge. She died when she was 83 and provided for Cecilia in her will. Elizabeth's daughter Louisa Christie, a widow who died at Eastbourne in 1886, was buried with the Moyses at Pett. The Moyses were an early example of people coming to the village in retirement, at a time when most residents were either farmers or agricultural labourers. Looking at his memorial in the church, no one would think that Choyce Moyses had been a bit of a rogue during his lifetime, as well as serving in the Royal Navy!

On the north wall at the west end of the nave is a list of Rectors produced by Miss Barbara Hill in 1958, and further along the wall are two coloured pictures in the same frame, one showing the 'Old Church Pett destroyed 1854' (the date is incorrect) and the other showing the 'Old Pett Rectory destroyed 1864'. These are copies of photographs painted by Evacustes A. Phipson and presented to the church in 1915. There is also a:

> Photograph of a water-colour drawing amongst the Burrell M.S.S. in the British Museum (Addl. MSS No. 5670). The artist was S.H. Grimm (or possibly Lambert), who executed a large number of drawings for Sir William Burrell, which are now in the British Museum. This photograph of the original drawing was taken at the British Museum by Mr J.E. Ray F.R. Hist.S. who gave this enlarged copy to Pett church – Easter 1926

On each side of the War Memorial, at the west end of the south wall of the nave, hangs a British Legion flag. Boards commemorating those who have died and who served on the Pett Life Boat are situated on the ledge on either side of the St Nicholas window on the north wall of the nave.

Many of the furnishings within the church have been the gifts of faithful parishioners and are a testimony to their love of and devotion to the church. Among them are the wall safe at the north west end of the church, given by Col. N. MacLeod; the Churchwardens' wands, given by Mrs H. Jury and Mr C. Barden; and a banner presented to the church by Mrs Marjorie Rowson and ladies from Fairlight. Mrs Rowson is the wife of the Rev. Frank Rowson, a Non-Stipendiary Priest who assisted the Rev.

The banner made by Mrs Marjorie Rowson and the ladies of Fairlight, first used during the Bishop of Lewes, the Rt Rev. Wallace Benn's Mission

Robin Balch for three years. The banner was made for the Bishop of Lewes' Mission – 'Walking the Way' – in 1999 and was placed in St Mary's Church, Rye, for the final service of the week's activities. It now has a permanent place in Pett Church on the north side of the chancel arch, facing the body of the church. The banner is a striking work of art depicting Pett Church on the hill, overlooking the sea – with fields, sheep and flowers, together with the beach, seaweed, shells and a star-fish. At the top are two sets of crossed keys, one each side of the word 'Pett' and in the centre is a large golden cross with the words 'Follow Me' embroidered in red upon it. Two small sign-posts direct the traveller to either Pett or Pett Level. Gold lines radiating from the central cross indicate God's presence across the parish and the whole banner is simply a delight to see.

So this then is a description of St Mary and St Peter Church, Pett. A rural parish church that has some obscure connections to two Prime Ministers – Henry Addington (between 1801 and 1804) and Robert Banks (between 1812 and 1827). A rather humble and ordinary parish church, but one that has been loved, has provided comfort and help, and has been a centre of public worship in the village for nearly 150 years. With the passing of time, we can certainly be sure of one fact – and that is that, long after the wood has become rotten and the stones and brick have crumbled, there will be abundant witnesses in Heaven to the Love and Witness Pett Church has given.

14

The Churchyard

The churchyard is probably the oldest and most sacred site in the parish. Prehistoric man considered it important to bury the dead close to monuments of religious, though pagan, significance. Since the sixth century, it seems to have been the practice for burial grounds to be attached to churches. This was contrary to the Roman practice of placing the cemetery outside the walls of the town. In fact it was in 601 when Pope Gregory advised that pagan shrines should not be destroyed but should be purified with holy water so that in time they might become temples of the true God. In many instances the level of a graveyard is higher than the road outside it. This can be an indication (but not, I think, at Pett) of repeated burials where numerous dead, buried through the centuries one on top of another, have raised the level of the ground whilst the road outside has worn down.

Enclosed churchyards were introduced in the 10th century. The north side of the church was often avoided and was seen to be the domain of the devil, fit only for the burial of unbaptised and illegitimate infants, suicides and criminals. Possibly the unpopularity of the north side was due to the fact that the shadow of the church fell on it for most of the day and evil spirits were believed to visit there. Of course these superstitious beliefs have not prevailed, and certainly not in the enlightened modern times following the coronation of Queen Victoria.

The churchyard was often the venue for village festivities and social gatherings, for dancing and commercial transactions. In many places it was used as a sort of village recreation field. Quoits, ninepins, marbles, wrestling and other sports were often played in the churchyard. Some of these games continued well into the 20th century and I can well remember, as a young choirboy in the 1930s, playing ninepins with wooden balls and pins after choir practice in the summer months in the grounds of St Michael and All Angels Church, Mill Hill (NW London). Only the ghosts from the past could tell us whether or not such games were played at Pett.

In the early days of Pett Church the poorer people were conveyed to the church in the parish coffin, which was probably wheeled on the parish bier or carried shoulder high, and were buried in a shroud. Only the well-to-do were buried in coffins. In 1668, in a worthy attempt to help the wool trade, an Act was passed making it illegal for the dead to be buried unless wrapped in woollen material. The penalty was a fine of £5 on the estate of the deceased. The law remained in force for 136 years. Coffins did not come into general use until the end of the 17th century and uncoffined burials took place up to the 19th century.

Gravestones were, in the main, a 17th century innovation and most date from the 18th century or later. By custom all grass contained within a churchyard belongs to the incumbent as part of his endowment, though in the past it was frequently grazed by the sexton's animals. Although the entire churchyard is now consecrated ground, this was not always so and there persisted into the 19th century the practice whereby the virtuous received burial on the salubrious south side away from the perpetual shadow on the north side of the church.

Writers may chill our blood with spine-chilling tales from beyond the grave. But the churchyard, despite its pagan roots, is a place both spiritual and benign, a sacred site at the heart of the village community.

Pett churchyard today is considerably larger than it was when the church was built in 1864. Originally it covered an area from the road to where the old boundary walls can be seen on the east and west sides. This was extended in 1907 when William Lucas-Shadwell made a gift of land south of the church. This is the extent of the present churchyard, though an additional piece of land on the east side (known as the 'Twitten') is now available for use, having been given by Mr Jones of Mill Cottage in 1950.

The earliest recorded burials in the churchyard are those of: John Teyler – 'husbandman, of the paroch of Pett', in 1539; Richard Cheeseman in 1543; Elizabeth Firlow in 1545–46; Thomas Bakeholder in 1548 and John Jones in 1552. They had all declared in their wills that they wished to be 'buryed in the churchyerd of Pett'. There must have been burials in the church ground long before this, probably as far back as the 13th or 14th centuries, but the earliest surviving Parish Records do not begin until 1606. The first entry in the register is particularly sad. On 25th March 1606 Richard Butler, son of John Butler, was baptised in the church and on the following day, 26th March, he was buried in the churchyard. What is more, five years later John's wife Joan died and was buried on 19th September 1611, having borne two other sons during that time.

There is no indication in the churchyard where these early graves are positioned and no gravestone exists from these far-off days. There is an ancient gravestone on the north side of the church, just east of the porch door. It is not known how old this stone is or what its original size was. The slab is a sculptured stone with two shafts springing from a base of four steps, all in relief. The shafts do not end in crosses but die into the stone. When Sir William Burrell visited Pett in 1776, the stone was there and Burrell made a sketch of it to add to his account of the church. It was recorded as being a double-cross gravestone, though there is no sign of a double cross now.

The oldest recognisable gravestones that are partially decipherable are as follows:

- A blackened, almost illegible, stone by the church door – 'In (all) memory of John Nabbs, yeoman who died April … 1757 aged 61 years, also in memory of Martha wife of John who died in 17… (the date is not clear, though in the Burial Register Martha, wife of John was buried on 6 March 1735).

- A white weathered marble gravestone on the north side of the north door, virtually illegible – this is the grave of Joseph Rhodes and his wife Mary and is dated around 1780.

- A brick box tomb with a Yorkstone top, by the south wall of the church – this is a Tilden tomb dating from the 1790s.

- A white marble stone, old and weathered by the middle of the north wall of the church – it reads, 'In memory of Christopher Dearing who died 6 of Nov. 1780 aged 71 years. "*Reader by whatsoever motive led to view these gloomy mansions of the dead. Remember lies no more than … . Tomorrow thou perhaps sleep in … .*" Also in memory of Penelope wife of Christopher Dearing who died the 31st July 1793 aged 71 years.'

There are one or two earlier stones dated around 1700, but it is very difficult to be certain in whose memory they were placed.

Some of the gravestones have words of comfort on them, most of these being typical of the Victorian age. Examples are:

- Charlotte Thorpe, wife of Christopher Thorpe (the younger), b.21.2.1817 d.29.1.1870 – '*In the midst of life we are in death. Therefore take heed, watch and pray. For we know not what hour the Son of Man cometh. Even so them also which sleep in Jesus will be coming with Him. Wherefore comfort one another with these words*'

- Mildred Gertrude, wife of James John Hills, died.13.6.1891 – '*Her end was peace. Death has been and borne away a sister from our side, just in the morning of her life though young and fair she died*'

- Frank Wickens of Gatehurst, Pett, died.3.2.1875 aged 18 years – '*Come and rejoice with me, for I was wearied sore, and have found a mighty arm which holds me evermore*'

- Samuel Hills, d.28.3.1866 – '*Love looks below with weeping eyes where her long cherished treasure lies. Our sweet companionship is o'er, our Pilgrim friend returns no more*'

ST MARY - ST PETER, PETT   and St Andrew, Fairlight

Engraving by Robert Heather – 2002. (Can you see 'Concorde' in the engraving?)

- Richard Griffen, d.23.2.1855 – *'Life is uncertain, death is sure. Sin is the wound, but Christ is the cure'*

There is only one gravestone where the words inscribed on it not only provide a timely message, but also contain just a grain of humour. This is the marble head of the coffin shaped tomb of Frances, wife of Spencer Davis, who died 21st February 1847 aged 43 years. The inscription reads:

All you who come my grave to see,
Prepare yourselves to follow me,
Repent in time make no delay,
For I in haste was called away.

Pett churchyard is one of those that have a wooden 'Leaping Board' or 'Dead Board' as a memorial. This is in the south west corner and is dedicated to Henry Whelpton, 1860–1935, and Edith Beatrice, his wife 1874–1952. A memorial of this type was called a 'leaping board' because of its shape; it consists of a plank suspended on its edge by two wooden supports and looks rather like a 'jump' for a small pony.

There is also an interesting tomb just south of the vestry that is an ornate box-tomb with eight polished pink granite pillars and lead inserted letters. This is the Young family grave and is of interest because one of the panels on the side of it has been refaced and had new lettering inserted. It is not possible by looking at the panel (on the west end) to see that any change has been made, but there is a photograph taken in the early 1900s that shows what the early inscription was. Originally it read:

Beneath this lie the remains of HENRY YOUNG of Essex Street and Russell Square, London and of Sudbury Grove Harrow, in the County of Middlesex. The Patron of the Rectory of this Parish. In the welfare of which his sincere interest was shown by the liberality of his contributions towards the expense of rebuilding this Church. He was born in Lambeth in the County of Surrey on Christmas Day 1797 and practiced for upwards of fifty years as a Solicitor in London where he died on the 1st of December 1869 leaving his widow and five Children by whom this monument is erected in affectionate regard for his memory.

After Henry's wife died the face of the panel was changed to read:

Beneath this lie the remains of HENRY YOUNG of Essex Street and Russell Square, London and of Sudbury Grove, Harrow Middlesex. Patron of the Rectory and of this Parish. Born at Lambeth, Surrey 25th December 1797 Died in London 1st December 1869. Also of MARIA, his widow. Born 26th February 1801 Died 27th December 1892.

I wonder how many other gravestones in the land have been altered in this way? It does seem a pity that much of the information about Henry Young is now missing from the tomb, but we are fortunate to have a record of it.

On the north side of the Young tomb, two panels are inscribed. The first is in memory of James Forbes Waring Young, fourth son of Charles Waring and Augusta Emma Young; the second of Charles Waring and his wife Augusta. On the south side there is a panel in memory of Henry's only daughter Jane Maria Young. The Rev. F.C.A. Young and his wife Eva Mary are buried on the south side of the church near the vestry; this grave and the Young tomb were enclosed by wrought iron railings, but as in many churchyards throughout the country the railings were removed as part of the War Effort in the 1940s.

There is a note in the Parochial Church Council minutes of 12th December 1929, which states that a letter from the War Graves Commission affirms that the 5/- (25p) per annum grant towards the upkeep of the grave of a body washed ashore at Pett during the Great War would be discontinued. This is not the only record of a body, or bodies, being found on the seashore. In January 1871, the British sailing brig *Equator* struck another vessel and the helmsman fell into the sea and was lost. His body was

Pett Church – looking across the fields from Rosemary Lane

discovered the next day off Pett Level. In December 1881, Johann Peters and August Fredricks were found drowned at Pett Level and were buried by the Rev. E.O. Bright. And a rather grisly record tells of a body part consisting of two femur bones attached to haunch bones, of a person unknown, that was found on the beach and buried in the south east corner of the churchyard on 12th November 1942 by the Rev. R.C. Wood.

Another tale about the Second World War involves Ada Florence Stott, who died on 16th December 1943, aged 70. Apparently her daughter, Mrs Carr, was registering this poor lady's death in Rye while there was an air raid taking place. A German plane was shot down and crashed with all its bombs still on board. The following explosion blasted Mrs Stott out of her coffin, much to the distress of her relatives who found her when they returned from Rye.

A grey granite War Memorial is situated on the north side of the churchyard near the Pett Road wall. It is in the form of a Celtic cross and is engraved with the names of the servicemen who lost their lives in the two World Wars. On the north face of the memorial a plate reads 'In memory of the men from this village who fell in the Great War 1914–1918', and above it 17 names are recorded. On the south side another plate reads 'And also of those who fell in the War of 1939–1945', with seven names engraved above. A complete list of these servicemen who lost their lives in the two wars is shown in Table 26 in the Appendix.

One recent feature of the churchyard is the Memorial Garden, which was dedicated by the Archdeacon of Lewes, the Venerable Nicholas Reade in May 2001. Because of the dwindling amount of space left for burials and the increasing practice of cremation, the PCC had decided to create a Memorial Garden for the sole purpose of the interment of ashes. The work involved in bringing the decision to fruition was great and was carried out by the Rector's wife, Mrs Eileen Balch. The final result is a lovely, simple garden with a seat and an inscribed stone indicating its presence and purpose, which will be available for the burying of ashes for many years to come.

Many churchyards are a haven for wildlife, and Pett's is no exception. Slow worms and common lizards could at one time be seen sunning themselves among the gravestones. Badgers and foxes use it as a highway and a place to hunt. Many different birds nest in and around the churchyard and can be seen perching on the stones and shrubs, searching for insects in the grass or berries from the trees. The most wonderful display that Nature provides is the plant life around the church. Between 1989 and 1990 Mrs Joan Medlock, the church organist and a keen naturalist, who has spent many hours keeping the grounds tidy, and Mrs Breda Burt, a former Botanical Recorder for East Sussex, carried out a botanical survey in the churchyard. They were able to identify over a hundred different plants and flowers. Table 12 in the Appendix lists what was found, with the English name first and the Latin name alongside it. Though this may not be the correct way to list plants it may be more helpful to those of us who are not botanists. What a huge variety of flora there is in such a small area, and what pleasure the plants and flowers give to visitors who come to see the resting place of their loved ones.

15

Parish and Other Records

A close examination of the old Parish Records gives a fairly good insight into the lives of the people of Pett, particularly in the 18th and 19th centuries. We have already seen the effects of plurality on the Parish in the 17th and 18th centuries and Table 3 in the Appendix shows the names of various curates who, during the period between 1606 and 1754, conducted most of the services for the incumbents, who were often far away from Pett. The records also give information about the occupations of the local people and illustrate the social conditions of the time by giving many details about families.

Table 13 in the Appendix gives descriptions of people buried at Pett, between 1626 and 1809, and these range from 'an unbaptised infant' to 'an old man'. One entry mentions Thomas Cooper, who was both an uncle and servant to Thomas Crowhurst. This is the same Thomas Crowhurst who was a churchwarden in the 1630s and who could not write his own name. Though illiterate, he must have been quite an influential person in the growing village in the 17th century. We do not know when this churchwarden died as there are no records between 1640 and 1667; it was during this period that England was torn apart by the Civil War.

Table 14 gives a list of occupations of fathers of baptised children in the 19th century. It can be seen that in Pett, as in most villages, there was a wide range of jobs that were typical of the time. Most men in the village were agricultural labourers who worked on the local farms and who rarely travelled far from the village. One entry in Table 14 is rather odd, and that is where the occupation 'Cheesemaker' has the word 'Paddington' in brackets alongside it. It would be interesting to know whether or not this gentleman originated from Paddington, or commuted to and from there (though this is unlikely), or perhaps had another establishment in London.

Most of the occupations are self-descriptive, but one is not as well known as the others – and that is a 'looker'. A looker is a person who looks, or observes, the sheep as they graze in the fields in order to check that the numbers are correct. Sheep are not too bright, and they do have a habit of straying away from the flock, falling into ditches, or getting their heads trapped in fences. The looker would check that the numbers of the flock remained constant and would also collect up any strays and casualties. They were not shepherds, and the 'lookering' job is still carried out today in some areas where the sheep roam free.

The growth of the village is indicated by various counts taken by the Church and later by Census returns. The Parish Records too give some idea how the number of births increased over 250+ years. Table 15 in the Appendix shows a comparison in 20-year groupings of the number of Baptisms, Marriages and Burials that occurred between 1606 and 1892. Though the number of marriages in the church did not change significantly, the number of baptisms increased. From the time of the Reformation most children were baptised soon after birth, a very different situation to that which exists today where fewer baptisms take place in church as each year passes. When studying Parish Records, it is necessary to remember that there was a lot of movement between the villages of Fairlight, Guestling and Pett and later, as transport facilities improved, people began to move more frequently both to and from the village of Pett. Though the population was slowly increasing, for each group of 20 years the number of burials did not change greatly. This may be due, in part, to the fact that as the centuries passed the life expectancy for both men and women increased.

Table 16 shows the families with six or more children. There are more than those listed, all of which are recorded in the Baptism Records. Between 1606 and 1891 many marriages produced sizeable families, and some of the parents listed are related to others shown in the table. From the very early days for which records are available most families consisted of more than one child and it was not uncommon for large families to occur. The same family surname can be seen in the records again and again and the Baptism records are an excellent place to start looking into a family history.

Like most places, Pett had its share of illegitimate children. Table 17 lists the names of spinsters who had children, all of whom were baptised in the church. Four of these ladies had more than one illegitimate child. Bastardy was a fairly public fact of life in medieval England and, under the law, a child born out of wedlock was not of inferior status but, since he was 'the sone of no one' (filius nullius), he could not be heir to his parents nor inherit their property. An Act of 1576 enabled Justices to imprison the parents of an illegitimate child and a further Act, of 1610, provided for a mother to be imprisoned unless she could provide securities for her good behaviour. An Act of 1733 obliged a mother to declare that she was pregnant with an illegitimate child and to reveal the father's name. Parish Officers would then attempt to obtain a bond of indemnity from the father that would provide for maintenance to be paid, either as a lump sum or by instalments. From 1844 mothers were permitted to apply to the courts for maintenance orders. The Parish Officers in Pett would have ensured that any children born out of wedlock would have been cared for.

Table 18 gives a list of names that appear often in the Parish Records with the first date of entry of any particular name. Most of these names have very strong links with the area and there are people in the village today who are direct descendants of some of the folk shown on this list.

Table 19 shows infant mortality for children under five years of age. There were no National Health Service or Children's Clinics in the 17th and 18th centuries. Conditions in many village homes were not nearly as good as they are today and infant mortality was high. The situation in Pett was not as bad as in some parts of the country, even though the chance of a child dying under the age of five was about one in five between 1606 and 1740, reducing to about one in ten in the 19th century. It can be seen from the table that 16 per cent of the children baptised between 1606 and 1811 died at an early age, most of them before they were three years old. Some mothers died soon after giving birth and, where this occurred, most died within two weeks of the confinement. Some families suffered the death of more than one tiny child. One couple, Thomas and Elizabeth Foster, had 12 children between 1740 and 1762, including two sets of twins. Four of the children died, including one of each pair of twins; five sons and three daughters lived on. The list of deaths of young people grows considerably when those who died before their teens are taken into account, but the rate is not as high as for those of more tender years.

Table 20 shows those residents of Pett who were both baptised and married in Pett Church. It seems strange that only 18 out of 188 marriages recorded between 1606 and 1811 were of couples that were baptised and married in St Mary and St Peter's Church. This indicates how people moved about the area, for, if the marriage records of Fairlight and Guestling are examined, the names of many folk baptised in Pett can be seen. With little transport this meant that people walked some distances to meet, get to know each other and carry out their courting. How different today when people get the car out to travel little more than a few hundred yards!

A number of marriages were conducted after a licence had been obtained from the Bishop. A licence normally allowed a marriage to take place without the calling of Banns and, before it was granted, one of the parties was required to swear that he or she knew of no impediment to the marriage and that the church in which the ceremony was to take place was that which was normally used by one of the couple (or that one of the couple had resided in the parish during the preceding 15 days). Most of the licences allowed to people from Pett were granted because they were either girls under age or widows; in each case two men of good standing had to give sureties, or act as sponsors.

This area has long been associated with smugglers and coastguards. The Baptism Records together with Census Returns for the period give much information about the families of the coastguards, many of whom lived in the eight Martello Towers that were situated on the beach between Winchelsea Beach and Cliff End, Pett Level. Table 21 lists the names of residents of the Martello Towers and the dates that they were known to be in the area. Though the towers were built in the early 19th century as a defence against the possible invasion of these shores by Napoleon, the first reference to coastguards living in them, as preventive officers against smuggling, is in the late 1820s.

Tower 31 was the first of the eight low-level towers that ran from Dog's Hill to Cliff End and was at one time installed with similar semaphore apparatus to that which was housed in Towers 4, 27 and 55. This was mentioned in the 1863 Coastguard Inspection Report and in the 1873 report on Coastal Defences. It was eventually undermined and consumed by the sea towards the end of the 19th century. There is in existence a photograph showing a large crack where the tower had split from the foundations to the parapet.

Little is known about Tower 32. It was mentioned in the 1873 report and was probably washed into the sea before 1900. There are the names of two families who lived in it during the middle of the 19th century.

The same applies to Tower 33. It is interesting to note from the 1851 Census that three families were living in the tower at that time. Altogether six adults and nine children shared the accommodation. The tower was still standing in 1873 but was undermined by the sea in subsequent years.

Again, nothing is known about Tower 34, which was last mentioned in the 1873 report before being undermined and washed away by the sea by the end of the 19th century.

Tower 35 was probably in danger from the sea when it was still being used as a residence. Its greatest claim to fame was in explosive trials on 27th April 1872, when it was used to determine whether the new gun-cotton, invented by a Mr Abel, would prove more effective than traditional gunpowder. Towers 35 and 38 were used for this experiment and Tower 35 was filled with 800 lb of the traditional gunpowder in barrels. The detonation of the gunpowder resulted in a loud explosion accompanied by a large column of rising smoke. The explosion was described in the 1872 edition of *The Graphic* as 'slow and sullen', the beams and stones of the tower being thrown up into the air. The tower lay in ruins long after the explosion.

Tower 36, too, was mentioned in the 1863 Coastguard Inspection Report, and a man was recorded as having been drowned in the sea nearby in 1864. The tower is thought to have slipped into the sea at some point between 1869 and 1872, and traces of it have been found at low tide as late as 1966.

Tower 37 had become unsafe due to the relentless undermining of the sea, and was blown up by the Royal Engineers in June 1866. Traces of this tower also were found at low tide in 1966.

Tower 38 was the last in line stretching across Pett Level, and was situated near the end of the extension to the Royal Military Canal. This tower was the other half of the experiment on the 27th April 1872 carried out to prove whether the newly invented gun-cotton was more effective than gunpowder. After Tower 35 was destroyed, three charges of gun-cotton, totalling 200 lb, were placed in Tower 38 and detonated by electric current from a distance of a quarter of a mile away. The resulting explosion produced less smoke than that which arose from Tower 35, but proved far more devastating. Tower 38 was shattered into small pieces with a charge a quarter of that of gunpowder. The second explosion was much sharper than the first and, as well as shattering the tower, spread the fragments laterally as opposed to vertically. It was a very satisfactory experiment.

A visitor to Pett Level today would never realise that in years past the whole expanse of the beach from Cliff End to Dog's Hill would have been dominated by the eight massive stone Martello Towers that never did serve their real purpose, but did survive for most of a century – against the constant invasion of the sea – acting as a deterrent to smugglers and providing accommodation for many families. As ever, the sea won in the end and the Martello Towers are no more.

Table 22 lists all the 'Coast Guards', often known as the Preventive Service, who are not shown in Table 21. Some of these men may have lived for a time in one or other of the Martello Towers and some lived in the Coastguard Cottages at either Pett or Fairlight (where this is known, the Fairlight men's names are followed by an F). All these men are mentioned in the Pett Baptism Register and all had at least one child christened at the church. The last mentioned Coastguard was George Richards, whose son Albert was baptised on the 16th June 1887. It should be said that these lists of names are not exhaustive, as it is known that others, not mentioned in the Parish Records, lived in the Martello Towers. Towards the end of their days, after the new Coastguard stations were built, the towers were let to civilians. Among these were the parents of Reginald Cooke, a well-known inhabitant of Pett Level, a great naturalist, ornithologist and broadcaster, who died in 1965. Reg joined HM Coastguard Pett Level as a volunteer in 1917 after being invalided out of the army and in 1923, when the Coastguard station at Pett Level was closed down, he formed the Pett Level Coast Life Saving Company, which was one of the first in the country. These companies are an integral part of the Coastguard Service and by 1950 there were over 700 around the coast of Britain. During the Second World War there was a permanent watch post (the 'Lookout') just above the beach at

Pett Level and now, in the 21st century, the Local Volunteer Company carries out a co-ordinating function linked to the Dover Coastguards.

Since 1923 32 members of the Cooke family and their in-laws have served over 600 man-years in the Coastguard Service and two of them, Reg and his son Lawrence (Lawrie), were awarded the British Empire Medal. In addition, during the period of years since 1923, 28 men have been awarded the 20-year long-service medal, seven the 35-year medal, and several have served over 40 years in the 'Service'. What dedication and example of service they present to us all!

It is interesting to look at some families who have lived and worked in the village for more than a hundred years, and I am indebted to Mr and Mrs John and Rosemary Moon for information about the Cooke family and to Dr Jillian Green, who has researched the Hills and the Colegate families.

Table 23 shows the three main strands of the Cooke family and the names of other local people linked to them by marriage. James Cooke (the elder) was the third son of William Cooke and moved to Pett Level about 1831. Here he became the innkeeper of the Ship Inn, taking over from Thomas and Ann Davis, three of whose sons married three of James's daughters; one of their daughters married one of James's sons (James the younger). This is not surprising as there were few people living on the Levels in the mid-nineteenth century and the marriages of four of each of the families' offspring would have given much joy to the parents. Both James (the elder) and his grandson Charles were at different times innkeepers of the Ship Inn before it was destroyed by the sea in 1932.

Locally the Cookes were associated with Braggs Farm, Black Hoth Farm and Gate-hurst Farm, but some members of the family moved away as far as the USA. James (the younger) and his sons used to buy up wrecks on the seashore and sell the timber to estate owners for fencing and building. Most of the fences on the marsh were made of wreck timber and many of the older houses had beams of timber from wrecks used in their building. Reg Cooke's notes about his grandfather tell of a wreck that occurred about 1860. The vessel was called the *James Brown* and had a cargo of tobacco and buffalo hides. The coastal folk received a shilling each for salvaging the hides, but there is no mention of what became of the tobacco.

James the younger's eldest son Alfred Henry moved to Winchelsea and there are two lovely stories involving him.

One Christmas Eve, Alfred had been out visiting friends and was on his way home across the churchyard. It was midnight and very dark. He suddenly saw a pale hazy light in the church porch. A silent grey-robed figure made its way slowly out of the church carrying a dimly lit lantern. Alfred followed the figure across the churchyard and out through the gate. At his house he stopped and watched the ghostly figure move on into Grey Friars. Was this apparition really a ghost, moving from the church to the ancient Grey Friars Chapel?

The other story also concerns a strange light in the church. Once again, on his way home late one night, Alfred saw a light on in the church, which should have been closed. He went to the church door and there found the Sexton, who had come to investigate. They could hear a tragic voice declaiming inside. On opening the door, they saw lights on the altar and the figure of a woman with upstretched arms, in the middle of the aisle, crying out as if in torment. As they stood there the woman fell flat on the floor. Alfred and the Sexton rushed to the prostrate form, only to find that it was the great Ellen Terry, rehearsing for the part of Lady Macbeth. Ellen Terry owned Tower Cottage near Strand Gate at that time and it is said that she enjoyed Winchelsea, where she was very popular. However, she frightened poor Alfred and the Sexton.

The Cookes married into other local families and more than one married a cousin. It has been said that if you lift up any stone on Pett Level beach a Cooke will be found under it! There is no doubt that the family loved and still love the area around Pett Level and we will notice this again in Chapter 17 where an article written by Reg Cooke is full of his appreciation of this very special part of the parish.

Tables 24 and 25 give details of the Hills and Colegate families. The Hills came to Pett in the 18th century, and over the years members of the family have settled in Pett, Guestling, Fairlight and other villages in the area. The table shows that a number of Richard Hills's descendants had large families and the links through marriage to other local families can be clearly seen. The children of Thomas and Sarah Colegate were born in Westfield; some moved to Icklesham and then early in the 19th century John Colegate (1791–1841) moved to Pett. This John had 12 children, most of whom lived to adulthood and a number married local folk. In the 1880s three of the Colegates married three of the Hills and in the generations that followed many people in the two families were (and are) related. Thomas Colegate (1721–1807), though not living in Pett, must have known the area as he witnessed the marriage of John Nabbs at Fairlight church in 1756, and later both the Hills and the Colegate families were very much associated with the church at Pett. A photograph taken of the Pett Church Choir in 1913 shows 21 people, most of whom are related in some way, with the majority originating from either the Hills or Colegates. George Hills (1794–1873) was Parish Clerk for 38 years, and George Henry Colegate (1856–1919) was a churchwarden for 25 years and also a powerful voice on the Parish Council during the First World War. These are not the only families in Pett that have a long history in the village; Table 18 lists some of the others.

Rector, Officers and Choir, St Mary and St Peter Church, Pett, 1913. 1. Mr Glazier – sexton; 2. Fred Harman (m. Mabel Colegate)*; 3. Thomas Colegate (m. Maude, No. 15)*; 4. Mr Catt from the Royal Oak, father of 16 children; 5. Not known; 6. Rev. F.C.A. Young; 7. Mr Thomas Gibbs; 8. William Gallop Colegate, son of George Henry, PCC secretary, treasurer and Churchwarden at different times*; 9. Alfred Harman, Churchwarden from 1892; 10. Eddy Weston; 11. Fred Barter; 12. Charlie Barden, blacksmith at The Forge; 13. George Henry Colegate, Churchwarden from 1892, builder*; 14. Cyril Weston; 15. Maude Colegate, daughter of George Henry*; 16. Florence Catt of the Royal Oak; 17. Miss Grace Peters, infant teacher at Pett School (her father was headmaster); 18. Miss Oweda Jenner; 19. Miss Winnie Davidson (?); 20. Sam Hills (son of James John)**; 21. Bert Barnes. A number of the people in this photograph were related (** See Table 24 in the Appendix; * See Table 25 in the Appendix)

The reason for including so many names in the tables is simple. These are some of the people who lived in Pett, farmed, worked and defended the land, gradually turning a small hamlet into a thriving village. These are the people who influenced the development of the local church and community that makes up this place. These people are part of our heritage, and each of them contributed to what we, in our time, enjoy today. It is well that they are remembered.

16

The Parish Magazine

The Parish of Pett has had a monthly magazine since about 1910. I have not been able to trace any of the original issues, the first in my possession being Vol. VI, No. 6, June 1915. The Rev. F.C.A. Young started the publication, which in its early days catered only for the parish of Pett. Later it became the magazine for both Guestling and Pett.

The first magazines were 7¼ × 9 inches in size and entitled *Church of S. Mary & S. Peter – Pett*. There was a photograph of the church, with two small girls in their smock dresses standing in front of it, and a list of the church services and officials on the front cover, which was pale green. Most of the content, four sides of paper, was written by the Rector and *The Sign* was inserted between the parish information and the covers. Local advertisements, helping to pay for the publication, filled the back cover and included such well-known tradesmen as W. Catt – The Royal Oak, Temperance Inn; Mrs G. Colegate – Country Furnished Apartments; A. Skinner – Post Office, Pett; Arthur Harman – Furniture Dealer & Undertaker; and Arthur C. Towner – House Furnisher and Furnishing Undertaker.

By the end of 1935 the front cover had changed. The page was headed *Pett Parish Magazine* and displayed three photographs, all titled. The largest was of St Mary and St Peter Church, on the top half of the page, and underneath this were two smaller pictures – one of the interior of St Nicholas chapel, Pett Level, and the other of the inside of St Richard's, Winchelsea Beach. This change followed the dedication of St Nicholas chapel and the introduction of services at St Richard's (see Chapter 10). The number of local advertisements had increased and now included: T.C. Colegate – Dairyman and Grazier, Gatehurst Farm; W.R. Baker – Groceries, Provisions and Off-licence; A. & F. Foster – Butchers and Dairymen, Two Sawyers, Pett Road; J.F. Earle – Saloon Car for Hire, Sea Bank, Chick Hill; and Frank Millet – Organ and Piano Tuner, Hastings (Mrs Millet was organist at the church in 1937).

A somewhat reduced magazine was published during part of the Second World War after a gap until September 1941. After the war the cover of the magazine changed once more. The photographs were no longer used and the front of the monthly magazine, now costing 3d per issue, displayed the names of the Rector and the church officials – including the Day School teachers. Advertisers still continued to help pay for the cost and included Barden & Sons – Builders, Decorators and Funeral Directors; Sea View Private Hotel, Pett Level; and Butler's Emporium, George Street, Hastings. This format continued until 1956 when the size of the insert, *The Sign*, changed to octavo. From then until the 1970s the size of the magazine remained constant and advertisers continued to display their goods and services. Each month the printer published a different photograph on the front cover of the magazine and the insert, *The Sign*, was still included.

Some time after Pett and Guestling became a plurality a new cover reflected the change with a splendid drawing of the tower and spire of Pett Church and the tower of Guestling Church. The magazine was entitled *The Two Spires*, cost 2½p, and inside the front cover it stated that this was 'The Parish Magazine of the Churches of St Laurence, Guestling and St Mary & St Peter, Pett'. Both the cover and the text were duplicated locally, reducing the publication cost and enabling more copy to be included.

There has been one further change to the cover of the magazine. A celebrated illustrator of wartime posters and the *Radio Times*, Cecil W. Bacon, drew a magnificent composite picture for the cover that has been in use since the early 1980s. A tanner's son, Cecil Bacon was born at Battle in 1905. He was educated at Sutton Valence School, St Lawrence College, Ramsgate and at Hastings Art School. In 1929 he began to produce posters, notably for the London Underground. From 1943 he worked for the Ministry of Information and at the end of the war began his long association with the BBC and took on commissions for publishers. He designed the covers of many books including Nevil Shute's bestseller *A Town Like Alice*. He and his wife were very well known in Pett (where his wife still lives) and his drawing for the cover of the *Parish News* has been admired by all who have seen it. Cecil Bacon died in 1992 and is remembered for his outstanding work and friendly manner.

The cover shows the three churches of Guestling, Pett and Pett Level, these being the only churches in the Benefice at that time. Surrounding the churches are sprigs of oak, hazel and chestnut, bramble, honeysuckle and holly, bluebells, primroses and wild roses – all of which can be found in the area. At the top right-hand side Hog Hill windmill is drawn and a little lower St Andrew's Church, Fairlight can be seen in the distance. A blackbird, a mallard, a swallow and a wood pigeon fly among the foliage and at the bottom of the picture Pett Level is shown with the old bridge spanning the canal. Cliff End and a flamingo (which appeared on Pett Pools for nine years) are depicted by the sea, the flamingo standing sedately in front of a stand of bull rushes. The drawing captures the ethos of this country seaside group of parishes, set in some

April, 2002

GUESTLING

PETT

PARISH NEWS

Pett Level

Cover of Pett and Guestling Parish Magazine, designed by Cecil W. Bacon

glorious countryside and associated for centuries with both the land and the sea. In one way Cecil Bacon's drawing was prophetic. No one imagined when it first appeared on the front of the magazine that by 1994 a United Benefice of Guestling, Pett and Fairlight would be created. Including Fairlight church in the drawing for the cover of Pett and Guestling's magazine was surely inspirational. Today the parishes work very closely together and the United Benefice has helped in the formation of many new friendships, and the magazine cover drawn by Cecil Bacon symbolises the strong links being forged between the three parishes. The magazine is now produced by photo-copying and the cost to its readers has increased from 10p an issue in the 1980s to 30p an issue (or £3 per year). Its title, the *Parish News* signifies that it covers not only Church news but also news and views from the two parishes, in other words, all aspects of life in this community. [See note at the end of the chapter.]

As would be expected, the content of the magazine has always been mainly Church based, but frequently there is a piece of writing or comment that is of much wider interest. Some articles managed to combine both local and national themes. Below are some extracts from magazines since 1915.

June 1915

Empire Day is to be held on June 11th, the Children's Service on that day will be held at 10.45 and Songs, Recitations and Saluting the Flag at 11 o'clock.

June 15th is the 700th anniversary of the signing of the Magna Carta and might be kept in memory of Stephen Langton. Church matters are dealt with in Clauses 1 and 18 of the charter. Clause 1, "Out of reverence and love for God I grant freedom to the Holy Church".

June 18th is the centenary of the Battle of Waterloo.

On the last day of May we lost our squire, William Lucas-Shadwell, his death is a loss to the whole parish and we offer our sympathy to his aged Mother, his Sisters and a Widow, Son and Daughters, and feel that we have lost a friend, and another link in the chain of friendship has been broken.

The Belgian Relief Fund is slowly growing and is now 17/6 (*87.5p*).

February 1938

A large quantity of bulbs have been planted in what will probably be identified as our 'Hyde Park' through the kindness of Major Eves. We are very grateful to him for the gift of the bulbs. Some fears have been expressed that the flowers may be 'picked', and it is only natural that children may be inclined to do so unless they are told not to do so. We hope that all parents will explain to their children that they are there for all to enjoy. (*Note: Hyde Park is the grassy bank on the side of Pett Road between Faith Cottage and Glebe House. In the 21st century the flowers still appear for us all to enjoy.*)

July 1966

A Look at 1946. In 1946 Walter Hammond headed up the first class batting averages and at Pett Mr Charles Barden's top score was 42. Better still, he was second in the village bowling averages and took 43 wickets for 157 runs. The magazine reports an enjoyable cricket season – 'the first more or less normal one since 1939'.

In the Women's Institute annual report it was announced that the membership had increased from 127 to 142 with an average attendance of 65. 377 articles had been sent to 'Help Holland' and the Jam Preservation Centre was the highest for East Sussex, having achieved 1,333 lbs of jam and 1,331 tins of fruit, as well as chutneys and pickles. Later in the year an appeal was read for 'Help Holland' asking for any discarded Home Guard uniforms.

December 1955

We read that television, according to some observers, is reviving home life and causing families to stay in together in order to watch the flickering screen. The tendency, they say, is most marked in America where, of course, television has so far made a much greater social impact than even here, for certainly one of the tragedies of the modern world is the partial disappearance of family life with the home as its centre. The rush and bustle of life today, National Service, work away from home, all tend to break up the family, but television or not, it is at no other time in the year that we become more conscious of the privilege and joy of family membership than we do at Christmas. (*This was part of the Rector's monthly letter to parishioners.*)

September 1965

For those of you who use the bus and have been unfortunate in missing it owing to it running early on several occasions recently, the East Kent Co. in reply to a letter I wrote them, informed me – 'that the matter was being taken up with the staff concerned. It is hoped that, as a result, your parishioners will have no further cause for complaint'. The bus in question is down to leave Pett P.O. (*the old Post Office near the church*) at 7.41 pm which should allow plenty of time, but any who wish to leave during the last hymn, please do. (*Note: This was in the days of regular Sunday Evensong service.*)

July 1956

Good news from the East Kent Bus Co. They have informed me that starting on the 17th June, the 7.15 pm bus from Hastings will leave at 7.20 pm, so making the time here approximately 7.45 pm. This will give a comfortable margin after the service in which to catch the bus.

August 1957

There is a little known story of the days when King George VI was serving in the Royal Navy. His personal messenger was instructed to visit his cabin at certain times every day. He was to knock and enter, and, if he found the young Prince engaged, stand to attention and wait. One day the messenger carried out his instructions and found the Prince on his knees, praying. A little embarrassed, the man stood and waited. After a few minutes the king-to-be rose to his feet, put an arm around the messenger's shoulders and said, 'If ever you find me on my knees, remember there is room for you at my side'.

September 1966

For several months the organ in the church has been very much out of tune, and in spite of the fact that the organ builders, Messrs Browne & Sons of Canterbury have from time to time been called in to give attention to the organ, it is still causing great concern to our organist and the choir. Messrs Browne & Sons have now reported that the cause of the trouble derives from the fact that the tuning stoppers have shrunk, and also to the softness of the pipe metal itself. The result is that when a dry or hot spell is experienced the stoppers drop, some more than others, and so the pipes become out of tune; owing to the looseness of the stoppers it is difficult to tune or guarantee that they will stay in tune. The remedy is for the stoppers to be recovered with chamois leather, the pipes to be reshaped and finally retuned. The estimated cost of this work is £25. Unfortunately church funds does not allow for an expenditure of this kind, and therefore the Parochial Church Council at a recent meeting proposed that an appeal should be made to the members of the congregation to assist.

August 1966, August 1967 and August 1968
The Rectory Garden Fete

1966: This was the twenty-fourth successive Fete to be held on the last Saturday in June – a date which has now traditionally become known as 'dry day'. Yes, the weather was kind again! The sun shone a little, the wind blew things over and away, but the rain kept off ...

1967: An early recollection of Fete day was the Rector sweeping the water away from the Rectory drive! This set the scene for the day. The morning just kept fine but shortly before 3 o'clock a thunderstorm broke over Hastings and the Rectory garden had some of the splashes ... even the rain didn't dampen our spirits ... We missed the sun and we missed the ponies; both kept away by the thunder clouds ... It was the twenty-fifth Fete and one old local parishioner was heard to say that it was the wettest 'last Saturday in June for forty-four years'.

1968: The last Saturday in June last year was the wettest for forty-four years, and the month of June in 1968 was one of the wettest ever. Even so, at the twelfth hour (as far as the month was concerned) the clouds cleared and the twenty-sixth Garden Fete was held in ideal garden-party weather ... The event, of course, was in the New Rectory garden which seemed to lend itself well to the fun and fellowship we have come to enjoy so much. We had moved down the road, as it were, but it was all here as usual – and in a few hectic hours the Fete raged and the sun shone.

March 1975

(*The beginning of the Rector's Editorial*) I listened recently, with incredulous delight, to one of those radio programmes on 're-cycling'. For why? Because it described a new source of protein for animal feed. Apparently, after pulping and chemical treatment, Government forms are ideal for this purpose! Will there come a time when forms are too valuable to be issued to us and are issued to cattle instead, even a time when, at one remove, ministers are glad to be able to eat their own departmental words?

March 1985

(*The first paragraph of the Rector's letter to his parishioners*) The Arctic conditions of mid-January caught everyone out, as of course they always do! They brought with them enormous problems for many, and not least the farmers of our communities whose entire time was taken up in keeping stock fed and watered in the face of freezing water systems and the necessity of taking provender to the beasts out in the fields. The cold conditions brought quantities of birds into our gardens and among them redwings and fieldfares. We so often overlook the fact that freezing conditions present a crisis for them too! One of the few happy aspects of the cold snap was the fact that villagers took to their feet, and the village's roads became a meeting ground and a place to talk, – so much nicer than just waving from a speeding car. The children of the parish enjoyed their enforced extension of holiday, some fantastic tobogganing was enjoyed, and those who did not possess a sledge found plastic sacks fast if not very comfortable. Another happy aspect was the tremendous amount of caring and helping that went on during that time – people just 'popping in' to see if another person was all right. It is so true that adverse conditions specially prompt excellent qualities though there are so many acts of kindness and help which go unseen in our communities all the time.

February 1994

(*A final extract in a lighter mood from the Editor of the time, Mr. D. Griffiths*) From the day one of my uncles was ordained, he was nicknamed 'the Pope' by his 'wag' brothers. This remained so, within the family, until his dying day. At that time, most parishes had a curate, and curates were 'fair game' in the marriage stakes among the young ladies. One of his brothers teased him with this rhyme:

> The farmer's daughter Mabel,
> As oft as she was able,
> Would kiss her date –
> The young cur-ate
> Who found it ag-ree-able.

Her name was not really Mabel, but she did become my aunt – who objected strongly to the nickname – but to no avail.

There are many gems hidden away in the old magazines. Like all Parish Magazines the one covering Pett and Guestling is an important means of communication that people look forward to receiving each month.

Note: Since this chapter was written, the 'Parish News' continues to exist as a magazine, but is produced by the Pett Parish Council for the residents of Pett, who receive it free of charge. 'The Benefice Magazine', published bi-monthly, incorporates the Anglican churches of Fairlight, Guestling and Pett, and is also distributed free of charge.

17

People and Pett

This chapter is about people, some who have visited the area and a couple of local folk that are typical of those who live here. It is not surprising that some well-known people have visited Pett and Pett Level. The beauty and charm of the area has attracted artists, authors and others, each gaining inspiration from this glorious East Sussex land.

Joseph M.W. Turner (1775–1831), one of England's most well-known landscape painters, used artistic licence in his painting of soldiers by the Royal Military Canal, with Rye in the distance. William Holman Hunt (1827–1910), famous for his picture 'The Light of the World', was a member of the Pre-Raphaelite Brotherhood and he hoped to work in solitude when he visited the area in the 1850s. His picture 'Our English Coasts' looks as if it was painted from the view at Cliff End looking towards Fairlight. Later, artists associated with the Slade School of Art in London visited Pett Level, some to live there for a time. Mark Gertler (1891–1939) came to Pett Level in the summer of 1914. He was a friend of Dora Carrington, with whom he had studied at the Slade School. In one of his letters to Dora he revealed that he was staying with Mrs Cooke; he also observed: 'The air is splendid and I am feeling much better'. One of his paintings is of the 'White House' on Pett Level, of which he said, 'I am working hard here – the first landscape which is nearly finished is of a black and white cottage – the foreground consists of a golden elder seen through another plant called pampas grass. The scene as it is in nature is most beautiful.' Augustus John (1878–1961) was in Pett Level around the same time as Mark Gertler. Apparently he was renowned for being short of money and sometimes paid off his debts by giving away drawings. At first they were thought to be originals but at least two turned out to be copies. These were of Dorelia, his wife, and Euphemia, the wife of the painter Henry Lamb. Sir William Orpen (1878–1931), a friend of Augustus John, visited Pett Level before he was appointed an official War Artist in 1917. Another painter from the Slade School of Art, Arthur Ambrose McEvoy (1878–1927) also painted here. It is thought that all the Slade School artists came to Pett Level through a Mr Knewstub, an art dealer with a gallery in London, who had a house in Hastings and would have arranged their stays here in the coastal area.

Sir Jacob Epstein (1880–1959), the famous sculptor, came to live in Pett in 1913 after being in Paris for some time. He rented 'Bay Point' at Pett Level and worked there for three years. He wrote: 'I could look out to sea and carve away to my heart's content without troubling a soul.' Whilst at Pett Level he carved some of his best known pieces: 'Venus', the three groups of doves, the Flenite carvings, the marble 'Mother and Child' – now in New York Museum of Modern Art – and 'Rock Drill'. He also kept rooms in London, which he would have needed to keep in touch with the various galleries and people wanting commissions. Epstein would have required a wagon and several horses to transport his work up Chick Hill and it must have been very difficult getting his finished sculptures to the capital.

Epstein complained about the Military Authorities, who seemed puzzled as to why 'an alleged sculptor' would want to live in Pett Level while a war was raging a few miles away across the Channel. The Zeppelin raid on the Level was the final straw that caused Epstein to move to London, which he did with regret. He said: ' … had I an income I would like to live in the country and keep in touch with Galleries, and others who might want my work. My three years at Pett Level, near Hastings, were productive of many carvings, but I had continually to run up to London to see if I could dispose of something or get a portrait to do.'

Jacob Epstein was a bit of a rogue and it was said that he always had some girl living with him at Bay Point, including his wife! Mark Gertler wrote in one of his letters that he was more at home and happy with the people of Pett Level than he had been for a long time. The one fault in his holiday, he said, was Epstein (Jacob). 'Somehow he puts me off working. So far I have done nothing. If it wasn't for Epstein I would settle here for some time.'

Pett still has a fascination for artists and many have made it their home. Another well-known and well-loved person had a temporary home on the Level. This was Gracie Fields, who had a caravan not far from the sea in the 1930s. And today, the comedian Paul Merton has a house in the locality.

When Britain was getting ready for war against the French at the beginning of the 19th century, an officer of the garrison here was the father of George Borrow (1803–1881). George adopted literature as his profession and toured through France, Germany, Russia, Spain and the East, studying the language of each country he visited. He was an agent for the British and Foreign Bible Society and wrote several books, among which were *Lavengro* (1851) and *Romany Rye* (1857). In *Lavengro* Borrow tells, among other things, of his childhood and an interesting adventure at Pett. George had an elder brother and they lived, for a time, with their parents under canvas with the garrison at Pett Level. The two young boys were playing one day in a sandy lane not

The Village Hall being opened by comedian Paul Merton – 30th March 2002

far from the camp (*possibly Elms Lane or Fox Earth Lane – off Pannel Lane*) as they were out for a walk with their mother. She was some distance behind the boys when all of a sudden an adder appeared gliding down the bank of the lane. Without thinking, George grabbed the beautifully marked snake by the middle. He goes on to say: ' … the object to the eye appeared so warm and sunlike. I did not drop it, however, but holding it up, looked at it intently, as its head dangled about a foot from my hand. It made no resistance; I felt not even the slightest struggle; but now my brother began to scream and shriek like one possessed. "O Mother, Mother!" said he, "the viper! – my brother has a viper in his hand!" He then, like one frantic, made an effort to snatch the creature away from me. The viper now hissed again, and raised its head, in which were eyes like hot coals, menacing, not myself, but my brother. I dropped my captive, for I saw my mother running towards me; and the reptile, after standing a moment nearly erect, and still hissing furiously, made off, and disappeared. The whole scene is now before me, as vividly as if it occurred yesterday – the gorgeous viper, my dear frantic brother. My agitated parent, and a frightened hen clucking under the bushes – and yet I was not three years old.' There are still adders to be seen in and around Pett, but they are cautious and avoid humans if possible.

Edward Lear (1818–1888), artist and author knew of and wrote about this area. Lear was a fine illustrator of birds and his *Family of the Psittacidae* is one of the earliest volumes of coloured plates of birds published in England. He gave lessons in drawing to Queen Victoria in 1846. In the same year he published his *Book of Nonsense* for the grandchildren of his patron, the Earl of Derby. In 1870 he published his third book of nonsense and included in it are the following limericks about this area:

Pett:
> There was an old person of Pett,
> Who was partly consumed by regret;
> He sate in a cart, and ate cold apple tart,
> Which relieved that old person of Pett.

Winchelsea:
> There was an old lady of Winchelsea,
> Who said, "If a needle or pin you see
> On the floor of my room, sweep it up with a broom!"
> That exhaustive old lady of Winchelsea!

The Marsh:
> There was an old man in a marsh,
> Whose manners were futile and harsh,
> He sate on a log, and sang songs to a frog,
> That instructive old man in a Marsh.

Rye:
> There was an old person of Rye,
> Who went up to town on a fly,
> But they said, "If you cough, you are safe to fall off!
> You abstemious old person of Rye!"

Dover:
> There was an old person of Dover,
> Who rushed through a field of blue clover;
> But some very large bees, stung his nose and his knees,
> So he very soon went back to Dover.

There are hundreds more limericks in the *Nonsense Books* and I wonder if Edward Lear visited each place mentioned in them. Perhaps he just sat and perused a book of maps of Britain, picking out the names of places that caught his eye. It would be nice to think that he did actually visit Pett!

This book mentions many people and their associations with Pett and Pett Level; but it would not be complete if more mention was not made of farmers and the life of folk at Pett Level. Several farms have been referred to and some of these have existed for hundreds of years, as farming has been the main means of making a living.

Lunsford Farm takes its name from William Lunsford, who probably acquired the land in the 1670s. William, described as a 'gentleman', was a man of substance, owning farms in the vicinity and land too in Ore and Battle. In 1672 William took on 18 acres of land in Pett, which included an eight-acre parcel called 'le Stench' – presumably an ill-drained site! Two years later he bought a barn and 60 acres called Keales Farm, near Shellies Green. Lunsford Farm grew in size. William and his wife Eleanor suffered several deaths from among their children and William Lunsford himself died when he was only middle-aged in March 1691. Eleanor kept the farm going and in 1724 was paying three shillings Land Tax on some of the land. This remarkable lady lived on till 1736, when she was over 95 – an extraordinary age for her time. The name Lunsford had once been common in this part of Sussex. In 1535 a John Lunsford had 'Wykam Roke' and William (of Pett) is thought to have been a kinsman of Colonel Thomas Lunsford, who fought on the side of the Royalists in the Civil War.

The farm changed hands several times and has changed in size too as fields have been bought and sold over the years. In 1851 it was being farmed by John Waghorne, followed by the Skinners, and in 1888 the Dunlop family became tenants, Andrew Dunlop of Church Farm, Hendon, taking on the lease for his son Robert. Robert died in 1894 and his younger brother Thomas took over the tenancy. Thomas bought the farm in 1917 when the Fairlight Hall Estate was sold, and, when he died in 1958, his son Andy took over. Thomas Parker Dunlop was very well known in the village; he served on the Parish Council for many years. He also kept diaries that contained entries about the daily work on the farm and the people with whom he came in contact. I am most grateful to Thomas's grandson, Andrew Dunlop, for permission to record some extracts of the diary for 1898 here:

Thurs. 6th Jan: Dry most of the day, but some showers. Will helped to tie straw – got 3 sacks and 300 hop poles from Rogers and load of bushes from 5 acres. All tying wheat straw. William and self put up hop poles round lodge in calves yard. One of own lambs died. Kept white heifers and cows in all day.

Mon. 17th Jan: Alf took 50 trusses hay to Stricklands, loaded back gas lime to heap in 3 acres. (*Stricklands was a corn merchant in Hastings. Gas lime was a by-product from the gas works and a good fertiliser*).

Thurs. 27th Jan: Work started on building the new Coastguard Station on Toot Rock.

Weds. 9th Feb: Mild dry day. S.W. light wind. Will, Jack, Dennis and self drilling beans. 4 of own and one of Mr. Wickens horses ran away with and broke our drill. Borrowed Mr. Griffen's – drilled about 2 acres. Harrowed once across before, twice after. Alf day off with sore arms.

Thurs. 24th Feb: Cold dry day. Wind N.N.W. Will harrowing and ploughing 5 acres – 4 hours up and down – iron plough. Alf put out dung to near side of big meadow. Self drove round farm with father – came down by 5 o'clock train from London and walked out. (*from Hastings station*)

Frid. 15th Apr: Cuckoo was heard. Parish Council meeting – elected as deputy chairman.

Mon. 20th Jun: ... Sold Mr. Daniel Smith; I barren ewe 42/-, 2 tegs 38/-, 3 lambs 26/-, 11 beasts (*cattle*) £15, the white home-reared steer being left out, 2 to be taken in July and 2 each month. (*A teg is a sheep in its second year. The price of a barren ewe would have paid Will's wages for nearly three weeks, now it wouldn't pay a man for one day.*)

Thurs. 7th July: Will finished Spring Meadow and about 1 acre near side of big meadow with Willett's machine. Self went up to see grandmother. Old cow calved – red heifer calf. Jack took 80 trusses of straw to Jackson.

Weds. 3rd Aug: ... Self drove Mr. Rogers to Rye then to Rolvenden. When on the road back saw Mr. Baffard's stack on fire, went to fire and waited till engine put it out. Drove 6 tegs to market – no bid – large market. (*So they would have had to walk them all the way home from Rye*).

Mon. 24th Oct: ... Mr. Wickens, Merricks, Tom Hilder and George shooting. 4 rabbits, 1 snake, 1 cat, 1 stoat, 1 rook and 1 landrail (*corncrake*).

Mon. 14th Nov: Dry, very fine day, warm. Will – Budds, self sowed, Jack harrowed. Jack got up bushes from Budds to lodge stable yard. Father and self moved 40 ewes, ram and strange ewe to bottom ground. Fred Standen drove white cow to Lanningtons near Black Horse, Battle.

Of course, these were the days of real horsepower – no tractors! Cash Accounts show that the wages per week were fairly low. Will and Alf earned 16/- (16 shillings equates to 80p today); Jack earned up to 6/-; Dennis between 4/6 and 5/6 (Jack and Dennis were boys); George Foster earned 12/- per week, David 15/- and George Standen 14/-.

The diary gives a clear picture of the hard life led by those whose livelihoods were involved with working the land. It is still hard today as livestock prices rise and fall, as disease is a constant threat, as the weather can either make or break a crop's success and as rules and regulations associated with farming become more complex and, sometimes very difficult to comprehend.

Thomas Parker Dunlop's son Andy (Andrew senior) grew up at Lunsford, and returned to farm after the Second World War. Andy could tell many a tale about the farm and the village. One story illustrates the hardship faced by the farming community and also describes an event that could have occurred anytime sheep were moved. Until the early 1930s there was a lagoon in the shingle on the beach at Pett Level opposite where the Colonel Body lakes now lie. As a condition of their tenancy, all those farming on the estate had to cart shingle to spread on the roads and farm tracks for maintenance. It was the continual removal of shingle from one spot which caused the lagoon to form. When, one day, as a small boy, Andy was helping to bring up some sheep from the marsh, a lamb took it into its woolly head to wander away from the flock and into the lagoon. The family could not afford to provide shoes for a young lad working on the farm and so Andy was barefoot. This being so he was the obvious choice to be sent to retrieve the stray lamb. It must have been quite frightening to a small boy to wade out into deepening water, but happily both lamb and boy returned safely, and the sheep were moved without further trouble.

Years later, Andy Dunlop had a good friend in Victor Prior. Vic was older than Andy and was a very good and skilled farm worker. As a youngster he worked near Appledore, and after the war came to Pett to manage Elms Farm for the Coopers. Andy remembers Victor's rustic sense of humour and tells the following story about him. Mr Prior had a Sussex bull and he used to lead it along the road on a halter at about the time the congregation was leaving the Parish Church after the Sunday morning service. Andy would have been on the cricket field – he played good cricket for Pett for many years – and he would meet Vic and discuss the finer points of the bull in front of the elderly lady churchgoers. Mr. Prior would poke the bull a bit to make him cavort about for the benefit of the ladies watching!

On another occasion, Vic had a heifer that he kept on the marsh for the summer. He asked Andy to help him get it off the marsh and the two of them, Vic and Andy, led the animal to the Beach Club, which in those days was where 'The Smuggler' is now. While Vic went in to order two glasses of shandy, Andy sat on the steps outside with the heifer. When he came out with the drinks, Victor began telling the visitors at the Club that the heifer was a dangerous bull – and they believed him, and ran off.

While at Elms Farm, some of Vic's calves got out early one morning. He saw them at 5 a.m. and phoned Andy for his help. On arrival at Elms Farm, Andy found Vic, in his pyjamas, trying to prevent the calves from going further down the road and Mrs Prior, in her nightie, guarding the other end of the lane. Vic always assumed that it was his job to help his farmer neighbours when they wanted assistance and took it for granted, too, that they would help him when he was in trouble. Andy said that Victor Prior was gentle and polite, but he told off one lad who called him Vic. 'Mr. Prior to you,' he said, 'and Vic to your father.'

There have been several mentions in this chapter of the marsh at Pett Level, used often for grazing livestock. The marsh is a special place, often mysterious, full of wonderful wildlife and always beautiful. The spirit of Pett Level, the marsh and its people is captured in a newspaper article by Reginald Cooke. Before he died in hospital in March 1965, Reg wrote of his reminiscences of Pett Level, and these were published in the *Hastings & St. Leonards Observer* in June 1969. I am grateful for the permission of the Cooke family and the Observer Paper Group to include the article here.

I have been asked many times, by many people, to write about Pett Level as it has been during the seventy years I have known it. It is difficult to know where to begin, but perhaps a general description of the area would make the best opening.

The western boundary is Chick Hill, and the eastern what is now known as Winchelsea Beach. The northern boundary is the Dimsdale Sewer and, of course, the southern boundary is the sea. I have always had a great interest in the sea and the foreshore, and during my lifetime have seen a great exchange in the latter; the sea has encroached about 200 yards over the whole distance since I first knew it.

As I first remember, an earth sea wall ran from Cliff End on the west side to the old Ship Inn at Winchelsea Beach. This wall was at least 200 yards behind the foreshore in some places, and times out of number the sea damaged it during gales and high tides. Keddle net fishing was almost an industry 60 years ago (*about 1900*) and was in operation from Cliff End to Jury's Gap, the other side of Rye Harbour. These nets were hung on poles and looked like large kettles from a distance, hence the name. They were used mainly to catch mackerel, which at times were caught in very large quantities: so many, sometimes, that the local farmers used to come down and cart them on to land for manure for their hops. Quantities of these mackerel were sent to London by the bigger Keddle net owners, but Hastings was the main market. The only means of transport was by farmers' wagons, and the fishermen paid 6d (*2½p*) a box for the carriage to Hastings. On many occasions the farmers made more money than the fishermen. As a boy, I well remember hearing the loaded wagons rumbling past our house at night, or very early in the morning, during the mackerel season, which is from May until August. In those days, in spite of slow transport, large amounts of mackerel were got rid of in local markets – much more than would be possible today.

On the beach, opposite each of the Keddle net stands, was a small hut with a flagstaff attached. When any of the nets had fish, a flag was run up on the staff to tell the local people of the fact and that help would be needed to wash and pack the fish. The inland villagers used to keep a look out during the season, and as soon as they saw a flag up at any of the huts they would flock down to the shore to help, getting fish as a reward for their trouble. I have actually seen as many as a hundred villagers on some evenings down at the nets. I am afraid things are vastly different these days. There are only two Keddle net stands operating now, and these are floated from cork floats instead of hanging on poles, whereas when I was a boy there were at least 20 stands between Cliff End and Rye Harbour.

The marshland, which extends to about 1,000 acres, belonged to several owners but was farmed by tenants, usually in blocks of not more than 50 acres. These parcels of land were all attached to the upland farms and were very good 'fatting' land, of great value to the upland farmers. The marsh was looked after by two or three men called 'lookers', who were paid 2 shillings (10 p) an acre for the job. Ditches were mown out sometime during the winter, and the mowings carted home to the bullock yards. The price for this job was 2 shillings a score of rods (110 yards) for mowing, lumping and raking ready for picking up. Thistles were kept down by spudding. It was seldom one saw a scythe used on this land, except in the winter ditch and rush mowing. I believe it was a condition of tenancy that mowing machines were not to be used on the marsh.

In 1940, the marshland was flooded, as part of the South-East England's defences. This was done by blowing breaches in the sea wall and letting in the sea. It was ruination of the land for several years, of course, but made the marsh a duck paradise. A good deal has already been written about the ducks on the flooded level, but perhaps a few notes here will not be out of place.

The largest number of ducks on the water at any one time was 6,000 – sometime in the winter of 1942. These were mixed species of the more common ones, usually more mallard than any other sort. Certainly, in the early part of the winter mallard predominated, but during the latter part of the winter wigeon were more plentiful. Teal, tufted duck, pochard, scaup, shoveller, pintail and shelduck were always present in some numbers. Garganey came, and a few pairs bred every year. There were other birds as well, of course – lapwing, snipe, sandpipers, ringed plover, and very large numbers of black-headed gulls, common and little terns. A few pairs of oyster-catchers bred each year. As far as I can remember, the only two rare birds I saw were a squacco heron and a cream-coloured courser.

The black-headed gulls and common terns bred in their hundreds, every small portion of dry land being occupied by both species. It was a remarkable sight to see these birds all sitting on their nests together. I occasionally put them off just to have a look at the eggs. The nests were so close together that it was impossible to walk about without treading on them. I have heard it said that these two birds will not nest near to each other, but here was a case defeating that argument. Many of the gulls eggs were taken for food by some of the local men: small blame to them in wartime. Lapwing and ringed plover nested on the dried mud or ditch banks in good numbers, and a few oyster-catchers also nested on dried mud. I believe this was the first time for almost a hundred years that oyster-catchers had bred in East Sussex.

My father kept the Old Ship Inn for several years up to 1887, and the customers then were mostly coastguards and the occupants of the Martello Towers. The towers were numbered from east to west, No. 31 being at Dogs Hill (Winchelsea Beach) and No. 38 at Cliff End. I think the last of the towers to be demolished was No. 38, about 1890. Occasionally, they were occupied by the military, then taken over by the Coastguard. After the Coastguard Stations were built, they were then let to civilians. In fact my parents lived at either No. 31 or 32, though I'm not sure which. My father was born in the old cottage near the Ship Inn which survived in a rather dilapidated state until the new sea wall was built recently. Oh, the happenings on the Level during the early days. I am dependent on what I was told by my father and mother.

In 1887, the wreck of the German ship *Seggeta* at Fairlight caused a great deal of interest for a week or two. This vessel had a general cargo which included gin and bottled beer, and I believe a few casualties occurred through people over-indulging and being drowned in the consequence. The Coastguards had a very busy time trying to prevent this cargo being taken from the beach.

A story my mother told me about getting the gin off the beach amused me. She had a rather hefty servant girl at the time, and in those days women wore very long petticoats that came down to the ankles. The girl used to sew two petticoats together at the bottom and put bottles of gin in between them, but the

Coastguard were not allowed to search her, although they knew full well what she was doing.

At this time my mother's father was a retired Coastguard, and he told her that there was to be a search for spirits in the district, also that the Ship Inn would be the first place they would suspect. My father and mother were consequently rather frightened, so they buried what bottles of gin they had in the shingle. When the excitement died down it took them a long time to discover where they had buried it. My father told me that for years afterwards, when mowing out the ditches in the marsh, they often came across hidden bottles of gin that had been forgotten.

My grandfather, and my father and his brothers used to buy up wrecks on the shore and sell the timber to estate owners for fencing and so forth. Nearly all the fences on the marsh were made of wreck timber, as I first remember. There must have been many wrecks around the coast when you reflect that the old houses within several miles of it have beams of wreck timber.

Another wreck that I heard of occurred about 1860. The vessel was, I believe, called the *James Brown* and had a cargo of tobacco and buffalo hides. The coastal people received a shilling each for salvaging the hides, but I never heard what happened to the tobacco. Yet another wreck I was told of was the *Madeleine*. She came ashore at Dogs Hill, but I don't remember what cargo she had. A Coastguard from Pett made history by throwing the heaving cane aboard and thereby effecting a rescue. Some verses were written about this event, supposedly by Anthony Aldridge, who was famous in those days. All I can remember of those verses is about two lines, which run, 'If you ever get caught in a storm, make straight away for Johnny Horn'. Johnny Horn was the Coastguard who threw the heaving cane aboard the *Madeleine*. The heaving cane was at that time part of the Coastguard life saving equipment. There were several other wrecks whose names I heard of but which had no particular interest; the *Billy Boy* and the *Anna Maria* being just two of them. I forgot to mention that I have an old muzzle-loading gun that came from the *Seggeta*.

The old sea road from Cliff End to Winchelsea ran for a large part of the way on the sea side of the sea wall, and at high tides it was often blocked by shingle, but never to make it impassable. There were several ponds in the shingle between the sea wall and the sea, some of them containing fish. I remember an occasion when my brother, cousin and self, during very rough weather, borrowed a drawnet and caught a lot of large plaice in the pond near the Ship Inn. We took them to Hastings Fishmarket where they sold very well indeed. As the weather had been too rough for some time for any boats to be able to get off, it puzzled the local fishermen where the plaice had come from. We didn't tell them, of course – at least, not the truth!

One of the shingle ponds about half-way between Cliff End and the Ship, was known as the 'Cocked Hat' because of its shape, and was absorbed by the sea in 1913. In fact most of these shingle ponds disappeared during the gales and high tides of March 1913, when the sea flooded a good deal of the marsh, drowning some sheep.

During the summer months a number of beasts were fatted on Pett Level and sent to Rye market. My father, the night before market day, would say to my brother and me, 'I shall want you to help me out of the marsh with a few bullocks in the morning.' The next morning we would drive down to the marsh and take a bullock or two out of several lots, get them up to the road when my father would say to us: 'Go home and get your breakfast. I shall manage now.' He would get up into his trap, and go off to Rye behind the bullocks, his dogs doing the necessary work. Looking back now, I remember what a simple little job it was, compared with what I sometimes see nowadays.

The old Ship Inn, as I first remember it, was rather a remarkable place. Almost everyone met in there, and there were some characters – artists, sculptors, authors and others, some of whom became famous. It's rather a pity I cannot mention names, it would make this far more interesting. My mother has told me that when father and she kept the Ship, their patrons were mostly Coastguards, and the officers had to have a separate room. They were not allowed to drink with the men. Whisky was 4d a quarter – about two doubles.

So ends Reg's article. Nearly 40 years have passed since these words were written about Pett Level and more changes have taken place. There are no hops grown on the local farms now, and there is no requirement for the upland villagers to go down to the Level to help with large catches of fish. However, Pett Level is still a wonderful place to explore; it possesses a special magic, and the folk who live there today have their own stories to tell – just as fascinating as those of the past.

Now, as the new millennium moves into its second year, the Internet 'surfer' can find out about Pett on the World Wide Web. The entry for the village begins:

Pett lies 4 miles east of Hastings on the Fairlight to Rye road. Its first mention is in the Domesday Book and it was known then as Luet. It consists of a collection of houses and bungalows that straggle along about 1½ miles of road, which swings steeply down at its East end to Pett Level, a wide expanse of land which is a haven for wildfowl.

It also states that the village is quiet and pretty. A few more notes are added, but none of them capture the real truth about the area. It is only by walking the fields, lanes, woodlands and beach as well as talking to the people who live and love it here that the visitor can really begin to fully appreciate this jewel in England's crown.

18

A Ghost and Conclusion

No pathway through history would be complete without a ghost story. Certainly no village should be without one and the story that follows really only touched Pett in passing. It is a love story and is well known in the Rye area as it concerns a monk from there. It all happened in medieval times when cruelty, superstition and fear were commonplace. Though it is not a proper Pett story, some of the events took place in the desolate local marshes and in one of the sea caves at Cliff End, sadly washed away by the sea. So with a little bit of licence we'll call it Pett's ghost story.

In the monastery at Rye lived a young monk whose fame spread far and wide because none could sing as sweetly as he. The young cleric had been placed in the monastery as a small boy, and when he grew up he took his vows knowing nothing of the outside world. He might have stayed happy and contented as a monk for the rest of his life, with his singing and his prayers, until the day came when he climbed up to peer over the monastery wall. Looking into the garden of the Dormy House next door, he saw a maiden busy among the flowerbeds. Her beauty smote him like a spear and his happiness suddenly deserted him. No saint nor angel, nor even the Holy Virgin, could satisfy him now that he had seen a real woman of such loveliness. Not knowing quite why, he began to find reasons to stand by the garden wall in the hope of seeking a glimpse of the girl who had stolen his peace and his heart. Because he had no other means of expressing himself, he sang and sang and all the hymns and chants he knew unconsciously became love songs. The girl in the garden heard him singing, and the music enchanted her until she could no longer resist the impulse to look upon the sweet singer. She sought for a niche so that she could climb the wall. Finally the two young people looked at each other – and fell in love.

The fate of a monk who broke his vows was perpetual seclusion and penance in a dungeon. The father of the girl could lawfully kill her, if he wished. Life was hard, rules were strict and a happy ending to the young couple's love for each other looked bleak. Regardless of this the two lovers made secret plans to run away together, and, when the opportunity arose, slipped away out of town. They were free at last, he from a life of rigid discipline in a monastery and she from a strict and forbidding father.

However brief their freedom might be, they were together. Not knowing which way to go, they headed into the marshes outside the town. They struggled over reed beds and bogs, forded streams and dykes and, as they became weary, the marsh still stretched into the distance before them. Behind them they now heard the baying of hounds and realised that they were being pursued. Gamely they pushed on until eventually they came to the seashore at Pett. There, wet and exhausted, they found shelter in a cave and huddled together. As the darkness closed in on this young man and girl who had defied the customs of their day, the baying of the fierce hounds grew stronger and the youngsters shivered in their dark and damp shelter.

The pursuers were led to the cave by their bell-voiced dogs and the lovers were caught, bound with ropes and dragged back to Rye. And there, it is said, they were both buried alive in the wall. While the monk was being walled within his tomb he sang of the joy of their day together, and of love and freedom. His ghost sings there yet, and it sings in the wind over the marshes and the lovers' voices whisper in the darkness of the cave in Pett.

A good story to finish with, and it tells us that it was away from the town that the young lovers were looking for a fresh start and a future together. Though they did not find it here and though they came to Pett Level by accident, not knowing which way to go, they did look for shelter here. Many folk have since come to the area looking for a place to live; perhaps to farm and bring up their families. We have met many of them in this history and it is proper that we should end by looking a little towards the years ahead.

What of the future? What will Pett be like in another thousand years? Will it still remain a village or will it be swallowed up by the gradual encroachment of the towns of Hastings and Rye? The people attending the Guestling Hundred Courts would have had no concept of the alterations to the area over the next eight or nine centuries, and Pett, with Pett Level, has changed almost beyond recognition since those far off days.

The beauty of the area, however, still exists. Each season continues to bring its own special attraction. In winter the fields can look bleak and covered with hoar-frost, with sheep huddled together in the winds, and fieldfares, redwings and other birds feeding on berries from the holly and the hawthorn trees. As spring approaches the woodlands are carpeted, first with wood anemones and later bluebells. The banks of the hedgerows become sprinkled with primroses and local folk listen eagerly for the first cuckoo. The long summer days bring out the bowls, stoolball and cricket teams, who with the keen tennis players enjoy the fabulous view from the recreation field down to the sea. Pett Level begins to attract the holiday visitors: children playing on the beach, ice-cream vans, plus the drawback of Jet-skis and power-boats creating huge waves and much noise. And of course, throughout the year, the 'twitchers' peer through their telescopes for sightings of rare birds on Pett Pools or on the sea-shore at low tide. The autumn sunlight enhances the colours of the changing leaves before they fall from the oaks, sweet chestnuts, birches and other splendid trees that stand proudly in and around the village. The migration of many birds gives the naturalist much to see and enjoy and soon the cold days of winter are back with us; the foxes mate and the badgers scavenge far and wide for food as it becomes more scarce. The gently rolling countryside is still a good place for walking and exploring and at every turn there is a magnificent view. The night sky is often full of bright stars that cannot be seen from an urban area and the air is always fresh and clean. Pett is a great place in which to live!

Though the church spire stands high over the village, its congregations have dwindled somewhat over the years. Now Pett is combined in a United Benefice with Guestling and Fairlight, one has to ask if the use of all the churches in the benefice will continue? Will St Mary and St Peter's Church still be standing in another thousand years? Will it still be open in another ten years? Because maintenance costs are high and worshipping at the village church seems to be less important now to many than it was a hundred, or even fifty, years ago, it is a great strain on the faithful few to raise the vast sums of money necessary to keep a village church in good repair and available for all who need it at some point in their lives.

The two major changes that have occurred since the far off days of the Guestling Hundred Courts are the number of houses in both Pett and Pett Level, and the growth in the population caused by people coming into the area to live. Pett Road infilling has taken place so that, on both sides of the road, there is now little space between the houses, and Pett Level is a strong community in its own right. Fortunately, the new houses fit well into the village, but in nearly every case the cost of a new house is far beyond the means of any young local couple trying to set up a home. There are some low cost houses rented out by the Rother Homes (plc) and these are fairly recent additions to the number of dwellings in Pett. A comparison of the number of houses and population between 1841 and 2000 is staggering. In 1841 there were 49 houses and the population was about 300; in 2000 there were more than 400 dwellings and the population must exceed 800 (there are more than 650 on the Rother Register of Electors). Because the cost of property is high, and the number of jobs in the area is very limited, there are more retired couples coming into the village to live than young people. However, the number of youngsters of school age in the village remains fairly stable. There is now no school in the village; Guestling Bradshaw C.E. Primary School takes in young children from the three villages of Pett, Guestling and

Fairlight. The village does, however, have a Toddler Group and a Play Group, and there are some thriving Baden Powell Groups.

Most local people would consider it disastrous if there were much more building of houses in the village, as it would begin to change the nature of Pett and remove some more of the fields and woodlands which help to make this such a special place. The local facilities, such as shops, are few, but the new Village Hall has brought fresh life to the social activities shared by the people of Pett. Transport to and from the village is not easy: buses are infrequent and few. Unless a person has his or her own transport the best way of getting about is by 'shank's pony'.

It is, as it has always been, the people of Pett and Pett Level that make this place what it is. Much of the beauty of the area is due to farmers' and landowners' conservation of the land. Many local people do all they can to ensure that Pett remains a place where they are proud to live. Pett people are friendly, make good neighbours and are very caring for one another. Each of them has his or her own story to tell and a book such as this can only scratch the surface of the wealth of tales that could be told. Each generation has added to the ethos which enfolds the village and that, I am sure, will continue well into the future. Let us hope that Pett and Pett Level are not swallowed up into becoming a suburb of Hastings. Pett is a companionable place, and has been so for more than five hundred years. No one knows what the future holds for the area, but it will not be surprising if the village is still attractive and a much sought after place to live in after another thousand years have passed.

Appendix

Table 1. Pett Church – Clergy (Rectors)

1285		Robert de Hastings	1615		Griffin Flud
1365		William Baron	1622		Peter Theobald
1391		Thomas Wardon	1660		John Eston
1397	ex	John Lawrence	1660		William Horner
1397		John Fox	1661		Zacharias Cradock
1398		John Walkyngton	1695		Thomas Rotheram
1404		William Hancock	1702		James Cranston
1405		Thomas Sampson	1726		Edward Levitt
1409		Osbert Done	1731		David Denham
1415–1416	r	John Kyne	1745		William Colbron
1415–1416		William Eston	1750		Augustin Diones Geere
1430	ex	Simon Kyng	1765		Johnson Towers
1430		John Knoyl	1772		Nathaniel Bristed
1439	r	James Chestre	1774		Diones Geere
1439		William Russell	1823		Henry Wynch
1444		Walter Nicholl	1853		Robert West
1504	r	John Stowe	1857		Frederick Young
1504		Richard Hersey or Horsey	1882		John Moore Fincher
1515		Robert Hodde	1909		Frederick Charles Ashburnham Young
1520		William Hode	1930		Herbert Ernest Moxon
1524		Richard Duckett	1941		Roland Clifford Wood (*)
1544		John Foster	1954		Ernest Algernon Parkins (†)
1550		Thomas Stunt	1971		George William Egan Manners
1554		Richard Dounton	1978		John Hanson Read (‡)
1556		Simon Suder	1984		Michael Butler
1560		William Garrett	1988		Norman John Charles Greenfield
1569–1570		Richard Gowge	1994		John Robin Balch (§)
1581		Thomas Mawdesley	2002		Bernard Edward Crosby

Notes: ex = exchanged; r = resigned.

(*) In 1941 Rev. Victor Charles Roberts was appointed Rector for Pett and served in the parish for about two months. Unfortunately he died before his induction. (†) Pett united to Guestling, 8th July 1968 (Plurality). (‡)United Benefice of Guestling and Pett, 1st June 1978. (§)United Benefice of Fairlight, Guestling and Pett, 8th September 1994.

Table 2. Patrons

ADVOWSON: the right of nomination or presentation to an ecclesiastical benefice. The advowson is held by a patron who may be an individual or institution, clerical or secular. The patron presents the candidate to the appropriate bishop for institution and induction. An advowson is a form of property that may be bought, sold or given away and is subject to civil law.

	Advowson held by
	Richard de Ore & his wife Cecily (in the reign of Henry III 1216 –1272)
1274	Roger de Mosewell and his wife Joan
	Cecily de Ore
1368	Henry Halle of Ore
1397 & 1405	Robert de Ore
1409 & 1444	John & William Halle
	(The advowson follows the descent of the manor till the end of the 17th century)
circa 1515	Elizabeth, d. of John Dudley and widow of Thomas Ashburnham
1529	Robert Haule
1544	Godard Haule
1569	Thomas Sackville Kt.
1574	John Thatcher
1581	George Courthope (before 1613 James Thatcher)
circa 1612	William Thatcher
1615	John Taylor
1622	Thomas Bennet
1618–1650	Manor sub-divided into shares. James Rootes and Anthony Morgan
1669	Elizabeth Morgan 3/7 shares
1698	Manor divided into 7 parts:
	Mary, widow of Peter Farmor (perhaps daughter of Elizabeth Morgan);
	Andrew Wharton (son and heir of Thomas Rootes) & Elizabeth – wife;
	Bartholomew Walmesley and John Jenkins;
	Edmund Boleworth and Grace: Mary Eyston (youngest of the original
	Thatcher sisters) & William, her son; Barbara Vincent and
	Nathaniel Pigott; Anthony Trumbell and Jordan Metham
circa 1700	Joseph Gage (*)
1717	Thomas Medley (*)
1702 & 1726	David Denham and Mrs Elizabeth Denham
1731	Everard Levitt
1745	Stephen Kennard
1750	William Hyland & John Alde
1765	Grace Geere
1772	Diones Geere
1823	George Wynch (of Winchelsea)
1835	Henry Wynch

Table 2 (continued)

	Patrons
1853	Sir Richard Thornton (of London)
1860s	Henry Young
1882	C.W. & F. Young
20th century	Vivian Edward Young & Ellen Waring Braithwaite
1937	Bishop of Chichester
1994	The Diocese (Bishops) and the Church Pastoral Aid Society

(*) Not patrons, but did hold the manor.

Table 3. List of Rectors, Curates and Churchwardens, 1606–1754

This list is taken from Baptism Records and the spelling of names is as written. The first recorded entry reads: '1606 25 March Richard the sonne of John Butler was baptised and buried ye nexte day following.'

Date	Rector	Curate	Churchwardens (*)
1606	Thomas Mawdesley	Griffin Flud	Richard Lewes, Nicholas Dandy
1607	Thomas Mawdesley	Griffin Flud	Robert Sheppard
1608	Thomas Mawdesley	Gryphin Flud	Clement Ward
1609	Thomas Mawdesley	Griphin Flud	John Bett(X)
1610	Thomas Mawdesley	Griphin Flud	John Bett(X), Robert Foster(X)
1611	Thomas Mawdesley	Griphin Flud	Edward Arnold, Robert Foster(X)
1612	Thomas Mawdesley	Griphin Flud	Edward Arnold, John Winchaden
1613	Thomas Mawdesley	Griphin Flud	John Butler(X), John Winchaden
1614	Thomas Mawdesley	Griphin Flud	John Butler(X), George Wrighte(X)
1615	Griffin Flud	None	George Swane(X),George Wrighte(X)
1617	Griffin Flud	None	Edward Gibson, Thomas Winge
1618	Griffin Flud	None	Ezechiell Snepp(X), Thomas Winge
1620	Griffin Flud (†)	None	John Winchaden, Robert Dabcon(X)
1622	Peter Theobald	None	John Boniface(X), Godward Foster(X)
1623	Peter Theobald	None	John Boniface(X), John Keale(X)
1624	Peter Theobald (‡)	None	John Manser(X), William Teylon
1625	Peter Theobald	None	John Manser(X), Samuel Theobald
1626	Peter Theobald	None	Thomas Taylor, Samuel Theobald
1628	Peter Theobald (‡)	None	William Wilson(X)
1630	Peter Theobald (§)	None	Goddard Foster(X)
1631	Peter Theobald	None	Thomas Avan
1632	Peter Theobald	None	Thomas Salman
1633	Peter Theobald	None	Thomas Crowherst(X)
1634	Peter Theobald	None	Thomas Crowherst(X), John Haywood
1635	Peter Theobald	None	Edward Gibson
1636	Peter Theobald	None	Edmund Purfle(X), William Boorder
1637	Peter Theobald	None	Thomas Avan, Edward Gibson
1638	Peter Theobald	None	Thomas Avan, William Burden
1640	Peter Theobald	None	Thomas Crowherst(X)

The next Bishop's transcript after 1640 is for 1667

1667	Zacharias Craddock	Anselm Mathilry	William Lunsford, William Rootes
1668	Zacharias Craddock	Anselm Mathilry	William Martin

Table 3 (continued)

The next transcript is for 1672

Date	Rector	Curate	Churchwardens (*)
1672	Zacharias Craddock	Thomas Brian	Richard Carpenter(X)
1673–1674	Zacharias Craddock	Thomas Brian (¶)	Richard Carpenter(X), Nicholas Myles
1675–1676	Zacharias Craddock	Thomas Brian	Simon Sharuall, Lawrence Houghton
1677	Zacharias Craddock	Thomas Brian	William Purfield
1678–1684	Zacharias Craddock	Thomas Brian	(No churchwardens mentioned)
1686	Zacharias Craddock	Thomas Brian	William Lunsford, Simon Shervell
1686–1688	Zacharias Craddock	Thomas Brian	Samuel Cromp, Abraham French
1689–1690	Zacharias Craddock	Thomas Brian	William Lunsford, Abraham French (Nicholas Myles deleted as Churchwarden)
1691	Zacharias Craddock	Thomas Brian	Abraham French, Nicholas Myles
1692–1693	Zacharias Craddock	Thomas Brian	Nicholas Myles
1694	Zacharias Craddock	Thomas Brian	Nicholas Myles, John Marten
1695	Thomas Rotheram	Thomas Brian	John Marten, Stephen Bennett
1696–1697	Thomas Rotheram	Thomas Brian	William Rich, Stephen Bennett
1698–1700	Thomas Rotheram	Thomas Brian	(No churchwardens mentioned)
1701–1702	Thomas Rotheram	Thomas Brian	Edward Atkin, Abraham French
1703	James Cranston	Thomas Brian	
1704	James Cranston	Thomas Denham	Nicholas Myles, Abraham French
1705	James Cranston	Thomas Denham (Minister of Pett)	
1706–1707	James Cranston	Thomas Denham	Nicholas Myles, John Marten
1708–1709	James Cranston	Thomas Denham	Thomas Nabbs, John Marten
1710	James Cranston	Thomas Denham	
1711–1712	James Cranston	Thomas Denham	John Marten
1713	James Cranston	Thomas Denham	John Marten, Richard Blackman
1714–1719	James Cranston	Thomas Denham	(No churchwardens mentioned)
1720	James Cranston	Stephen Frewen (Vicar of Fairlight 1701–1726)	John Marten, Thomas Nabbs
1722–1723	James Cranston	Stephen Frewen	John Marten, Joseph Rhodes
1724	James Cranston	Edward Dyson	John Marten, Joseph Rhodes
1725	James Cranston	Edward Dyson	
1726	Edward Levitt	Thomas Denham	
1727	Edward Levitt	John Frewen (Rector of Guestling 1736–1743)	Stephen Nabbs
1728–1730	Edward Levitt	John Frewen	(No churchwardens mentioned)
1731–1741	David Denham (#)	(No Curate)	(No churchwardens mentioned)

Table 3 (continued)

Date	Rector	Curate	Churchwardens (*)
1742	(No minister mentioned)		
1743	(No minister mentioned)	Edward Innes	
1744	(No minister mentioned)	H. Woodward (Vicar of Fairlight 1743–1749)	John Bean, Richard Weller
1745–1746	William Colbron	H. Woodward	Joseph Rhodes, J. Kennard
1747	William Colbron	H. Woodward	Joseph Rhodes, John Bean
1748–1749	William Colbron	H. Woodward	Joseph Rhodes, Edward Jarret
1750	Augustin Diones Geere	H. Woodward	Joseph Rhodes, George Booth
1751	Augustin Diones Geere	W. Hickes Coppard	Joseph Rhodes, George Booth
1752	Augustin Diones Geere	Thomas Edwards	Joseph Rhodes, George Booth
1753–1754	Augustin Diones Geere	Lewis Jones	Joseph Rhodes, George Booth

(*) (X) indicates a cross instead of a signature.

(†) Griffin Flud was buried at Pett, 6 Jan. 1623.

(‡) Peter Theobald and his wife Ann had a daughter Ann, baptised 29 Aug. 1624 and another daughter Eleanor, baptised 8 Jan. 1628

(§) From 1630 to 1636 Peter Theobald is shown as Minister and from 1637 to 1640 as Rector.

(¶) Thomas Brian and his wife Mary had a son, baptised at Pett 27 Mar. 1673

(#) Anne, wife of David Denham was buried at Pett, 28 Jun. 1733

Table 4. East Sussex Land Tax 1785

Extract from: Sussex Record Society, Vol.77 p.168 and 169 – for Pett

Owners	Occupiers	Lands	Rental
			£ - s
Ashburnham, Sir William Bart, & Chichester Lord Bishop	Hoad, Crunden, Suter Veness and White	-	59 - 0
do	Messrs. White, Daniel	-	33 - 15
Stonestreet, Mr	Jewhurst, Stephen	-	40 -10
Tilden, John & George	Tilden, George	-	40 - 10
Turner, Mr	do	-	40 - 10
Jackson, Henry, esq.	Standen, John	-	27 - 0
Milward, Edward, esq.	Fairlight Parish	-	3 - 10
Little, Mr	Dearing, Christopher	-	6 - 0
Geere, Rev Mr	himself	-	75 - 0
Murray, General	Linfield, Mr	-	27 - 0
Tress, Mr	himself	-	40 - 10
Medley, George, esq.	Farncombe, William	-	149 - 0
do	Collins, Mrs	-	101 - 0
do	Thorp, John	-	54 - 0
do	Field, Messrs	-	27 - 0
do	Davis, John	-	20 - 0
do	Cloak, Moses	-	7 - 0
Rootes, Mr	Hill, James	-	6 - 10
H.M. Customs	Stevenson, John	-	60 - 10
Reed, John	-	-	33 - 10
do	do	Pett Barn land	37 - 0
Gibbons, Mrs	-	-	49 - 0
Morfey, Messrs	Harman, Richard	-	2 - 0
White, Mr	Standen, Thomas	-	2 - 0
Pulford, Mrs	-	-	2 - 0

Assessors and collectors: George Tilden, John Reed

Total collected: £187 2s 8d

Table 5. Extract from Pett Poor Books
(East Sussex Record Office: PAR 442 30/1 & 30/2)

The earliest Pett Poor Book (where details of income and distribution are recorded) is dated 1723.

The Overseers Accounts 1723–1770: Extracts

1730	April.	For writing 'Poore' Books this year	2s 0d
1733	March.	'Disburssments' of Thomas Foster of the 'Oversees of the Poore For the year 1733' – including – May 17. Paid to Henne Sloman 4 weeks pay	8s 0d
1746	Sep. 20.	paid for repairing 'pannel bridge'	£3 13s 0d
1748	Jan. 25.	paid a bushel of wheat for Foster	4s 0d
1755		For 'straw and thatching'	6s 0d
1758	Dec. 21.	Pound of yarn	1s 10d
1762		To a journey to Rye and expenses for the examination of Dame Harman	8s 6d
		For sending man and horse to Rye for Doctor to Dame Foster	3s 0d
		Foster's nurse	12s 0d
		Mrs Cramp for laying Dame Foster	7s 6d
1767		to John Clive – in need	1s 0d
1769		paid to Rev. M Gybson for 11 Registers	16s 0d

1770–1797 (second book)

Overseer Accounts Assessment made by the Churchwardens, Overseers and other inhabitants of Pett in the County of Sussex for a Monthly Relief of the poor of said parish for the rate of one shilling in the pound full rent.

1770		To Robert Cloke for keeping of the boy 50 weeks @ 1/6 per week	£3 15s 0d
1772		Dame Potter for clothes for boy	7s 0d
		To a bottle of wine, sugar and rolls	2s 3d
		To sending to Hastings for a shroud for Sloman	1s 6d
1789	Dec. 8.	Journey to Battle with Militia list	5s 0d
1793		To Doctor Cropper as the bill for 'Jos. Issacs'	£6 12s 0d
1794		Journey and expenses to Battle	7s 6d
		Two hocks of mutton	7s 0d
		A pair of shoes	3s 6d
		A pint of wine	1s 3d
		Two shirts	6s 3½d
Plus:-		provided for a woman and two children in distress	1s 0d
		Gave a poor man in want	6d
		relieved a blind man	1s 0d

Table 6. 'Sussex Proceedings of Meeting of Deputy Lieutenant for the internal Defence of this County – 1801'

Extracts from list prepared in preparation for Napoleon's invasion detailing the inhabitants of the Guestling Hundred (E.S.R.O. LCG/3/EW1 and 2)

'An Abstract of the Returns of the Churchwardens and Overseers of the Poor of the several Parishes in the said Rape (*Hastings*) pursuant to the Resolutions of a General Meeting of the Lieutenancy held at the Star Inn in said County (*Sussex*) for carrying into execution an Act of Parliament made and passed in the 38th year of the reign of his present Majesty (*George III*) intitled An Act to enable his Majesty more effectively to provide for the Defence and Security of the Realm during the present war and for indemnifying Persons who may suffer in their Property by such measures as may be necessary for that purpose.'

	Pett	Guestling	Fairlight	Icklesham
Men/boys between 15–60 capable of active service	36	59	84	70
Men/boys between 15–60 incapable of active service	4	–	2	6
Men over 60 capable of active service	4	–	11	3
Men over 60 incapable of active service	–	1	4	6
Men over 60 capable of removing themselves	–	1	3	1
Men over 60 incapable of removing themselves	4	6	5	1
Women & girls over 7 capable of removing themselves	63	90	106	93
Women & girls over 7 incapable of removing themselves & women with children at the breast	6	70	40	51
Boys under 7	9	45	34	30
Girls under 7	12	31	34	20
Serving volunteers – Yeoman	–	–	3	–
– Infantry	–	2	3	15
Aliens and Quakers	–	–	–	–
Fattening oxen	135	53	24	24
Cows	34	107	85	105
Steers: heifers: calves	214	249	131	220
Colts	6	4	8	3
Sheep	2040	1056	1879	7108
Lambs	202	2331	627	4621
Hogs	93	102	92	40
Sows	5	20	27	20
Pigs	54	70	30	42
Riding horses	5	17	11	25
Wagons	11	34	30	29

Table 6 (continued)

	Pett	Guestling	Fairlight	Icklesham
Carts	19	59	40	46
Other carriages	1	3	4	5
Draft Horses	31	87	77	58
Windmills	–	–	1	1
Watermills	–	–	–	–
Quantity of corn they can grind in 24 hours in bushels	–	–	80	60
Bakers	–	–	–	–
Private: amount they can bake in 24 hours (*see Note*)	177	101	135	1507
Implements:				
Felling ax	1	21	5	9
Pick ax	–	16	1	7
Spade	2	4	2	8
Shovel	–	10	–	3
Billhook	–	17	1	2
Saw	1	–	–	–
Persons 15–60 willing to act as drivers of cattle	11	13	23	14
Persons 15–60 willing to act as drivers of teams	10	16	19	24
Persons 15–60 willing to act as drivers of sheep	13	10	10	20
Persons 15–60 on horse willing to fight	–	2	3	8
Persons 15–60 on foot willing to fight	–	6	–	–
Arms:				
Sword	–	2	3	6
Pike	–	4	3	6
Flintlock	–	6	–	–
Pike	–	6	–	–
Persons 15–60 willing to act as pioneer labourers	2	27	15	30
Number of persons appointed to remove horse wagons conveying such as are capable of removing themselves	8	24	24	28
Number of overseers app. to superintend the service	2	4	4	3
Number of persons appointed to remove cattle	8	30	19	25
Number of overseers app. to superintend the service	2	4	3	5
Number of persons appointed for the removal of sheep and other livestock	10	30	3	26

Table 6 (continued)

	Pett	Guestling	Fairlight	Icklesham
Number of overseers app. to supervise the service	2	4	3	5
On service-persons on horse	–	–	2	–
On service-persons on foot	–	–	–	1
Cavalry sword	–	–	2	–
Cavalry pistol	–	–	2	1

Number to be given arms at place of assembly – Phillips has made return of neither service or stock.

Icklesham has not a sufficient number of men to man wagons in case of invasion. It is not in the power of the inhabitants to assist the government with anything but request the assistance of the government.

Government agent for parish to requisition carriages, Guestling – Moses Cloke.

Fairlight Down Mill – 10 sacks of flour milled in 24 hours. Will provide wheat.

Icklesham Mill will provide wheat.

Pett – not half the stock entered but returned in other parishes the occupiers reside.

Note: Pett 177 bushels of flour, Guestling 101 bushels of flour, Fairlight 135 peck loaves, Icklesham 1507 gallons of flour.

Table 7. Specification of Works Required in Creating a Church at Pett Near Hastings from a Design and under the Superintendence of B. Ferrey Esq. Architect. March 1864

Mason Bricklayer:

Build the walls in the best manner with sound stone facings of the local stone slightly hammer dressed and securely bonded to an internal lining of brickwork.

The several windows, arches, buttresses, quoins, string courses, copings and base course to be executed in the best Bath stone, the whole work to be well set and bonded together. Such stonework from the old Church as may be approved by the Architect may be used again where directed.

All the passages and Chancel to be paved with ½ inch tiles of red and black laid diagonally upon a sound concrete foundation.

Provide and fix 2 cwt. of wrought iron hooping to be built into the walls of the Church as may be directed.

Carpenter and Joiner:

All the timber to be of the best yellow Memel Riga or Danzic free from sap.

The Roof and Spire to be constructed as shown by the drawings with timbers wrought and framed and of the scantlings thereon marked.

The flooring under the seats to be 1¼″ deal boarding laid on joists and sleepers of sufficient dimensions.

The whole area to be fitted with open framed benching according to the plans.

The doors of the Church to be of 2″ framing filled with 1¼″ boarding fitted with proper stock lock, drop handle bolt, etc.

The Spire to be constructed as shown on the drawings and to be covered with oak cleft shingles securely fastened to the boarding of the Spire.

Painter:

All the timber exposed to view to be lightly stained and varnished.

Plumber, Smith and Glaziers:

The gutters at the base of the Spire to be laid with milled lead 7lbs. to the superficial foot.

Lead flashings of 3lbs. lead to be put wherever necessary.

The Windows to have Iron Casement and strong saddle bars.

The Doors to have Smiths' made ornamental hinges.

The Windows to be glazed throughout with diamond quarries set in stout Church Window lead.

4″ eaves gutters and stack pipes to be fitted to the Eaves.

Table 7 (continued)

Tiler:

The Roofs to be covered with well burnt plain tiles, alternated with such old tiles as may be found fit to use again, the whole to be fastened with oak pegs, and neatly pointed, having sufficient bond.

Plasterer:

The internal faces of the walls of the Church and Chancel to be finished in rough stucco.

Notes:
1. The original document was hand written on three pages of foolscap. Punctuation shown is that on the original, as is the use of capital letters.
2. Memel, Riga and Danzic are all ports from which came good quality pitch-pine. Memel, now called Klaipeda, an ice-free Baltic port in Lithuania. Riga, Baltic port on the west coast of Latvia. Danzic, now Gdansk, Baltic port in Poland.
3. The detail included in the specification is much less than that required for a similar building today. Building regulations have changed a great deal since the middle of the nineteenth century.

Table 8. List of the Names of Some of the Fields in the Parish of Pett

The names shown below are those that were in use at the end of the 19th century. Some of the fields no longer belong to the farms mentioned, as there has been considerable change in ownership over the years.

French Court Farm:
1 Frankenfield
2 Cotton Pot
3 Leach Pit
4 Springfield
5 Godlins
6 Front Field
7 Round Wood
8 Clay Banks
9 Hop Gardens
10 Back Field
11 Allotment Field
12

Church Farm:
13 Shop Field
14 Nine Acres
15 Brook
16 Seven Acres
17 Two Acres
18 Eight Acres
19
20
21 Five Acres
22

Lunsford Farm:
23 Spring Meadow
24 Big Meadow
25 Crisford's Kraft (corruption of Crisford's Croft)
26 Eight Acres
27 Poor Field
28 House Field
29 Hollow Field
30 Eastlands
31 Five Acres
32 Long Field
33 Three Acres
34 Snake Wood
35 Front Field (originally Little Buds, referring to calves)
36 Buds

37 Upper Chick Hill
38 Primrose Dell
39 Coneybanks (Coney = rabbit)
40 Slip
41 Cliff Piece
42 Ellis Field (corruption of Alehouse Field)
43 Ellis Brook
44 Horse's Marsh
45 Middle Field
46 Three-cornered Field (44–46 Cloke's Marsh)
47 Starve Crow
48 Catstail
49 Canal Bank
50 Road Field
51 Middle Field
52 Bullocks Field (collectively Field's Ground, originally went with Cherry Gardens Farm to the Field family)

Dennet's Farm: (53–57)
53 Big Horns
54 Long Six Acres
55 Lower Horns
56 Pilrags
57 Wall Field
58 Wall Field (one of the "Innings" walls)
59 Pett Barn Ashes

Carters Farm:
60 Acre Spot
61 Marl Pits
62 Fifteen Acre
63 Ten Acre
64 Twelve Acres
65 Six Acres
66 Pen Field
67 Rushy Brook

Other Fields:
68 Little Frankhams
69 Canal Bank
70 Frankhams
71 Drawbridge
72 Long Brook
73 Short Brook
74 Rick Field
75 Malthouse Field
76 Bowling's
77 Hop Garden
78 Chapel Meadow
79 Middle Ward
80 Knights
81 Rectory Field
82 Little Wards or Pineys
83 Big Wards
84 Ketlock
85 Brick Yard
86 Pony Field
87 Kiln Field
88 Dimsdale

Gatehurst Farm:
89 Church Field (Meadow)
90 Sixteen Acres
91 Four Acres
92 Six Acres
93 Eight Acres
94 Twenty Acres
95 Chick Hill Bank
96 Jacques (Inner Chick Hill)
97 Little Parlour Field
98 Big Parlour Field
99 Big Wards
100 Little Wards
101 The Quarries
102 Lower Brook
103 Middle Brook
104 Top Brook
105 Fifteen Acres
106 The Hawth
107 Lower Chick Hill

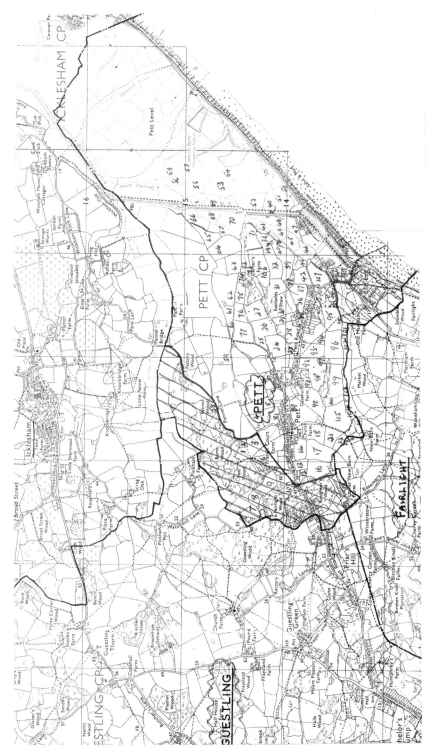

Pett Parish and its boundaries. Shaded area transferred to Pett from Fairlight Parish, July 1980; Pett Parish and Guestling Parish a Plurality from 8th July 1968; United Benefice of Pett and Guestling formed 2nd June 1978; United Benefice of Fairlight, Guestling and Pett formed 8th September 1994. Fields are numbered – see Table 8 [Reproduced by permisssion of Ordnance Survey on behalf of The Controller of Her Majesty's Stationery Office, © Crown Copyright 100043101]

Table 9. Extracts from the Catalogue of the Sale by Auction of the Outlying Portions of the Fairlight Hall Estate, near Hastings, Winchelsea and Rye, in the County of Sussex, with a Coast line of 5 miles

3,680 acres in the Parishes of Fairlight, Pett and Icklesham – in 75 Lots.
Sale by Auction by Messrs. John D. Wood & Co. at the Castle Hotel, Hastings,
24th November, 1917

Lot 18: A valuable Small Holding together with Shop – in all about 19a. 2r.13p. and known as:-
PETT GROCERY AND STORES
Comprising good brick and tiled House containing Shop, with Store behind, Living Room, Scullery and
Six Rooms over. Large Garden. Well of water
Let to Mr W.G. Colegate at £30 per annum.
Apportioned Outgoings: Tithe, 1917, about £7 2s 4d

Lot 21:A Well-placed Mixed Farm known as:-
ELMS FARM
Extending to 98a. 3r.19p. and including sound pastures and excellent arable, now used for Dairying
Purposes. The Picturesque Farm House – (suitable for a Gentleman's residence) with its steep tiled roof
and hanging tile upper storey and porch is enclosed in a garden with lawns and flower beds, with dwarf
wall in front, and contain: Entrance, Drawing Room and Dining Rooms with oak beam ceiling and
window seats, Larder, Dairy, Scullery, Store Room, Cellar, Kitchen, with oak beam ceiling, and Five Good
Bed Rooms with oak beams and woodwork. There is a brick and tiled building with ovens, Piggeries, and
timber and tiled Apple Store. Lawn, Flower and Kitchen Garden at rear, and Paved Yard. From the
Garden, extensive land and marine views are obtained.
THE HOMESTEAD
Comprises timber and tiled Cow House for four with Calf Pen, Open Shed, timber and galvanized Cow
Shed for 12, Open Shed on Outer yard, stone and tiled Oast-house and Buildings, stone, timber and
thatched Barn, brick and slate Nag Stable for two and Trap House, timber and thatched Granary partly
tiled, timber and slated Open Cart Shed, stone, brick and slated Cart-horse Stable for four with lean-to
Cow House for five cows, Yard and two-bay Cattle Shed, and timber and slated lean-to Implement Shed.
One arable field let to Mr Dunlop. Apportioned Rent £13 10s 0d.
The remainder to Mr Dennett with other lands. Apportioned Rent £102 10s 6d.
Apportioned Outgoings: Tithe, 1917, about £29 19s 11d.
The right to a supply of water from the well is reserved to Lot No. 28

Lot 22:An important and Profitable Mixed Farm known as:-
GATEHURST FARM
150a. 3r. 32p. with extensive frontage to Pett Road and Chick Hill, lying on the Southern slope, and
including excellent Sheep and Stock Land; together with a few acres of Woodland known as Magpies Hill.
The Superior Farmhouse occupies a magnificent situation and could readily be converted into a
Gentleman's Residence (*"Gatehurst" built circa 1650*). It lies adjacent to the village of Pett, and with the
Buildings forms a very attractive grouping of brick and tile. The house contains a Small Hall, Sitting Room
with beam ceiling, another Sitting Room, Dining Room, Kitchen with kitchener, Dairy, Pantry, Apple
Room, Scullery and cellar below. Above are seven Bed Rooms. There is a shaded Garden in front and a
Vegetable Garden and orchard at side.

Table 9 (continued)

The Farm Buildings comprise Stone and Tiled Hovel, Brick and Slated Five-bay open Cow Shed, Piggery, Post and Thatch Shed, Stone Tiled and Part-thatched Barn and Range of Timber and Tiled Buildings round Yard, Stone, Brick and Tiled Range of Open Sheds, Hop Oast and Store (*now The Roundels*), Cow Shed for ten and calf Pen, Implement Shed, Large Brick and tiled Barn and Open Shed adjoining, and also a Stone, Brick and Thatched Cottage. A valuable sub-stratum of Blue Stone underlays this lot.
The wood is let to Mr Gibbs at 2s 6d per annum, the remainder being let to Mr J.D. Cooke.
Apportioned Rent: £104 19s 3d. Apportioned Outgoings: Tithe, 1917, about £34
Land Tax, about £2 9s 5d.
Water Scot (average 10 years) £4 12s 9d.

Lot 23: A Compact Mixed Farm of very fine land with Valuable Marsh Pastures known as:-
LUNSFORD FARM
163a.1r.8p. including a small piece of woodland known as Eastlands Shaw in the Parish of Pett
The Farmhouse occupies a nice elevated position, is brick cemented with tiled roof, and contains; Entrance Lobby, Drawing Room, Dining Room with oak beam ceiling, Small Sitting Room, Workshop, Kitchen, Scullery, Larder, Three Bed Rooms, Box Room and Three Attic Rooms. Inside W.C. There is a Small Garden in front and Large Vegetable Garden and Orchard. The Buildings comprise brick and tiled Cart-Horse Stable for five, brick and thatched Shed, Piggeries, Trap House and brick and tiled Three-stall Stable, Open cattle Lodge, peat and thatch Open Shed with Cow Lodge behind, Out-house and Store used as Cow House for....., Yard and stone, brick and thatch Open Shed, timber and thatch Implement Shed and large timber and tiled Barn, Two Cottages with large gardens.
The Woodland is in hand. One Cottage is let to Mr Griffen (weekly) at £5 4s. per annum, Landlord paying Rates. Marsh pastures let to Mr J. Field. Apportioned Rent, £18 and the remainder is let to Mr. T.P. Dunlop, with other lands. Apportioned Rent: £165 5s.
Apportioned Outgoings: Tithe, 1917, about £38
Land Tax, £1 9s. Water Scot (average 10 years) £39 11s 6d, Timber, £29 10s.

Lot 24: A Compact Mixed Farm known as:-
CARTER'S FARM
Of very fine land, producing heavy crops of Hay, Hops and Roots, and extending to an area of 160a. 3r. 7p. including 56 acres of Marsh Pasture along the old Military Canal.
The House of brick, half-timbered and thatch, contains: Hall, Sitting Room, Living Room, Kitchen, Scullery, Dairy, Cellar and Pantry, together with Four Bedrooms, Box Room and Two Attics. The Buildings comprise Stables for four, Chaff house, Four-bay Cattle Shed, Three-bay Timber and corrugated iron Cattle Shed, Two Yards, Cow House for nine, another for five, Barn with Granary, Four-bay Wagon Lodge, Hop Oast and Store.
Two pastures are let with other lands to Mr. T.P. Dunlop: Apportioned Rent, £19 5s. and the remainder to Mr Griffen, Apportioned Rent, £141
Apportioned Outgoings: Tithe, 1917, about £38 14s 4d.
Water Scot (average 10 years) £8 0s 4d.

Notes: a. = acres: r. = rods: p. = perches. Scot is a payment corresponding to a modern tax, rate, etc. Thus Water Scot is, in effect, the Water Rate.

Table 10. Extract from "Pett Parish Magazine", Vol. XXVII No.4, for St Mary and St Peter, Pett; St Nicholas, Pett Level; St Richard, Winchelsea Beach – April 1936

EASTER OFFERING – A Message from the Churchwardens:

In accordance with the request of the Lord Bishop, the Churchwardens have decided to hand to the Rev. H.E. Moxon, the collection made on Easter Day at all services on that day in the Parish Church, and in St. Nicholas and St. Richard, together with any further sums that may be sent to them. The following statement will show the present official income of the above, and will enable those who feel disposed to contribute to judge for themselves how far an increase is desirable:-

Gross Income of the Living of Pett in 1935:

	£	s	d
Tithe Rent Charges	494	9	6
Rent of Glebe	110	0	0
Dividends etc.	11	0	0
Fees	1	0	0
	£ 516	19	6

Deductions:

	£	s	d
Rates and Taxes	51	12	4
Cost of Collection and deductions made by Queen Anne's Bounty	74	1	6
Dilapidations and Pension	45	5	0
Ecclesiastical Insurance	6	8	1
	£ 177	6	11

NETT INCOME:- £339 12s 7d

A budget for the Parish of Pett (1936) would work out as follows:	£	s	d
1. Maintenance and Insurance of the Church Fabric	20	0	0
2. Furniture and Ornaments (including Organ tuning and insurance)	5	0	0
3. Requisites for public worship (music, altar requisites, etc.)	5	0	0
4. Salaries (including insurance)	32	10	0
5. Cleaning, lighting and heating	20	0	0
6. Maintenance of the Churchyard	6	0	0
7. Expenses of the Church Council	5	0	0
8. Sunday School (including treats and prizes)	3	3	0
9. Quota	14	0	0
	£ 110	13	0

Morally the council is bound to arrange for financial support for the work of the Church overseas and for religious and philanthropic organisations; but no definite amounts can be stated as regards the moral obligations and therefore they should not be included in the budget...

Table 11. The Young Family – Major Benefactors of Pett Parish Church

Henry Young   b. 25 Dec. 1797, d.1 Dec. 1869, Patron and Benefactor *
Helped to raise money for the new church, built 1864
Memorial: West window

Maria Young   b. 26 Feb. 1801, d. 27 Dec. 1892, Wife of Henry Young *

Frederick Young   b. ? d. 28 Oct. 1882, Son of Henry Young and Rector of Pett 1857–1882.
Gift of oak lectern, helped raise money for the organ and some of the church plate.
Memorial: St Nicholas window

Anne Young   b. ? d. 29 Oct. 1862, 1st wife of Frederick Young*
Memorial: East window

Caroline Maria Young   b. ? d. ? 2nd wife of Frederick Young

Jane Maria Young   b. 1826 (?) d. 13 Oct. 1871 (age 45) Daughter of Henry Young*
Memorial: S.W. window in nave

Charles Waring Young   b. 1827 (?) d. 22 Feb. 1899 (age 72) Younger son of Henry Young*
Gift of Office Prayer Book (Book of Common Prayer)

Augusta Emma Young   b. 16 Dec. 1836, d. 17 May 1907, Wife of Charles Waring Young*

Herbert Edward Waring Young   b. 1 Mar. 1866, d. 9 Mar. 1895, Son of Charles and Augusta*

James Forbes Waring Young   b. 2 Sep. 1867, d. 28 Apr. 1869, 4th son of Charles and Augusta*
Memorial: N.E. chancel window

Henry Arthur Byron Young   b. 8 Sep. 1868, d. 9 Mar. 1870, Son of Frederick and Caroline*
Memorial: N.W. chancel window

Marion Caroline Young   b. 26 Dec. 1860, Daughter of Frederick and Caroline

Erica Mary Young   b. 16 Jun. 1866, Daughter of Frederick and Caroline

Ethel Flora Young   b. 16 Dec. 1872, Daughter of Frederick and Caroline

Byron William Douglas Young   b. 9 Jan. 1880, Son of Frederick and Caroline

Frederick C. A. Young   b. 14 Jul. 1867, d. 11 Sep. 1938, Rector of Pett 1909–1930 *
Son of Frederick and Caroline
Gifts: Electric light, two standard candlesticks, silver chalice

Eve Mary Young   b. 12 Oct. 1870, d. 22 Feb. 1909, Wife of F.C.A. Young*
Gift: Kneeler with hinged lid, Memorial: Vestry window

Alan, Derek, Kathleen & Edie   Sons and daughters of F.C.A. Young and his wife Eve Mary

V.A. Young   *Gift of ivory and wooden Crucifix above pulpit*

Miss G. R. Young   *Gift of four Antependia (frontals for pulpit)*

Note: Entries with * indicate that the person concerned is buried in the churchyard at Pett.

Table 12. Botanical Survey of St Mary & St Peter Churchyard. Carried out in 1989–1990 by Joan Medlock and Breda Burt (Former Botanical Recorder, East Sussex)

English Common Name	Latin Name
Barren Brome	*Bromus sterilis*
Bent, Common	*Agrostis capillaries*
Bent, Creeping	*Agrostis stolonifera*
Bent, Black	*Agrostis gigantea*
Bindweed, Hedge	*Calystegia sepium*
Birch, Downy	*Betula pubescens*
Bird's-foot-trefoil, Common	*Lotus corniculatus*
Bird's-foot-trefoil, Greater	*Lotus uliginosus*
Bitter-cress, Hairy	*Cardamine hirsute*
Bittersweet	*Solanum dulcamara*
Black Horehound	*Ballota nigra*
Black Medick	*Medicago lupulina*
Black Spleenwort	*Asplenium adiantum-nigrum*
Blackthorn	*Prunus spinosa*
Bluebell	*Hyacinthoides non-scriptus*
Bracken	*Pteridium aquilinum*
Bramble	*Rubus fruticosus*
Buddleia (Butterfly Bush)	*Buddleia Davidii*
Burnet-saxifrage	*Pimpinella saxifraga*
Buttercup, Bulbous	*Ranunculus bulbosus*
Buttercup, Creeping	*Ranunculus repens*
Buttercup, Meadow (Butter-flower)	*Ranunculus acris*
Campion, Red	*Silene dioica*
Cat's-ear	*Hypochoeris radicata*
Celandine, Lesser	*Ranunculus ficaria*
Centaury, Common	*Centaurium erythraea*
Cleavers	*Galium aparine*
Clover, Alsike	*Trifolium hybridum*
Clover, Red	*Trifolium pratense*
Clover, White (Dutch)	*Trifolium repens*
Cock's-foot	*Dactylis glomerata*
Comfrey, Russian	*Symphytum x uplandicum*
Couch, Common	*Elymus repens*
Cowslip	*Primula veris*
Crane's-bill, Dove's-foot	*Geranium molle*
Cress, Thale	*Arabidopsis thaliana*
Daisy	*Bellis prennis*
Daisy, Oxeye	*Leucanthemum vulgare*
Dandelion, Common	*Taraxacum officinale*

Table 12 (continued)

English Common Name	Latin Name
Dead-nettle, Red	*Lamium purpureum*
Dead-nettle, White	*Lamium album*
Dock, Broad-leaved	*Rumex obtusifolius*
Dock, Curled	*Rumex crispus*
Dog's-tail, Crested	*Cynosurus cristatus*
Elder	*Sambucus nigra*
Fescue, Red	*Festuca rubra*
Flax, Fairy	*Linum catharticum*
Foxglove	*Digitalis pururea*
Foxtail, Meadow	*Alopecurus pratensis*
Ground elder	*Aegopodium podagraria*
Ground ivy (Ale-hoof)	*Glechoma hederacea*
Hart's-tongue, Fern	*Phyllitis scolopendrium*
Hawk's-beard, Smooth	*Crepis capillaris*
Hawkbit, Autumn	*Leontodon autumnalis*
Hawkbit, Lesser	*Leontodon taraxacoides*
Hawthorn	*Crataegus monogyna*
Herb Robert	*Geranium robertianum*
Hogweed	*Heracleum sphondylium*
Holly	*Ilex aquifolium*
Ivy	*Hedera helix*
Knapweed, Black (Hardheads)	*Centaurea nigra*
Male fern	*Dryopteris felix-mas*
Mallow, Common	*Malva sylvestris*
Maple, Field	*Acer campestre*
Meadow-grass, Annual	*Poa annua*
Meadow-grass, Rough	*Poa trivialis*
Mouse-ear, Common	*Cerastium fontanum sub. glabrescens*
Nettle, Common (Stinging)	*Urtica dioica*
Oak, Pendunculate (English)	*Quercus robur*
Oat-grass, False	*Arrhenatherum elatius*
Oat-grass, Yellow	*Triseturm flavescens*
Orchid, Green-winged	*Orchis morio*
Parsley, Cow (Queen Anne's lace)	*Anthriscus sylvestris*
Pearlwort, Annual	*Sagina apetala*
Pearlwort, Procumbent	*Sagina procumbens*
Plantain, Greater	*Plantago major*
Plantain Hoary	*Plantago media*
Plantain, Ribwort	*Plantago lanceolata*
Privet, Wild	*Ligustrum vulgare*

Table 12 (continued)

English Common Name	Latin Name
Ragwort, Common (Stinking Willie)	*Senecio jacobaea*
Redshank	*Polygonum persicaria*
Rose, Dog	*Rosa canina*
Rye grass, Perennial	*Lolium perenne sub. perenne*
St John's-wort, Common	*Hypericum perforatum*
Selfheal	*Prunella vulgaris*
Sorrel, Common (Sour Leaves)	*Rumex acetosa*
Speedwell, Common-field	*Veronica persica*
Speedwell, Germander (Bird's-eye)	*Veronica chamaedrys*
Speedwell, Slender	*Veronica filiformis*
Speedwell, Wall	*Veronica arvensis*
Sow-thistle, Perennial	*Sonchus arvensis*
Sow-thistle, Prickly	*Sonchus asper*
Sow-thistle, Smooth	*Sonchus oleraceus*
Star of Bethlehem, Common	*Ornithogalum umbellatum (naturalised)*
Stitchwort, Greater	*Stellaria holostea*
Stitchwort, Lesser	*Stellaria graminea*
Sweet Vernal-grass	*Anthoxanthum odoratum*
Sycamore	*Acer pseudoplatanus*
Tansy	*Tanacetum vulgare*
Tare, Smooth	*Vicia tetrasperma*
Thistle, Creeping	*Cirsium arvense*
Thistle, Spear	*Cirsium vulgare*
Vetch, Bush	*Vicia sepium*
Vetch, Common	*Vicia sativa sub. segatilis*
Vetch, Tufted	*Vicia cracca*
Vetchling, Meadow	*Lathyrus pratensis*
Wall rue	*Asplenium ruta-muraria*
Water-droplet, Hemlock	*Oenanthe crocata*
Willowherb, American	*Epilobium ciliatum*
Willowherb, Hoary	*Epilobium parviflorum*
Woodrush, Field	*Luzula campestris*
Yarrow (Bloodwort)	*Achillea millefolium*
Yorkshire Fog	*Holcus lanatus*

Note: Some of these plants are no longer to be found in the churchyard of St Mary and St Peter.

Table 13. Descriptions of People Buried in Pett Churchyard. Data from the Parish Registers 1626–1809

1626	16 Apr.	John Butler, an old man
1627	14 Mar.	Henry Lewes, youth (son-in-law to Robert Foster)
1627	16 Mar.	John Carpenter, parish clerk
1629	23 Aug.	Eleanor Theobald, widow, a stranger
1632	15 Jan.	Thomas Cooper, uncle and servant to Thomas Crowhurst
1633	26 Jun.	Dennis Lurkins, a maid *(?)*
1634	6 May	Joan Siggs, a poor widow
1634	7 Oct.	William Bett, unbaptised infant
1635	9 Aug.	Katherine Kilner, an ancient maid
1636	14 Apr.	Robert Foster, yeoman
1636	19 Oct.	Nicholas Unstead, sawyer of Playden
1637	6 Jan.	John Sheaphard, a poor labourer
1639	11 Feb.	William Singleton, a poor man
1639	10 Mar.	William Christford, a poor old man

After 1640 householders, maidservants and manservants were noted

1681	1 Jan.	Joan Dulve, a maiden
1683	11 Feb.	Nicholas Powell, a poor stranger
1689	9 Jan.	John Cheesman, apprentice
1690	7 Jan.	Thomas French, (son of Abraham) a child
1691	29 Sep.	Richard Dean, miller of Guestling
1692	25 Apr.	Edward Apse, carpenter

After 1700 a number of labourers and widows were noted

1702	2 Oct.	Stephen Houghton, a poor minor
1721	5 Jan.	Edward Chapman, mason
1771	13 Nov.	Alice Williams, a traveller's child
1806	30 Jul.	Thomas Porter, of the 'Waggon train'
1809	7 Feb.	Unknown male, washed on shore

Table 14. List of Occupations of Men – Fathers of Baptised Children. Data from Bishops' Transcript of the Baptism Registers 1813–1892

Artist	Looker (1824 and 1827)
Baker	Mariner
Bricklayer	Mason
Builder	Master of Pett School – 1860 Philip Turner
Butcher	Milkman
Cabinet Maker	Mounted Coastguard
Carpenter	Music Seller (1875)
Carrier	Ordnance Overseer
Carter	Painter
Cheesemonger (Paddington)	Preventive Service
Clerk	Private, Royal Artillery
Coachman	Postman
Coastguardsmen (incl. Officers)	Publican †
Dairyman	Rector
Draper	Sailor
Engine Driver (1856)	Sergeant, Royal Artillery
Farmer	Servant
Farrier	Shepherd ‡
Gamekeeper	Shoemaker
Gardener	Shopkeeper
Gentleman	Smith (Blacksmith)
Gilder (Hastings)	Smith and Farrier
Grazier	Soldier
Grocer	Upholsterer
Ironmonger	Watch Maker (Hastings)
Labourer *	Yeoman
Lieutenant R.N.	Yeoman Farmer

* Many entries are for 'labourers', most of whom would have been agricultural labourers.

† Publicans: During this period three were listed: 1814 Thomas Davis; 1823 James Field (Innkeeper); 1824 William Foot.

‡ Richard Fellows was shown as a shepherd in 1824.

Note: It was only between 1813 and 1892 that the occupations of the fathers of baptised children were regularly entered into the Baptism Register.

Table 15. Numbers of Baptisms, Marriages and Burials Recorded. From Transcripts of Parish Registers 1606–1892

Dates	Baptisms	Marriages	Burials
1606–1620	40	17	65
1621–1640	93	22	84
1641–1680*	27	11	39
1681–1700	60	22	69
1701–1720	54	23	78
1721–1740	83	21	64
1741–1760	88	6	45
1761–1780	94	16	41
1781 – 1800	151	19	56
1801–1820	179	17 to 1812	35 to 1811
1821–1840	242		
1841–1860	169		
1861–1880	239		
1881–1892	82		

* There are gaps in the Registers between 1641 and 1666 and from 1669 to 1671.

Note: Where possible data is shown within groups of twenty years

Table 16. Families with Six or More Children – Data from Transcript of Baptism Registers 1606–1892

Parents Names	Between Dates	No. of Boys	No. of Girls	Total Children
Butler, John	1606–1624	5	1	6
Hobben, John & Alice	1632–1641	5	1	6
Westbourne, Richard & Elizabeth	1676–1688	-	7	7
Nabbs, Thomas & Deborah	1687–1700	4	3	7
Myles, Nicholas & Mary	1693–1728	3	5	8
Webb, William & Elizabeth	1694–1706	4	2	6
Marten, John & Alice	1701–1714	7 (incl. T)	2	9
Sloman, Henry & Mary	1722–1736	3	4	7
Hill, Richard & Susanna	1732–1742	4	2 (T B/G)	6
Potter, Thomas & Elizabeth	1738–1757	4	4	8
Foster, Thomas & Elizabeth	1740–1762	7 (incl. T)	5 (incl. T)	12
Rhodes, Joseph & Elizabeth	1744–1756	6	2	8
Ston(e)ham, Benjamin & Mary	1745–1764	4	3	7
Baker, Andrew & Alice	1748–1757	3	4	7

Table 16 (continued)

Parents Names	Between Dates	No. of Boys	No. of Girls	Total Children
Steel, James & Mary	1749–1758	5	1	6
Collins, Thomas & Elizabeth	1762–1774	4	2	6
Kennard, John & Judith	1762–1784	6	5	11
Buss, Thomas & Mary	1768–1777	4	3	7
Limbhurst, Richard & Sarah	1777–1793	2	4	6
Kennard, John & Mary	1787–1803	2	4	6
Hills, James & Ann	1778–1794	1	6	7
Harmer, Thomas & Sarah	1778–1797	2	5	7
Standen, Thomas & Ann	1778–1788	2	4	6
Booth, James & Martha	1783–1792	3	3	6
Dearing, Christopher & Judith	1783–1793	4	2 (T)	6
Baker, John & Ann	1783–1797	3	4	7
Nabbs, John & Susanna	1788–1805	5	5 (incl. T B/G)	10
Gibbs, William & Jane	1794–1812	4	2	6
Cloake, John & Lydia	1795–1812	5	3	8
Hills, James & Ann	1804–1815	1	6	7
Hills, Robert & Mary	1813–1827	4	2	6
Thorpe, John & Charlotte	1814–1825	2	4	6
Barden, William & Mary	1815–1835	8	2	10
Edwards, Thomas & Margaret	1817–1833	3	6	9
Kennard, George & Elizabeth	1819–1833	4	3	7
Foster, George & Elizabeth	1827–1843	5	2	7
Fellows, Thomas & Ann	1830–1841	2	4	6
Foster, Robert & Harriet	1831–1849	5	6	11
Fellows, George & Georgiana	1836–1852	5	2	7
Thorpe, Abraham & Sophia	1838–1854	3 (incl. T)	3	6
Harman, Alfred & Eliza	1859–1880	3	5	8
Judge, James & Sarah	1860–1876	5	2	7
Skinner, Adolphus & Sarah	1861–1873	4 (incl. T)	3	7
Standen, George & Harriet	1871–1891	6	3	9
Catt, William & Elizabeth	1879–1891	3	4	7

Note: (T) = Twins; (T B/G) = Twins – 1 boy and 1 girl

Between Dates = Span of dates during which the children were born, e.g. Alfred & Eliza Harman had 8 children between 1859 and 1880.

Table 17. List of Spinsters who had Illegitimate Children Baptised between 1603 and 1892. From Bishops' Transcripts of Baptism Records

1617	base sonne of Thomas	1784	Jane	1833	Anne
1633	Elizabeth K.	1785	Emma (b)	1836	Harriet
1635	Elizabeth W.	1785	Cordelia	1839	Jane
1687	Joan M (widow)	1787	Emma (b)	1839	Frances
1721	Elizabeth	1788	Elizabeth	1840	Sarah
1737	Elizabeth B.	1788	Susannah	1841	Charlotte
1745	Mary	1791	Mary	1843	Dinah
1767	Mary H.	1794	Sarah	1846	Agnes (d)
1768	Jane	1803	Sarah M.	1849	Harriet
1768	Anne	1805	Hannah	1853	Hannah
1769	Elizabeth	1810	Harriet	1854	Agnes (d)
1775	Sarah	1814	Mary (c)	1855	Maria
1776	Mary (a traveller)	1816	Maria	1855	Sarah Ann
1779	Martha (a)	1816	Mary (c)	1876	Ann
1780	Hannah H.	1818	Delia	1881	Sarah
1783	Martha (a)	1820	Elizabeth	1882	Mary Elizabeth

Note: Letters in brackets indicate ladies who had more than one illegitimate child

Table 18. Names Appearing Frequently in Parish Registers and Date of First Entry

Baker, C and B	1609	Collins, C	1762	Miles/Myles, C	1668
Barden, B	1738	Colegate, M	1812	Nabbs, M	1684
Barnes, C	1695	Dearing, B	1748	Rhodes, M	1716
Blackman, M	1704	Edwards, M	1686	Stevens, M	1607
Booth, C	1756	Foster, C	1608	Thorpe, M	1635
Bourn, M	1682	Harman, C	1609	Turner, M	1738
Burgess, C	1704	Hills, C	1732	Webb, M	1682
Butler, C and B	1606	Jenner, M	1720	Wickens, C	1692
Chapman, C	1714	Kennard, C	1751	Woodhurst, M	1770
Christford, C	1639	Martin/Marten, B	1610		

Note: C = Baptism: M = Marriage: B = Burial

Table 19. Infant Mortality 1606–1811. Data from Bishops' Transcripts of Baptism and Burial Registers

(a) Children under Five Years of Age.

Dates	Total Baptised	Total Buried	% Died	Time elapsed between Baptism and Burial for children who died under the age of five										
				Under: 2w	1m	3m	6m	1y	2y	3y	4y	5y	Inf
1606–1620	40	8	20	4	–	2	–	2	–	–	–	–	–
1621–1640	92	27	29	8	–	2	4	6	4	1	1	–	1
1641–1660	1	1		–	–	–	–	1	–	–	–	–	–
1661–1680	26	(T) 6	23	2	–	–	1	1	1	1	–	–	–
1681–1700	62	15	24	4	1	2	2	3	1	–	1	1	–
1701–1720	53	11	21	8	–	1	–	–	1	–	1	–	–
1721–1740	81	(T) 13	16	2	–	3	2	1	2	1	1	–	1
1741–1760	80	12	15	1	1	1	2	2	2	3	–	–	–
1761–1780	94	10	11	2	1	1	–	2	3	1	–	–	–
1781–1800	153	14	9	–	2	1	2	2	5	2	–	–	–
1801–1811	75	3	4	–	–	–	2	–	–	1	–	–	–
Totals	757	120	16	31	5	13	15	20	19	10	4	1	2

Notes: Dates in groups of twenty years – where possible. Gaps in Registers between 1641 and 1666 and between 1669 and 1671.

(T) = Twins – in one case there was an interval of four years between the burials.

Inf = Infant – in one case there is no Baptism date and the other infant was not baptised.

w, m, y = weeks, months, years

(b) Mothers who died at Childbirth, or soon after the Baptism of her Infant

Mother's name	Date of Burial	
Eleanor Baker	7 Apr. 1609	5 days after c. of Jane
Denise Butler	4 Feb. 1625	6 months after c. of Barnaby
Mildred Theobald	26 Sep. 1629	6 days after c. of Elizabeth
Margaret Medhurst	30 Oct. 1630	6 days after c. of Robert
Susan Lewis	14 Nov. 1632	2 weeks after c. of Elizabeth
Deborah Nabbs	16 Feb. 1687	Same day as c. of Stephen
Elizabeth Marten	25 Jul. 1696	9 days after c. of Thomas
Mary Myles	8 Sep. 1728	5 months after c. of Nicholas and 1 month after his burial
Mary Sloman	23 Sep. 1730	10 days after c. of Thomas
Elizabeth Paris	14 Jun. 1772	3 months after c. of John
Mary Woodus	10 Sep. 1772	2 weeks after c. of Mary
Elizabeth Stevens	10 Dec. 1791	Same day as c. of John

Note: c. = date of baptism

Table 19 (continued)

(c) More than one child, under the age of five, buried from the same family

Name	Dates of Burials	Other Children in the Family
Sheapherd	1629 (G), 1633 (B)	3 (B)
Hobben	1632 (B), 1635 (B), 1637 (B)	2 (B) & 1 (G)
Crowherst	1634 (G), 1638 (B)	2 (G)
Burden	1638 (B), 1640 (B)	1 (G)
Allen	1638 (B), 1638 (G), 1641 (B)	1 (G)
Houghton	1672 (G) (G) – Twins	
Lunsford	1677 (G), 1686 (G) – both named Judith	2 (B) & 1 (G)
French	1685 (B), 1690 (B)	1 (B) & 1 (G)
Westbourne	1686 (G), 1688 (G) – both named Sarah	5 (G)
Marten (Martin)	1702 (G), 1703 (B), 1703 (B), 1704 (B), 1712 (B)	3 (B) & 1 (G)
Myles	1703 (G), 1728 (B)	2 (B) & 4 (G)
Nash	1728 (B), 1730 (G)	3 (G)
Foster	1741 (B), 1744 (G) – one of twins, 1750 (B) – one of twins	5 (B) & 4 (G)
Marten (Martin)	1753 (B), 1764 (B)	1 (B) & 2 (G)
Tilden	1787 (G), 1788 (G)	1 (G)
Booth	1787 (G), 1793 (B)	2 (B) & 2 (G)
Marten	1788 (G), 1795 (G)	1 (G)
Gibbs	1795 (B), 1803 (B)	2 (B) & 2 (G)

Table 20. Residents of Pett who were both Baptised & Married at St Mary & St Peter Church: 1606–1811. Data from Bishop's Transcripts of Baptism and Marriage Registers

Of the 188 marriages recorded between 1606 and 1811 only 10% were where one of the couple was Baptised in Pett Church. They are given below.

Date Baptised	Date Married	Years	Names of Couples	Date of Baptism of First Child
3 Oct 1608	7 Jul. 1628	20	Jane Foster m. Edmund Burden of Fairlight	
29 Mar. 1612	1 May 1626	14	Elizabeth Arnold m. John Reeve	
10 Aug. 1679	22 Apr. 1703	23	Lucy Westbourne m. Edward Marten	G 1705
20 Dec. 1691	22 May 1716	24	Mary Nabbs m. Joseph Rhodes	B 1718
4 Jan. 1698	8 Apr. 1724	26	Nicholas Myles (Miles) m. Mary Richardson (wid.) by licence	G 1725
19 Dec. 1699	23 Apr. 1716	16	Mary Webb m. Henry Slo(w)man	G 1722
2 Jun. 1700	16 Apr. 1722	21	Elizabeth Cleave m. Richard Head of Fairlight	B 1724
25 Sep. 1720	20 May 1746	26	Mary Rhodes (d. of Joseph and Mary) m. William Weston of Battle, at Fairlight*	
23 Jan. 1721	29 Dec. 1737	16	Elizabeth Martin m. Thomas Potter	G 1738
1 Oct. 1732	7 May 1758	25	Joseph Hills m. Elizabeth Mathews	G 1762
14 Dec. 1746	15 Apr. 1770	23	Mary Foster m. William Woodus(t)	G 1772
21 Feb. 1762	17 Sep. 1787	25	Hannah Hills m. Stephen Marshall	G 1788
11 Jan. 1778	6 Apr. 1802	24	Sarah Hills m. William Kennard	
25 Dec. 1778	12 Dec. 1792	14	Ann Standen m. Thomas Overy by licence	G 1793
8 Apr. 1781	23 Dec. 1806	25	Daniel Edwards m. Hannah Malgon	
25 May 1783	25 Oct. 1804	23	Mary Kennard m. Andrew Lian	
8 Jun. 1783	30 Apr. 1804	20	James Hills m. Ann Jarret	G 1804
18 Sep. 1785	24 Jun. 1806	19	Mary Stevens m. William Simmons by licence	

Notes. Date Baptised – relates to the name of the first named person of the couple marrying.

Years – time (in years between date of baptism and marriage). Baptism usually took place soon after the birth of a child.

Date of Baptism of First Child – as recorded in the Baptism Register, B = Boy, G = Girl.

* Not married in Pett Church.

Table 21. Martello Towers on Pett Level Beach – Residents – Coastguards etc. Data from Baptism Registers and Census Returns

Tower No.	Date	Residents
31	1840	George and Hannah Pearn & family
	1843	William and Anne Hutchins & family
	1851	George and Ann Burtchell & six children (Chief Officer)
	1851	David and Eliza Coughlan & five children (Chief Boatman)
	1881	John and Susannah Philip & three daughters
	1881	William and Mary Ellis & one daughter
	1881	William and Hannah Woodly & four children
	1881	William and Bridget Callaghan & five children
	1881	John and Rebecca Hood & son
	1881	James and Elizabeth Kerridge & three daughters
32	1843–1851	John and Jane Wallace & seven children
	1851	William and Mary West & five children
33	1831	William and Ellis Shallard & family
	1833	Thomas and Elizabeth ? & family
	1839	Richard and Emma Symes & family
	1843	William and Jane Arnold & family
	1851	George and Jane Anthony & four children
	1851	James and Margaret Wicks & five children
	1881	James and Margaret Wicks
34	1835–1841	James and Charlotte Davison & five children
	1847–1851	George and Jane Teague & two children (Boatman)
	1851	William and Sarah Mundy & four children (Boatman)
	1881	George and Clara Cunn & child
	1881	Joseph and Jane Egerton & three children
35	1831	Joshua and Lucy Blakely & family
	1835	Richard and Mary Ann Buck & family
	1846	James and Mary Coates & family
	1851	John and Elizabeth Menear & five children (Boatman)
36	1827	Francis and Frances McLennon & family
	1834	Thomas and Mary Barnesley & family
	1846	Richard and Rachel Phillips & family (Preventive Service)
	1851	William and Ann Hawkes & two children
	1881	Albert and Agnes Gidley & three children (Chief Boatman)
	1881	John and Harriet Hudson & five sons
	1881	Henry and Sarah Howard & two sons
37	1828	John and Elizabeth Barton & family
	1835	Andrew and Jane Reedon & family
	1851	Robert and Mary Newson & two children (Boatman: Mary worked on Braggs farm)

Table 21 (continued)

Tower No.	Date	Residents
38	1833	Evan and Elizabeth Williams & family
	1834	Donald and Margaret Cooper & family
	1834	John and Margaret Martin & family
	1846	William David and Mary Matilda Jordan & family
	1851	Charles and Sarah Russel & four sons
	1851	Jane Monger, wife of a Coastguard and her son were visitors

Table 22. Other Coastguards (Preventive Service) Mentioned in Baptism Records 1830–1887

1831	John Tremble		
1832	Thomas Quested		
1833	Thomas Critchell	William Driver	
1834	Stuart White	Robert Yetts (F)	John Buckle (F)	Alexander Brown (F)
1835	Samuel Colbreay	Thomas Arnor	William Stacey	Edward Rochet
1836	Robert Topping	John Smith	Hugh Rainy	Robert Barrett
	Benjamin Buckkel (PS)		
1837	Richard Andrews	Joseph Fabone	John Colberry
1838	Robert Anderson (F)	Robert Newsom	Joseph Foot
1839	William Fabone (M)	William Stapleton	Samuel Coalberry (PS)
1840	John Mathewson	William Dennis	
1841	Charles Crone	William Lewis	Thomas Dinman (M)
1842	William Prophet	Robert Barrett	Richard Woodruffe
1845	William Smith		
1848	James Williams		
1851	William Sheppard		
1852	George Hodge		
1857	Thomas Jones	James Pullen	Charles Cable	Alexander Tremble
1858	Henry Stay	William Gilbert	John Rogers
1859	George Wells		
1861	David Burgess		
1862	John Alfred James	Daniel King	
1863	John Leggatt	William Joyce	
1865	Thomas Penny	William Cummings Bull (C Off)	
1866	Christmas Patteson		
1867	David Adams	James Ward	George Balcombe

Table 22 (continued)

1868	Isaac Silbick	David Douch	William Knox	
1869	John Hicks	George Paddon	Alfred Laker (F)	
1871	Thomas Gibbs	William Reed (C Off F)	William Padden	Daniel Powell
1872	John Handford	Thomas Kensey Pope	James Johns Terrell	
1873	John Chalker			
1874	Charles Knight			
1875	George Burridge	Joseph William Bartlett		
1876	Charles Reynolds	Joseph James Brown		
1877	James Walker			
1878	Daniel Piper (F)	John Brown	Charles John Symms	
1879	Samuel Griffiths (C Off F)			
1887	George Richards			

Note: Dates shown are of the earliest entry in the Baptism Register. The spelling of names is as recorded.

The abbreviations are as recorded in the registers: F = Fairlight, PS = Preventive Service, M = Mounted, C Off = Coastguard Officer, C Off F = Coastguard Officer Fairlight

Table 23. The Cooke Family

Showing the three main strands of the family associated with Pett, and the names of other local families linked to the Cookes by marriage:

William Cooke   1742–1812 Farmer – Ticehurst, Hertsmonceux, Penhurst, and Ashburnham
m. Elizabeth Vigear. They had 18 children, all of whom survived childhood, 13 boys and 5 girls. The third child was *James* 1772–1841 (see A)

A. James Cooke   b. 16 Dec. 1772 d. 1841, aged 69. m. Mary Wright of Ashburnham
Came to Pett Level about 1831. Innkeeper of Ship Inn

8 Children:	Mary	1808–1851 m. Davis – Pett grazier
	Elizabeth	1812–1900 did not marry
	Frances	1814–1847 m. Davis – Pett labourer
	James	1816–1910 (see B)
	Sarah	1818–1907 m. Hawkins – Guestling carpenter
	Matilda	1820–1883 m. Davis – Pett labourer
	Henry	1823– ?
	Emily	1825– ?

(*Note*: All three of the Davis men were brothers, sons of Thomas and Ann Davis of Pett Level)

B. James Cooke   b. May 1816 d. 3 Jun. 1910
m. Dinah Davis (daughter of Thomas and Ann Davis)

6 Children: Alfred Henry Davis   1843–1928 m. Paine – Winchelsea
(one of their daughter's m. Jury)
Albert Davis   1845–1908 m. Ann Smith – Coastguard's daughter
(2 of their children m. into the Merrick family)
Albert was a looker in Pett parish and later a shepherd
Emmeline   1846–1924 m. Wicks – Coastguard at Pett
(one daughter m. Goodsell – Rye joiner – later Pett)
George Frederick   1850–1927 m. Hawkins – Guestling
(one daughter m. Fellows – Guestling)
Charles Thomas   1852–1933 (see C)
Joseph Davis   1855–1936 m. Turner – Guestling

C. Charles Thomas   b.29 Jan. 1852 d. 4 Sep. 1933
Cooke   m. Eliza Ann Wicks – No. 33 Martello Tower

13 Children: Eliza Annie   1875–1959 m. Harman – Pett labourer
Frederick James   1877–1915 killed at sea on H.M. Trawler *Briton*
Ellen Louise   1879–1955 m. Osborne – Pett labourer
(daughters m. Cloke, Willard, Goodsell)
Lucy   1880–1950 m. Coastguard from Hampshire
Charles Thomas   1882–1974 (one daughter m. Griffen)

Table 23 (continued)

Walter	1883–1957
Alice	1884–1948 m. Osborne – Ewhurst labourer (grandson m. Cooke – cousin)
Joseph	1885–1938 emigrated to USA
Mildred	1887–1975 emigrated to USA and Canada
William Clyde	1889–1971 emigrated to USA
Reginald	1890 – 1965 m.(i) Gladys Begbie, (ii) Lydia Henson (daughters m. Goodsell, Shearer – Fairlight)
Emily Janette	1895–1964 Lived in Canada and Pett Level
Mabel Madeline	1897–1970 m. Cooke – cousin

Table 24. The Hills Family

Showing the names of other families linked to the Hills by marriage – including the Colegates:

Joseph Hills   – Udimore m. 1705 (at Catsfield) Sarah Corby (c. 1677) son *Richard* (see A)

A.   Richard Hills   b. 1706 (Hastings) d. 1791 (Pett) m. (i) 1727 Ann Gardiner – daughter Sarah had a son *James* (see B) by William Colbrun
m. (ii) 1731 Susanna Barden – had 5 children,
the eldest Joseph 1732–1821 m. Elizabeth Matthews – had 3 children

B.   James Hills   1754–1803 (son of Sarah and William) m. Ann Guy (Fairlight)

7 Children:

Sarah	1778– ? m. 1802 William Kennard
Ann	1780– ? m. 1806 Mark Rigby
James	1783–1816 m. 1804 Ann Jarret (drowned at Boulogne) (had 8 children – one son m. Hunt (Pett) & a daughter m. Holman)
Robert*	1785–1816 m. Mary ? (6 children all born in Pett)
Pilbe (Phyllis)	1790– ? m. Henry Gorham (Fairlight)
Mary	1792– ?
George	1794–1873 (see C) Proprietor of 'Royal Oak' & Parish Clerk for 38 years

C.   George Hills*   1794–1873 m. Hannah Knight

6 Children:
Hannah

Charlotte	1817–1870 m. Christopher Thorpe
	1819–1901 m. Henry Harman
Thomas	1822–1883 (see D)

+ William 1825–1826 : Alice 1827–1849: Ann 1832–1846

D.	Thomas Hills	1822–1883 m. Shelomith Oliver	
	8 Children:	Ann	1852– ? m. 1874 Albert Edwin Skinner
		Thomas George	1854–1922 m. 1882 Ann Winifred Colegate, 3 children†
		Shelomith	1856 – 1870
		Alice	1858–1939 m. 1886 George Henry Colegate†
			(see Table 25)
		James John	1861–1941 m. (i) 1886 Mildred Gertrude Colegate,
			2 children†
			m. (ii) 1892 Caroline Maria Colegate, 9 children†
			(James John and Caroline's children's spouses included Catt,
			Baker, Green, Griffin and Jury)
		Charlotte	1863–1938 m. 1882 George Turner
		Sarah	1863–1880
		Harriet Lucy	1872– ? m. 1897 Walter Harry Gibbons

* Robert and George Hills are shown in the Register of Electors of 1847–1848 as being entitled to vote as freeholders. Only eight people in Pett had the right to vote at that time.

† Thomas George, Alice and James John Hills all married into the same family; who were children of Jesse and Cordelia Colegate (see Table 25). James John married sisters, Mildred, the younger, in 1886 and Caroline, an elder sister, in 1892.

Table 25. The Colegate Family

Showing the names of other families linked to the Colegates by marriage – including the Hills:

	Thomas Colegate	– Sedlescombe c. 1691 m. 1717 Sarah Body	
		(9 children, 4 boys & 5 girls, most lived in Westfield)	
	Eldest child	Mary	1718– ? had 2 children, *John* (see A) and Mary
	2nd child	Thomas*	1721–1807 (Westfield & Icklesham)
			m. 1763 May Henley
A.	John Colegate	1749–1831 m. 1772 Elizabeth Guy (7 children, most lived at Icklesham)	
	7th child	*John*	1791–1841 (see B)
B.	John Colegate	1791–1841 m. 1812 (at Pett) Winifred Harman	
		(12 children; 7 boys & 5 girls, most lived at Pett)	
	4th child	Charlotte	1819–1839 m. 1838 Charles Turner
	5th child	*Jesse*†	1821–1900 (see C)
	8th child	Thomas	1829–1919 m. 1859 Noakes (Guestling) – 2 girls
	9th child	John	1831–1927 m. (i) 1861 Emma – 2 children,
			(ii) 1873 Eliza Selmes
	10th child	Richard	1833–1884 m. 1859 Rosina Hawkins

C. Jesse Colegate	1821–1900 m. Cordelia Gallop	
	(9 children; 3 boys & 6 girls – lived in Fairlight or Pett)	
2nd child	Mary Lydia	1851–1873 m. Horace Noakes (Guestling)
3rd child	Ann Winifred	1853–1916 m. 1882 Thomas George Hills‡
4th child	George Henry	1856–1919 (25 years Churchwarden) m. 1884 Alice Hills‡
		(2 children, William Gallop§ and Maude Alice¶)
5th child	*Albert John*	1858–1921 (see D)
7th child	Caroline Maria	1862–1915 m. 1892 James John Hills‡
8th child	Mildred Gertrude	1865–1891 m. 1886 James John Hills‡
9th child	Margaret Louisa	1867–1946 m. 1895 Charles E. Jury

D. Albert John Colegate	1858–1921 m. 1879 Mary Elizabeth Barden (4 boys & 2 girls)	
1st child	Thomas Crampton	1890–1962 m. 1915 Maud Alice Colegate (cousin)¶
3rd child	Mabel Mary	1881– ? m. 1904 F.C. Harman
4th child	William Gallop	1884–1973 m. Annie Elizabeth Gardener (2 children)§
5th child	Albert John	1887–1979 m. Kate Madeline Sadler (2 children)

* Thomas Colegate 1721–1807 was witness at John Nabbs' marriage at Fairlight.

† Jesse Colegate 1821–1900 is shown in the 1847–1848 Register of Electors as being entitled to vote as a freeholder. There were 29 people entitled to vote at Guestling.

‡ See Table 24. Ann Winifred, George Henry, Caroline Maria and Mildred Gertrude all married into the same family, who were children of Thomas and Shelomith Hills. Both Caroline and Mildred married James John Hills.

§ In the line from Jesse Colegate 1821–1900 there are three William Gallops, one of whom was the uncle of the other two, who were both born in the year following their uncle's death.

¶ Thomas Crampton Colegate married his cousin Maud Alice, their fathers, Albert John and George Henry, being brothers.

Note: The name Griffen or Griffin appears throughout the book, as well as in Tables 23, 24, 25 and 26. Until the mid 19th century all members of this family were born Griffin. For some unknown reason the surname was changed to Griffen. Both spellings occur in the book.

Table 26. Rolls

Roll of Honour – First World War: 1914–1918

John Beeching	H.M.S. Aboukir, 22 September 1914
Arthur James Fleet	Royal Sussex Regiment, 7 November 1914
Frederick James Cooke	H.M.A.T. Britain (Briton), 24 July 1915
Henry Beeching	2nd Royal Sussex Regiment, 27 August 1915
William Brooman	H.M.A.C. India, December 1915
George F. Cooke	H.M.S. Queen Mary, 31 May 1916
Fred Osborne	13th Royal Sussex Regiment, 3 July 1916
George R. Jenner	2nd Lieutenant, East Yorkshire Regiment, 2 August 1916
Preston T.F.T. Dennett	2nd Lieutenant, 4th Queens Royal West Surrey Regiment, attached to Royal Flying Corps, 4 August 1917
Henry P. Griffen	Royal Sussex Regiment, 16 August 1917
Albert Cox	Royal Engineers, 15 January 1918
George E. Weston	Queens Royal West Surrey Regiment, missing 21–23 March 1918
Henry S. Batehup	Lance Corporal, 9th Royal Sussex Regiment, Lewis Gun Station, 22 March 1918
John Hutchinson	Lance Corporal, 11th Royal Sussex Regiment, 26 April 1918
James A.B. Foster	Signaller, Royal Naval Division, 27 September 1918
Owen Fellows	2nd Royal Munster Fusiliers, 4 October 1918
Sidney E. Fleet	Machine Gun Corps, 30 April 1920

Table 26 (continued)

Muster Roll – First World War: 1914 – 1918

John W. Barnes	2nd Royal Sussex Regiment
Amos F. Batehup	Royal Field Artillery
Frederick J. Butler	Royal West Kent Regiment
William O. Catt	Army Ordinance Corps
Percy J. Catt	Royal Fusiliers
James R. Catt	Royal Marines
James W. Cloke	Machine Gun Corps
William G. Colegate	Royal Engineers
Thomas C. Colegate	Royal Naval Air Service
Leonard Cooke	Royal Naval Air Service
Reginald Cooke	5th Royal Sussex Regiment
Raymond Foster	Royal Field Artillery
Samuel G. Glazier	Royal West Kent Regiment
Spencer Glazier	Royal Navy
Percy J. Morris	Royal Naval Air Service
Albert Standen jnr.	Royal Field Artillery – Transport Section
Llewellyn H.C. Stephens	Victoria Rifles
Reginald F. Weston	A.Co.84178, 3rd Platoon, 23rd Training Reserve Battalion
Henry Winchester	2nd Queens Royal West Surrey Regiment
Florence M. Catt	Munitions
Ouida Jenner	V.A.D.
Beatrice Lucas-Shadwell	Canteen Work
Violet Lucas-Shadwell	V.A.D.

Roll of Honour – Second World War: 1939–1945

Douglas Barden	Royal Engineers
Jack Barden	Royal Berkshire Regiment
Harry Barnes	Sergeant, Royal Air Force Volunteer Reserve
Preston John Ebbutt	Lance Corporal, Queens Royal West Surrey Regiment
George Edward Glazier	Royal Scots Fusiliers
Gilbert A.C. Newton	Lieutenant, Royal Artillery
Jack Warnes	Sergeant, Royal Air Force

BIBLIOGRAPHY

'Biographies'. Manuscript by T.B. Brett, 1828–1864. Available in Hastings Library.

Black's Guide to Hastings, 1861. Adam and Charles Black, London.

The Builder Vol. XXXIX No. 1961, 4 Sep. 1880.

The Building News, 3 Sep. 1880.

Chichester Diocese Clergy Lists – compiled by Rev. George Hennessy BA.

The Cinque Ports and Romney Marsh. Margaret Brentnall, 1980. John Gifford, London.

A Companion to the English Parish Church. Stephen Friar, 1996. Sutton Publishing, Stroud.

A Concise Historical and Topographical Sketch of Hastings, Winchelsea and Rye, including several other Places in the vicinity of these Ancient Towns. Fred W.L. Stockdale, 1817.

Crockford's Clerical Directory – Various editions.

A Dictionary of Dates Relating to All Ages for Universal Reference. Joseph Haydn, 11th edn 1863. Edward Moxon, Dover Street, London.

The Dictionary of National Biography.

East Sussex Record Office: PAR 442 1 – 30 Parish of Pett – East Sussex; P 442 Pett Parish Council Minutes; LCG/3/EW1 & 2 Sussex Proceeding of Meetings of Deputy Lieutenant for the Internal Defence of this Country 1801.

The East Sussex Village Book. Rupert Taylor, 1986. Countryside Books, Newbury.

East Sussex Sentences of Transportation at Quarter Sessions.

The Hastings Guide or a Description of that Ancient Town and Port and its Environs. James Barry, 3rd edn 1804. London.

A History of the Church in England. John R.H. Moorman MD, DD – Lord Bishop of Ripon, 1953. Black, London.

'History of Hastings'. Manuscript by T.B. Brett, 1828–1864. Available in Hastings Library.

A History of Pett. Zoe Vahey, 1991.

'A History of Pett Parish Church'. Richard A.S. Parkins, published in *Pett Parish Magazine*, 1956.

History of Sussex. Vol. 2. M.A. Lower, 1870. Lewes.

The History and Antiquities of the Town and Port of Hastings. W.F. Moss (Draughtsman to His Royal Highness The Duke of Cambridge), 1824. London.

History, Antiquities and Topography of the County of Sussex. Vol.1, pp.213 and 463–477. Thomas Walker Horsefield, 1835. The Sussex Press, Lewes.

'History of the Parish Council'. In *Local Council Administration.* Charles Arnold-Baker, 2nd edn. 1981. Butterworths, London.

An Historical Atlas of Sussex. Edited by Kim Leslie and Brian Short, 1999. Phillimore, Chichester.

Illustrated English Social History. G.M. Trevelyan, 52nd edn, 1949. Penguin, Harmondsworth.

Kelly's Directories – 1862, 1887, 1895, 1899, 1909, 1915, 1927, 1938.

King Offa's Charterlands – from The Bexhill Charter.

Let there be Sculpture: an Autobiography. Jacob Epstein, 1940. Michael Joseph, London.

Many a Bloody Affray. Kenneth M. Clark, 1968. Rye Museum Publication No. 8.

Mark Gertler: Selected Letters. Edited by Noel Carrington, 1965. Rupert Hart-Davis, London.

Martello Towers, A Brief History. Geoff Hutchinson, 1994. Hastings.

Martello Towers 1805–1815. Village Net History. See www.villagenet.co.uk.

Martello Towers – The South Coast. See www.martello-towers.co.uk.

'One Hundred Nonsense Pictures and Rhymes' from *The Complete Nonsense Book*. Edward Lear, 1994. Castle Books.

'Pett Church – the Aumbry'. (i) An article by Rev. John Read. (ii) An inventory compiled in 1930. (iii) Parish Registers for Baptisms, Marriages and Burials from 1606.

'Pett – and a Nice Keddle of Fish'. Fred Skinner. *Sussex Life* Feb. 1975.

'Pett Records'. V.J. Torr, published in *Pett Parish Magazine,* 1961–1962.

Place Names of Sussex. Part 2. *The Rapes of Lewes, Pevensey, and Hastings*. A. Mawer and F.M. Stenton. Published for the English Place Name Society by Cambridge University Press, Cambridge.

*Pett Parish Magazine*s. Various between 1915 and 2000.

Population – Pett, Guestling, Icklesham – from various Census Reports, both National and Ecclesiastical – 1831, 1841, 1842, 1851, 1861, 1871, 1881, 1891.

Post Office Directories – 1855, 1867, 1878, 1894.

'Reminiscences of Pett Level' In *Hastings & St. Leonard's Observer*, 28 Jun. 1969.

The Rector and his Daughter: Rev. Henry Wynch and Florentia Lucas-Shadwell. Joyce Wheatley.

The Retired Naval Lieutenant and his Wife: Choyce and Elizabeth Moyses. Joyce Wheatley.

The Royal Military Canal, a Brief History. Geoff Hutchinson, 1995. Hastings.

The Royal Military (Romney) Canal. See www.canals.btinternet.co.uk.

Sir Stephen Glynn's Description of Pett Church. Vol. 100, Folio 88. Flintshire Record Office, Hawarden, Flintshire CH5 3NR.

St Mary & St Peter Church, Pett: Monumental Inscriptions. Compiled by Mrs Benita Wickens, August 2000. Hastings and Rother Family History Society.

Strangers Guide and Commercial Directory to Hastings & St. Leonard's – 1852.

Sussex Archaeological Society. Vols. 1, 6, 9, 10, 11, 16, 17, 35, 45, 53, 55, 61, 68, 76, 104, 106, 116.

Sussex Notes and Queries. Vols. VI, VIII, X, XV.

Sussex Record Society. Vols. 1, 2, 4, 6, 7, 10, 14, 20, 23, 25, 26, 37, 43, 45, 50, 51, 56, 78, 81.

Sussex Express and County Herald. 17 January 1975.

A Thousand Years of the English Parish. Anthea Jones, 2000. Windrush Press, Moreton-in-Marsh.

Universal British Directory 1793 – 1798. Vol.3 Part 1.

Unknown Sussex. Donald Maxwell, 1923. J. Lane The Bodley Head, London.

The Victoria History of the County of Sussex. Vol. 9. *The Rape of Hastings,* 'The Guestling Hundred'. Edited by L.F. Salzman, 1937. Published for the University of London Institute of Historical Reasearch by Oxford University Press, London.

'The War in East Sussex, 3 Sep. 1939 – 7 May 1945'. Compiled by the *Sussex Express and County Herald –* August 1945.

Wealden Iron. Ernest Straker, 1931. G. Bell & Sons, London.

William Lunsford and his Family. Joyce Wheatley.

Winchelsea – A Port of Stranded People. Malcolm Pratt, 1998. Malcolm Pratt, Bexhill-on-Sea.

'Zeppelin Dropped Bombs in Pett, 16 March 1917'. *East Sussex News* 9 June 1983.

Index